Women's Caring

Women's Caring

FEMINIST PERSPECTIVES ON SOCIAL WELFARE

edited by
Carol T. Baines,
Patricia M. Evans,
and Sheila M. Neysmith

M&S

Canadian Cataloguing in Publication Data

Main entry under title :

Women's caring : feminist perspectives on social welfare

Includes bibliographical references.
ISBN 0-7710-1046-X

1. Social problems – Sex differences. 2. Sex role.
3. Women – Attitudes. 4. Caring. 5. Feminism.
I. Baines, Carol. II. Evans, Patricia M.(Patricia
Marie), 1944–   III. Neysmith, Sheila M.

HV541.W65 1991   362.042   C90-095741-7

McClelland & Stewart Inc.
The Canadian Publishers
481 University Avenue
Toronto, Ontario
M5G 2E9

Printed and bound in Canada

Contents

Contributors

Jane Aronson received her Ph.D. from the University of Toronto in Community Health. Her area of interest is informal care of the elderly, particularly as it relates to women giving and receiving care. She is currently an assistant professor at the School of Social Work, McMaster University.

Carol Baines is a professor of Social Work at Ryerson Polytechnical Institute. Her research interests and publications have focused on the history of women, social work, and child welfare, which were the basis of her doctoral studies at the University of Toronto.

Pat Evans is an associate professor at the School of Social Work, Atkinson College, York University. She received her doctorate from the University of Toronto and is currently working on a comparative study of work and welfare policies for single mothers in Canada, the U.S., and Great Britain.

Evelyn Ferguson is completing her doctoral dissertation in social work at the University of Toronto with a study of child care. Her areas of interest also include family policy and feminist social work practice, and she has written on private adoption. She is an assistant professor in the Faculty of Social Work, University of Manitoba, and the mother of a pre-schooler.

Sheila Neysmith is a professor with the Faculty of Social Work at the University of Toronto. She received her doctorate in Social Welfare from Columbia University and her research and writing has focused on social policies and programs affecting women as they age in Canada and Third World countries.

Marge Reitsma-Street is an associate professor at the School of Social Work at Laurentian University and holds a doctorate from the University of Toronto. She is working in the areas of child poverty, juvenile justice policy, and correctional practice with young people and adults. A particular interest has been the development of conformity and delinquency in girls and women.

Karen Swift is a social policy analyst in Toronto and has recently received her doctorate from the University of Toronto. Her research and publications are in the area of child welfare and she is currently working on knowledge development in social work.

Imogen Taylor is a research fellow for the Department of Social Work at Bristol University, England. She has been an instructor at Ryerson and the University of Toronto, where she received her MSW, and continues to work in the area of violence against women.

Preface

This book is about women's caring. In it, we trace the implications of this invisible work, particularly as it connects to women's poverty, vulnerability, and disadvantage. Although literature that is both feminist and Canadian is expanding, this book is intended to contribute to the emerging debate about caring and to focus on the Canadian experience. We believe that a perspective on caring uncovers the complexities and ambiguities of women's relationship to the welfare state and their experiences as they negotiate the social service system. The themes and issues addressed here, while important to the field of social work, are also highly relevant to women's studies and to those individuals who are teaching, working, and studying in the fields of education, nursing, and child care.

This book represents the work of a number of women, but we offer it as more than a collection of individual essays. The focus and shape of the book developed from a series of lively and productive discussions among the three of us in the winter of 1989. The individual contributors responded with enthusiasm to the suggested framework and, in turn, made important comments and suggestions. Despite the cautionary tales we heard of the difficulties inherent in producing a book to which a number of people have contributed, we can only say that our experience could not have been better. We owe a very large debt of gratitude to our five contributing authors. Each one has used her expertise and research to enrich the literature on caring and social welfare and has helped the development of our thinking. On a more pragmatic level, we are also grateful for what must be a record - not one of them missed a deadline during this entire process, and each was open to our suggestions and editorial comments.

There were others who have also had an important role. Michael Harrison of McClelland & Stewart has, from the beginning, been a source of excellent advice and encouragement. The reviewers were extremely thoughtful and thorough, and we have done our best to incorporate a number of their very helpful suggestions. The end product, whatever its limitations, has been strengthened by their anonymous contribution as well as by colleagues who commented on specific chapters. We would also like to thank our families, who helped, and cared, in so many tangible and intangible ways.

Carol Baines
Pat Evans
Sheila Neysmith

Toronto
November, 1990

CHAPTER I

Caring: Its Impact on the Lives of Women

Carol T. Baines
Patricia M. Evans, and
Sheila M. Neysmith

INTRODUCTION

The work women do in providing care to others both within and outside of families is only beginning to be examined. Caring refers to the mental, emotional, and physical effort involved in looking after, responding to, and supporting others. In our society, most of this work is done by women in varying forms throughout their lives. It is done as mothers, daughters, and wives in the context of individual relationships, in the community as volunteers, through the professions of nursing, social work, and teaching, and as low-wage workers in hospitals, child-care centres, and homemaking services. The cared-for are usually persons whom we view as dependent, that is, they are children, individuals with mental or physical handicaps, and the frail elderly. However, within the family, recipients may also be independent male adults.

Women's caring work is largely invisible and is thus not considered part of our current definitions of labour, leisure, and parenting (Pascall, 1986; Daniels, 1987). An understanding of the complexities involved in caring and its accompanying costs and benefits has not been incorporated into the design of our social policies and formal services, nor has it been reflected in our expectations about families.

Feminists identify the family not only as the locus of personal attachments but as the central arena of economic and power relationships. A division of labour has evolved in which women have the major responsibility for caring while men take on the primary role of economic providers. This gendered division of labour creates a socially constructed dependency that, paradoxically for women, is the consequence of providing care to others, rather than the outcome of receiving care (Graham, 1983). The work women do within the family is often mirrored in their work outside the home: as child-care workers, as domestic and office cleaners, and as waitresses and factory workers in food preparation plants. The "caring" professions of teaching, nursing, and social work are those in which "the 'woman's touch' has been formally incorporated into the job specification" (Graham, 1983: 16). In the home, the work is unpaid and undervalued; in the workplace it is poorly paid and undervalued.

The price paid for caring is reflected most sharply in the lives of poor women who must absorb its costs without the buffer that the purchase of babysitting, cleaning, and other supplementary services provides. The services poor women do receive often flow through a welfare state, and these services frequently reinforce rather than diminish the negative consequences of caring. The accumulated impact on poor women of our current social construction of caring is a major focus of this book.

The contributions in this book cover a variety of topics, but all document the centrality of caring in women's lives, the way in which the obligations and expectations embodied in the imperative of caring shapes women's opportunities, and has significant costs and consequences for them. Policies, programs, and professional practice assume that caring is a female mandate, yet services are organized in ways that do not respond to, or take account of, the daily realities of women's lives. All of the chapters demonstrate how the welfare state has served as a powerful reinforcer of women's caring. Women already vulnerable and usually caring for others as single mothers, delinquent girls, elderly or abused women are all too often revictimized through the underlying familial ideology of the welfare state, which emphasizes the importance of women providing care but limits their ability to express their own needs for care.

The first section of the book develops theoretical and historical perspectives on women's caring. The ordinary expectations of women's caring are explored throughout the life cycle in the second section, with chapters on mothers caring for children, adolescents learning to care, and daughters caring for aging mothers. In the third section, three major issues that most clearly illustrate the intersection between women's caring, the family, and social welfare are examined in more detail – these are women's poverty, wife battering, and child neglect. The final chapter discusses several aspects of the current social construction of Canadian programs and policies, which must be changed if responsibility for providing care to vulnerable groups in our society is to be shared more equitably.

This book begins to develop a Canadian literature on caring. From the specific perspective of each author drawing on her own area of expertise, women's caring is examined in a variety of settings, its outcome on women caregivers and consumers is assessed, and the necessary changes in attitudes, services, and policies to recast the current division of caring responsibilities are explored. The impact of caring on the well-being of women is elaborated by examining how it shapes our private lives within the family as mothers, daughters, and wives, as well as our public roles as care providers and service users. The importance of integrating an ethic of care as an essential dimension in our analysis and development of social policies, programs, and professional practice is emphasized.

In this opening chapter we explore the concept of caring and examine the reasons why women are the primary caregivers. The intent is to uncover the complexities and contradictions of caring from the perspective of women. Women's experiences as clients, caregivers, and care providers within and outside the family have been different from men's experiences. Typically, however, the male perspective shapes the identification, development, and interpretation of knowledge and, as a result, women's experiences have been marginalized and rendered largely invisible. Correcting this androcentric view of human experience means more than filling in gaps with missing information. Rather, it requires a shift in theoretical perspectives, research methodologies, and agendas (for further discussion, see Hawkesworth, 1989; Jaggar and Bordo, 1989; Harding, 1987; and Keller, 1985).

CARING: WHAT IS IT?

Gillian Pascall (1986: 70) defines caring as human service work – "people work" – but it has not been recognized as work. Janet Finch and Dulcie Groves (1983) suggest that caring involves both love and labour, and it is precisely this combination that underlines its conceptual complexity. The provision of comfort and nurturing to children, an elderly mother, or a disabled member of a family is arduous work, but it is usually undertaken in a network of personal relationships in which emotions of affection are mixed with resentment, and norms of family responsibility and obligation are intertwined. Because caring is provided in the context of a supposedly freely entered relationship and regarded as "natural" for women, the labour involved is often rendered invisible.

It is possible to distinguish several contexts within which caring occurs (Waerness, 1984; Croft, 1986). First, *caregiving* frequently denotes situations in which someone may suffer or even die if not provided with care. These relationships usually involve one healthy adult while the other is a child or a

sick, elderly, or disabled person. However, another pattern of
care is *personal service*, in which caring takes place between
persons who can help themselves, although one partner
continually gives more practical help and emotional support
to the other. A third situation can be labelled *support among
friends* and is characterized by an equivalence of power.
Practical help and emotional support are given to each other
without counting on being "repaid" in equal amounts (Ve,
1984). Only in the latter situation is the relationship based in
mutuality. The first two situations, which reflect the current
circumstances of so much of women's caring, provide the
primary focus of the research presented in this book. The
potential for choice and the absence of power differentials
that typify the third context of care suggest a standard
against which the contemporary realities of women's caring
can be compared.

A further important distinction is made between the dimensions of caring *for* and caring *about* (Dalley, 1988; Tronto,
1989). The first refers to the instrumental and tangible tasks
involved in caring; the latter encompasses its expressive and
affective dimensions. As Hilary Graham (1983) suggests, the
special relations of caring are defined by both caring-as-
feelings and the transaction of goods and services. While the
notion of caring incorporates both labour and love, the assumption that they are inseparable can call into question the
integrity of a woman's caring *about* when she is no longer able
to care *for*. This is illustrated in the reaction toward mothers
who are perceived as neglectful, and the guilt experienced by
individuals who must relegate care of their aged or disabled
relatives to institutions, themes explored by Karen Swift in
Chapter VIII and Jane Aronson in Chapter V.

Most caring work occurs within families, but the demand
for caring services has increased. This demand is particularly
evident with respect to the very young and the very old,
although, as we shall see in Evelyn Ferguson's discussion of
child care in Chapter III and Sheila Neysmith's assessment of
long-term care policies in Chapter IX, the response is still
very limited. Women are the principal care-providers in the
commercial (for-profit) organizations, in non-profit agencies,
and in publicly funded institutions providing services for the

young, individuals with handicaps, and the elderly. The pattern in which poorly paid women provide care to vulnerable populations has been evident throughout the development and expansion of health and social services in Canada and it continues into the present. The most common reason young women enter the human service professions is a desire to help others and serve society, and indeed nursing, social work, and teaching have recognized the importance of a commitment to an ethic of care in recruiting members to their professions. Therefore, the entanglement of caring for and caring about extends to situations of formal caregiving. Foster mothers, for example, who pressure to obtain better wages to care *for*, are likely to be challenged for not adequately caring *about*.

An exploration of the concept of caring is not an easy task – Gillian Dalley (1988: 8) suggests that it is surrounded by "a minefield of confusion." Part of this confusion derives from the way the dual nature of caring – the aspects of labour and love – has been divided and fragmented according to disciplinary boundaries. Sociology traditionally has divided work and family into separate analytic categories, while psychologists have focused on the emotional and psychological aspects of women's caring but ignored its physical and tangible demands (Pascall, 1986; Graham, 1983). The challenge that Pascall (1986: 71) poses is the development of an "analysis which can contain both love and labour, which can take seriously both the emotional and material understandings of caring and of why women do it." The next section outlines some of the major explanations for women's caring that are found in the literature, followed by a discussion of the interconnected influences that have shaped the female ethic of care. These include patriarchy, the "family ethic," and socialization. The section ends with a consideration of the differences between the caring men do and women's caring.

WHY DO WOMEN CARE?

Women's caring has traditionally been viewed, not as work, but as a form of relating to others that comes naturally to women, arising from the biological differences between men and women. These differences have provided a pervasive and persistent rationale for circumscribing women's role to the home. In the past, equality was viewed as a danger to women's health and reproductive capacities (Sayers, 1982). Similar arguments were used to reinforce women's role as nurturers and carers and to discourage women from entering medicine and higher education (Strong-Boag, 1979). While biological differences between the sexes do exist, Pat Armstrong and Hugh Armstrong (1984) point out that there has been little consistency in the implications that these differences have had for men and women over time and across cultures. In addition, technological innovations in the production process have reduced the significance of physical strength, while advances in birth control have given women increased control over their bodies.

Today the message of biological determinism continues to be echoed in the concerns of what Eichler (1988) calls the "patriarchal family movement." Although the contemporary messages are not delivered with the same level of consensus, explicitness, or vigour as in the past, all the authors contributing to this volume, from a range of perspectives and different foci, reveal the contemporary strength of the imperative to care and detail its attendant costs. An understanding of why the messages of caring are directed to women involves an appreciation of the inextricable linkages between socialization, patriarchy, and the relations of family and labour in advanced industrialized societies.

The notion that caring comes "naturally" to women fails to consider the significance of the socially patterned roles and the processes of socialization through which sex is translated into gender as women and men learn to incorporate into their behaviour and attitudes, assumptions related to masculine and feminine roles. Important dynamics differentiate the socialization of girls and women from boys and men. It is women who learn to take their place in society as informal caregivers to children and elderly relatives, and who transfer this to the public sphere and provide formal caring services as cleaners, child-minders, and teachers. Unlike their male counterparts, females are encouraged to identify with others and to develop altruistic patterns of interaction (Noddings, 1984). Nancy Chodorow (1978) reminds us that it is primarily women who mother, that daughters identify with their mothers, and thus relational issues assume a greater importance for girls. In contrast, boys learn to separate from their mothers in order to identify with their fathers, and in this process they become less concerned about emotional attachments. Jenny, one of the college students interviewed by Carol Gilligan (1982: 136), comments on what she learned from her mother:

> If I could grow up to be like anyone in the world, it would be my mother, because I've just never met such a selfless person. She would do anything for anybody, up to a point that she has hurt herself a lot because she just gives so much to other people and asks nothing in return. So, ideally, that's what you'd like to be, a person who is selfless and giving.

As Carol Gilligan's (1982: 160) interviews with women indicate, their "identity is defined in a context of relationship and judged by a standard of responsibility and care." Marge Reitsma-Street's research, presented in Chapter IV, invokes a similar theme – she finds that by the time a girl is a teenager, the mandate to care is firmly established.

Women's focus on interpersonal relationships has been viewed as limiting their development as rational adults, while our culture's prevailing theories regarding moral development have evolved with reference to men. Piaget's research on rule-making in children's games, for example, was developed from patterns of behaviour observed in boys, but was assumed to apply equally well to girls. The same criticism is made of Kohlberg's stages of moral development, which emphasize a male-oriented objective and abstract approach to moral reasoning while relational and contextual aspects are neglected. These are examples of how knowledge has been shaped from the male perspective. The result is that not only are women measured with reference to male criteria but women's patterns of interaction are not examined or understood (see Gilligan, 1982; Caplan, 1985, for a thorough critique of male bias in psychological theory).

The ideology of motherhood and femininity also supports and transmits the ethic of care. As Ann Duffy (1988: 114) points out, it is not simply economic inequality and the burdens of domestic labour that account for women's subordinate position: "Prevailing ideas about women's lives, including the dogma of romantic love and the cult of maternalism, are so pervasive and powerful that they discourage women from exploring alternative ways of living." By examining the socialization of women, we may begin to understand the process by which girls and women assimilate the expectations and norms that surround caring in our society, and we can as well appreciate how the ethic of care is transmitted. However, such an examination does not explain how this ethic originated and the reasons why it is attached to women rather than men. To address this, we must situate women's caring within the patriarchal relations that characterize advanced industrialized societies.

The concept of patriarchy is not new, although its use has become more frequent as feminists have worked to develop a theoretical base from which to understand the subordinate position of women. While there are many differences in the way the term is used, a common element is a focus on "men's power, authority or dominance" (Dahlerup, 1987: 95). Patriarchy is a term used to describe those "near-universal social forces" that result in a general dominance of men over women, although its particular form may vary over time and place (Dalley, 1988: 37–38). Feminist historians find considerable evidence to support the enduring nature of patriarchy (Lerner, 1986). The justification for terming a society "patriarchal" is provided by a Danish feminist, Drude Dahlerup (1987: 97–98), whose country has in many respects progressed much further than ours. She comments:

> The answer is that in our society on average women earn much less than men, that in general women advance less than men and hold inferior jobs, that women carry a double burden of work, are raped, battered, and subject to physical violence by men and to sexual harassment at work; that political institutions, the political parties and trade unions are dominated by men and finally that girls and women are

deprecated by men – and by themselves. Girls' and women's lower self-esteem is general. These are some of our reasons to label it a patriarchal society.

Particularly important to an understanding of patriarchy is women's role in reproduction – giving birth and rearing the next generation – although feminists differ in their interpretations and emphases. Radical feminists find the roots of patriarchy in women's reproductive capacity and the control men exercise over it. They have been particularly concerned with issues of abortion, contraception, and forms of male violence, including wife abuse and pornography. Their focus has been on the domination of men over women's lives in the private sphere. Because of their emphasis on the universality of women's experience, they have been criticized for verging on biological determinism and failing to consider how class, race, and ethnicity intersect with patriarchy to produce important differences among women (Abramovitz, 1988; Beechey, 1987).

Marxist and socialist feminists centre their analyses on understanding the relationship between capitalism and patriarchy, and have directed their attention to the significance of women's unpaid, reproductive labour. Thus they extend a Marxist analytic framework beyond its emphasis on production to examine reproduction – the bearing and rearing of children – and the nurturance given to those already in the work force. Its emphasis on women's role in reproducing and maintaining the work force has been criticized for an "economistic tendency to see the human results of reproduction solely as labourers in the capitalists' vineyards" (Pascall, 1986: 22). However, this perspective helped to bring women's labour out of the household closet, explored its connections to other forms of work, and began to integrate domestic labour into a feminist analysis of the family, the economy, and the state. It is not possible to understand the structural roots of caring without giving attention to the interrelationship of patriarchy and capitalism, the way they play out in women's labour at home and in the workplace and influence our expectations of the roles and obligations of different family members.

The development of modern industrial society shaped contemporary expectations regarding women's caring. Unlike pre-industrial societies in which men, women, and children all contributed to the family economy, capitalism created a sharp divide between the public world of men centred in the waged labour market and the locus of women's domestic labour within the private domain of the household. The market economy's emphasis on the "productive" value of men's work helped to obscure the significance and visibility of women's work and contributed to the emergence of a nuclear, autonomous family model dependent on the wage of a male "breadwinner." This gendered division of labour has important implications for the undervaluing of women's participation and experience in the labour market. Women were not expected to be primary breadwinners, although there were periods, such as the Second World War, when the work of women in the paid labour force was required. However, when the war ended and their use as reserve labour had finished, the newly created day nurseries were closed and the men returned to the factories while women went back to the home. The view of women as temporary workers, working for "pin money," is still used to justify their relegation to the low-paid and insecure secondary labour market. The connection between women's work in the home, their employment, and their poverty is explored by Pat Evans in Chapter VI.

Mimi Abramovitz (1988: 2) has identified those norms that govern the contemporary sexual division of labour as the "family ethic," which "articulates the terms of women's work and family roles." The family is often regarded as the fundamental unit of patriarchy, and it is certainly the central locus for the caring work women do. Particularly important to feminist theory has been the analysis of the political (power) and economic relations embedded in the social construction of the family. As one writer (Rayna Rapp, cited in Epstein, 1988: 161) comments:

> One of the more valuable achievements of feminist theory has been its effort to 'deconstruct the family as a natural unit, and to reconstruct it as a social unit' – as ideology, as

an institutional nexus of social relationships and cultural meanings.

Ann Duffy (1988) identifies four common themes in feminist analyses of family ideology (sometimes referred to as familism) that are important to this reconstruction. These are that: (1) the family's economic and social structure is rooted in and supports the power of the husband/father; (2) the roles of wife/mother serve to restrict women's lives; (3) the prevailing norms deny women real choices in their decisions regarding marriage and child-bearing; and (4) the subordination of women within the family extends to a generalized loss of power in the larger society. This is a helpful framework to explain why the ideology of the family ethic remains a powerful image in spite of the fact that fewer than one-quarter of Canadian families with children conform to the breadwinner/dependant model (Boyd, 1988).

Women, of course, are not the only ones who provide care. Although some men provide care, there are important differences. They generally have more choice about the caring work they do. There is no paternal equivalent to the concept of "maternal" bonding that has fueled the ideology of motherhood, helping to equate "bad" children and a disadvantaged environment with maternal deprivation (Mandell, 1988). While some men do care for elderly and disabled relatives, they do not take on primary responsibility in the same numbers that women do. Moreover, when sons take on the care of elderly parents, they are viewed as exceptional and are likely to receive more services from the formal sector than their sisters (Guberman, 1988; Arber *et al.*, 1988). For men, the caring *about* is more easily separated from the caring *for*. As Dalley (1988) points out, the expectation for men to care about is generally exercised through taking responsibility for arranging the provision of care. As the family breadwinner, for example, he may provide care by purchasing paid help or offering the services of his wife. For women, caring *for* and caring *about* are usually entangled in a web of emotions, socially constructed expectations, and their own sense of obligation.

Some suggest that the gendered expectations of caring are

changing, although they may be masked at times by contradictory trends in fathering. That is, we see the emergence of the "good dads," who are more involved than ever before, and the "bad dads," who find it easier than ever before to sever the connections with their children (Furstenberg, 1988; Holter, 1984). While it is true that maternal employment is no longer conventionally regarded as "deviant," there is little to suggest that husbands are more significant participants on the domestic labour front. A Canadian study found that husbands with wives employed full-time spend 1.32 hours per day on housework and child care, in comparison to the 1.09 spent by the husbands of non-employed women (Canadian Advisory Council on the Status of Women, 1987). In short, while some men take responsibility for caring, their identities and their opportunities are not structured and shaped by the same behavioural norms regarding caring with which women contend. The assumption that men do and should have primary responsibility for providing care to those around them is not likely to be reflected in their own expectations, the expectations of those around them, or in policies and services.

This section has sketched out some of the major analytic perspectives that inform our understanding of women's caring. The interaction between patriarchy, the organization of the market economy, and the idealized form of the nuclear family can only be briefly addressed here, and our discussion can only hint at some of the debates that characterize the literature. The development of the caring literature builds on feminist analyses of women's unpaid labour. It extends, however, beyond a strictly functional view of this labour, and while not diminishing attention to the costs of caring, the important social and affectional relations embedded in caring are acknowledged, as well as its personal significance to women.

CARING AND SOCIAL WELFARE

Women, caring, and social welfare are linked in three important ways. First, many social welfare policies and programs are rooted in the assumption that women are primarily responsible for the care of family members: the mother is the usual focus for intervention in child welfare; the wife tends her aging spouse; the daughter is called on to care for elderly parents. At the federal level, our inability to come to terms with the need for a national child-care policy reflects just how strongly entrenched is the moral imperative for women to care and the costs it imposes on them. In most provinces, women who live with men are eligible for social assistance only as dependants. In the field of aging, the growing emphasis on "community care" rarely acknowledges its reliance on the availability and readiness of women to provide care.

Because it is assumed that a person's need for care should be met within the family, services designed to replace or supplement this care are minimal, stigmatizing to the care recipient, and rationed according to the availability of female kin. A second link between women, caring, and social welfare is now apparent: when caring is provided by the state, the work is usually done by women as poorly paid child-care workers, nursing attendants, and homemakers. As Carol Baines explores in Chapter II, women's early efforts to expand their public role were based on an ethic of care now embedded in the professions of social work, teaching, and nursing.

Finally, women, most often poor women, are the primary consumers of social services (Andrew, 1984; Davis and Brook, 1985), although the services they seek are frequently required on behalf of children, husbands, and other relatives (Lewis, 1986; Rose, 1986). The reasons for this, and its implications for women, are an important theme of this book, a theme we believe is best understood through a perspective that recognizes the centrality and impact of caring in women's lives.

Social welfare policies and services, the cornerstones of a welfare state, are supposed to reflect principles of social justice, fairness, and equity. These concepts, as currently defined and operationalized, have not incorporated gender and thus do not reflect the priorities and experience of women. The critical stream of social policy literature that emerged in the last decade (Walker, 1983, 1984; Mishra, 1984; Djao, 1983; LeGrand, 1982; Moscovitch and Drover, 1981;

George and Wilding, 1976; Gough, 1979) developed in response to what is now known as the "fiscal crisis" of the state. This focus has tended to marginalize both gender and race as causal factors for explaining inequalities in the distribution of resources. Gender and race are noted as important dimensions for understanding the effects of the inequities that riddle a market economy, forces the welfare state attempts to ameliorate, however unsuccessfully. However, the fundamental problem is seen as being located within a political economy based on the precepts of free enterprise and capital accumulation.

In contrast, feminist analysis starts from quite a different premise. Economic systems, whether capitalist or socialist, may shape the forms of oppression that women experience but they are not its cause. Patriarchal relations create inequities that interact with specific economic systems to produce a dominance of men in the economic and domestic workplace. These relations must be directly challenged if women are to become full partners in Canadian society. It is not surprising, then, that the feminist perspective has identified mutuality in relationships and collective co-operation as the values conducive to redistributing the costs and benefits of caring between men, women, and the state.

Analyses of social policies typically examine rules and practices used in the distribution and redistribution of society's resources, and attempt to weigh the costs and benefits to various groups. However, the identification of problems and needs and the determination of their costs and benefits will reflect particular values and attitudes, depending on the arena or target group selected for attention. Programs, for example, are routinely examined for their impact on families. Feminist writers have pointed out that families are made up of individuals and that what is good for the family as a social institution is not necessarily equally good for its individual members (Eichler, 1988; Wilson, 1983). Jane Aronson in Chapter V unravels the stresses and strains on both aging mothers and caregiving daughters and critiques community care policies that assume family care is the best care. In Chapter VI, Pat Evans discusses the impact of the "breadwinner" model of the family on women's poverty, while Imogen Taylor demonstrates in Chapter VII how women's efforts to protect themselves and their children from violence are impeded by caring commitments as well as economic dependence, values that underpin our concept of "the family."

Women's relationship to the welfare state is an ambivalent one. It is the source of both protection and control, but the latter aspect has received less attention. Mimi Abramovitz (1988), in her examination of the relationship between women and social welfare policy in the United States, suggests that the particular targets of control and regulation have been women who have veered from their traditional role as guardians of the home – those, for example, who were viewed as not providing proper care to their children. Karen Swift's chapter examines this emphasis on the "neglecting" mother and the experiences of women as clients of the child welfare system.

Social control as exercised by the state has been an important influence and regulator of caring in women's lives, but women are not simply passive victims. Linda Gordon (1988), in her analysis of case records of social agencies in Boston between 1860 and 1960, documents the strengths women brought to bear in their efforts to deal with problems of violence and child neglect. They frequently sought intervention from child protection agencies and were instrumental in shaping the policies of these agencies. They also developed their own strategies of resisting what they considered unfair treatment within the family and community, strategies Marge Reitsma-Street identifies and conceptually develops in her discussion of delinquent and non-delinquent girls.

DEVELOPING SERVICES TO PROVIDE CARE

For women as clients and providers, the professionalization of health and social services has involved gains and losses. In the early phase of social work, as Carol Baines discusses in Chapter II, Canadian women were instrumental in initiating and managing services for women and children. As the twentieth century unfolded, private voluntary services gradually became part of the bureaucratic and professional technology of the welfare state. The incorporation of caring services into the welfare state has produced a hierarchical bureaucracy and a division of labour that reflect the traditional demarcation of roles in families. Nursing, social work, and teaching, frequently designated as "semi-professions," all reflect the subordinate role of women who have provided the direct service under the control of male managers.

Providing care is the *raison d'être* of an increasing proportion of health and social services. Some services target persons with transitory dependencies who are viewed as on their way to becoming independent, contributing members of society. These include services to children, individuals in acute-care hospitals, and adults who require short-term therapy. Many persons, however, such as the chronically ill and individuals with physical and developmental handicaps, need long-term care in order to fulfil even the basic activities of daily living. The young and temporarily disabled have formed the client base upon which teachers, nurses, therapists, and social workers have developed their professional models of practice. The success of several traditionally female occupations in articulating skills and specifying interventions with such client groups has allowed them to lay claim to a knowledge and expertise that formed the basis for demands for better wages and working conditions. While professional workers have gained more status, however, front-line caregivers, such as child-care workers, homemakers, and residential workers, remain among the lowest paid, and many of the people doing this work belong to the most disadvantaged groups in our society, immigrant women and women of colour.

The issue of "community care" as an important alternative to large-scale institutional care for the physically and developmentally handicapped has placed the provision of care for those viewed as dependent firmly in the public arena. Although the negative effects of large institutions were a motivating factor, the move to deinstitutionalize was also fueled by a desire to contain costs (see Angus, 1987, for Canadian data, and Estes *et al.*, 1983, for U.S. data). This has produced a disjuncture in the language, the outcome of which is the realization that "deinstitutionalization" is not the same as "community care."

An extensive North American literature documents the effects of what is now referred to as "the burden of care" on the well-being of female family members who care for physically and/or mentally incapacitated elderly persons (see, for example, Cantor, 1983; Brody, 1985; Brody et al., 1987; George and Gwyther, 1986). Despite this accumulating evidence, services continue to reflect traditional assumptions regarding the expectations of women and the provision of care (Fitting et al., 1986; Quayhagen and Quayhagen, 1988; Pruchno and Resch, 1989; Morycz, 1985). For example, a variety of programs are available to support family carers: respite care, day care, support groups, home helps. The evaluation of these services has consistently been positive on the part of family carers (Lawton et al., 1989). It is important to note, however, that these services build on and reinforce family-based care. They cannot operate unless a family carer is available. As Jane Aronson's chapter so graphically depicts, this image of family care as the ideal locus of care is so powerful, most women never consider that they have a choice.

Feminist social policy literature recognizes that the current emphasis on community-based care really refers to care given by the family – and that means care given mostly by women. Yet this is occurring at a time in which demographic changes and the increasing participation of women in the paid labour force are limiting the traditional supply of unpaid caring labour. This has contributed to the attention that caregiving is receiving. By the mid-eighties a feminist literature was developing in response to the exploitation of the unpaid care provided by women. Finch and Groves's A Labour of Love (1983) was the first major feminist work addressing the costs of caring to women. This was quickly followed by other writing critical of community care policy (see, for example, Land and Rose, 1985; Pascall, 1986; Dalley, 1988; Qureshi and Walker, 1986; Hooyman, 1990). Several British books developing a feminist research and policy agenda on caregiving have recently appeared (Ungerson, 1987; Dalley, 1988; Lewis and Meredith, 1988). This book contributes a Canadian perspective to this literature.

Although we are primarily concerned with the way in which caring shapes the lives of women providing the care, an examination of caring cannot be separated from the consequences it has for those who are cared for. The demands placed on women's caring and the lack of support and recognition it receives seriously impede the relationship between those caring and those in need of care. The devaluation of caring, coupled with its invisibility, can place those who are cared for, whether family members or clients of human service organizations, in a position of extreme dependency on others. Thus it is not caring that becomes the problem but the burden of caring experienced both by women who care and by those who are cared for. A feminist approach to caring seeks to provide an analysis of the ideological context that shapes the relationship between the cared for and the carers and identifies strategies allowing women choices and control over their lives.

TOWARD AN ANALYSIS OF CARING

The discussion thus far has portrayed caring as a responsibility women bear, and it would be difficult to overemphasize the strain this has placed on women's lives. The increase in numbers of women in the labour force, for example, has drawn attention to the "double" or "triple" day, as women take on employment without a concomitant reduction in household and community responsibilities. It is increasingly recognized that policies directed at diminishing the inequalities women face in the labour market will have little effect unless there are changes in their domestic and child-care responsibilities. The costs of caring are similarly documented in the literature, which identifies the physical and emotional strain borne by those women who care for elderly and disabled family members. Individual chapters in this book add to this literature by exploring how this continues to shape women's lives in both the private and public worlds. Several recurrent themes emerge. All the authors highlight the relative invisibility of women's caring, the implicit assumption that it is natural for women to care, the lack of attention paid to the complexities involved in caring, and the contradictions caring poses for women. Committed to a belief that it is their duty to care, women find the need to express their own individuality and exercise choices in their lives is limited. This is not only at great cost to women themselves but to the larger society as well.

The caring of women, whether for children, the elderly, or other vulnerable groups, includes both the practical day-to-day work of running households and the invisible emotional work of identifying and anticipating the needs of others. Combining the affective dimension of caring for young children with the often tedious work of attending to their physical needs is highlighted in the child-care crisis in Canada, discussed by Evelyn Ferguson in Chapter III. Juggling the needs of family members takes an incredible toll on women's lives both in a material way, as Pat Evans explores in relation to the poverty of women in Chapter VI, and in the emotional domain, as Jane Aronson argues in Chapter V in her discussion of the high expectations placed on women to be "dutiful and undemanding."

The lack of validation for women's caring obscures the work involved and reinforces the idea that this is the natural work of women. In a society that values paid work in the public sphere, the work of women's caring in the private sphere has received little attention. The resultant costs for women who fail to conform to the expected ethic of women's caring fall heaviest on those who are deemed neglectful, as illustrated by Karen Swift in Chapter VIII, on those who are abused, as Imogen Taylor discusses in Chapter VII, and on young girls who challenge the traditional feminine role, as Marge Reitsma-Street examines in Chapter IV. The costs to middle-class women who have entered the women-dominated professions have also been evident, as Carol Baines explores in the historical perspective she provides in Chapter II. When caring is transferred to the public sphere, it continues to remain invisible and undervalued and the status of women who are responsible for public caring is only marginally enhanced.

Addressing the burden of women's caring is complicated by the reality that caring is also a labour of love and involves relationships of profound importance to those who do the caring, as well as to those who are cared for. Gillian Pascall (1986: 72) comments: "The unsharing of caring can be counted and costed; but those who bear that cost are not clamouring to hand their children or their mothers over to the government." We can understand caring as a manifestation of love when it is given to another within the private sphere of personal and family relationships. We can also understand it as a form of tending to the needs of strangers when it is provided in the public sphere as a service.

An analysis of women's role in caring needs to examine the ways in which the private and public worlds of women intersect. Women experience these boundaries as artificial. Despite the problems that the polarization of the public and private worlds have posed for women, the chapters in this book demonstrate the various strategies different groups of women use in their attempts to negotiate this problematic divide.

The concept of separate spheres may hinder rather than further our understanding of activities that involve both labour and love. Such a classification clarifies some of the divisions that exist today but it does not necessarily help us to transcend the traditional dualism of public/private, paid/unpaid work, and family/state. In an attempt to bridge these worlds, the analyses in this book reflect a theoretical perspective on the part of the editors that is both woman-centred and attempts to step outside of traditionally male-oriented paradigms. At this moment in time the social construction of caring in our society affects the quality of women's lives in a very different way from that of men. As feminists we also recognize the challenges and dilemmas inherent in advocating for expanded choices for women at the same time as we are committed to building a more caring society.

The final chapter builds on this perspective as it examines options for the future. What are the implications of developing models of care that do not impose disproportionate costs on women? It will mean more than shoring up and compensating the caregiving endeavours of female kin or expanding services and instituting good wages for paid service providers. Rather, Sheila Neysmith suggests that caring must be moved to centre stage in future policy discussions, change has to occur simultaneously on several fronts, and the separate-spheres concept is best used as the starting point rather than the conclusion of the debate.

REFERENCES

Abramovitz, M. 1988. *Regulating the Lives of Women: Social Welfare Policy from Colonial Times to the Present*. Boston: South End Press.

Andrew, C. 1984. "Women and the Welfare State," *Canadian Journal of Political Science*, xvii, 4: 667–83.

Angus, D. 1987. "Health Care Costs: A Review of Past Experience and Potential Impact of The Aging Phenomenon," in Coburn, D'Arcy, Torrance, and New, eds., *Health and Canadian Society*, Second Edition. Toronto: Fitzhenry and Whiteside.

Arber, S., G. Gilbert, and M. Evanrou. 1988. "Gender, Household Composition and the Receipt of Domiciliary Services by Elderly Disabled Persons," *Journal of Social Policy*, xvii, 2: 153–75.

Armstrong, Pat, and Hugh Armstrong. 1984. *Double Ghetto: Canadian Women and Their Segregated Work*. Toronto: McClelland and Stewart.

Beechey, V. 1987. *Unequal Work*. London: Verso.

Boyd, M. 1988. "Changing Canadian Family Forms: Issues for Women," in N. Mandell and A. Duffy, eds., *Reconstructing the Canadian Family: Feminist Perspectives*. Toronto: Butterworths.

Brody, E. 1985. "Parent Care as a Normative Family Stress," *Gerontologist*, xxv: 19–29.

Brody, E., M. Kleban, P. Johnsen, C. Hoffman, C. Schoonover. 1987. "Work Status and Parent Care: A Comparison of Four Groups of Women," *Gerontologist*, xxvii, 2: 201–08.

Canadian Advisory Council on the Status of Women. 1987. *Integration and Participation: Women's Work in the Home and in the Labour Force*. Ottawa: CASSW.

Cantor, M. 1983. "Strain Among Caregivers: A Study of Experience in the United States," *Gerontologist*, xxiii: 597–604.

Caplan, P.J. 1985. *The Myth of Women's Masochism*. New York: E.P. Dutton.

Chodorow, N. 1978. *The Reproduction of Mothering*. Berkeley: University of California Press.

Croft, S. 1986. "Women, Caring and the Recasting of Need – A Feminist Reappraisal," *Critical Social Policy*, #16: 23–39.

Dahlerup, D. 1987. "Confusing Concepts – Confusing Reality: A Theoretical Discussion of the Patriarchal State," in A. Showstack

Sassoon, ed., *Women and the State: The Shifting Boundaries of Public and Private*. London: Hutchinson.

Dalley, G. 1988. *Ideologies of Caring: Rethinking Community and Collectivism*. London: Macmillan.

Daniels, A. 1987. "Invisible Work," *Social Problems*, 34, 5: 403–15.

Davis, A., and E. Brook. 1985. "Women and Social Work," in Brook and Davis, eds., *Women, the Family and Social Work*. London: Tavistock.

Djao, A. 1983. *Inequality and Social Justice*. Toronto: John Wiley and Sons.

Duffy, A. 1988. "Struggling with Power: Feminist Critiques of Family Inequality," in N. Mandell and A. Duffy, eds., *Reconstructing the Canadian Family: Feminist Perspectives*. Toronto: Butterworths.

Eichler, M. 1988. *Families in Canada Today: Recent Changes and Their Policy Consequences*, Second Edition. Toronto: Gage.

Epstein, C. 1988. "Toward a Family Policy: Changes in Mothers' Lives," in A. Cherlin, ed., *Changing American Family and Public Policy*. Washington, D.C.: Urban Institute.

Estes, C., R. Newcomer, and Associates. 1983. *Fiscal Austerity and Aging: Shifting Government Responsibility for the Elderly*. Beverly Hills: Sage Publications.

Finch, J., and D. Groves, eds. 1983. *A Labour of Love: Women, Work and Caring*. London: Routledge and Kegan Paul.

Fitting, M., P. Rabins, M.J. Lucas, J. Eastham. 1986. "Caregivers for Dementia Parents: A Comparison of Husbands and Wives," *Gerontologist*, xxvi, 3: 248–53.

Furstenberg, F. 1988. "Good Dads – Bad Dads: Two Faces of Fatherhood," in Cherlin, ed., *Changing American Family and Public Policy*.

George, L., and L. Gwyther. 1986. "Caregiver Well-being: A Multidimensional Examination of Family Caregivers of Demented Adults," *Gerontologist*, xxvi, 3: 253–59.

George, V., and P. Wilding. 1976. *Ideology and Social Welfare*. London: Routledge and Kegan Paul.

Gilligan, C. 1982. *In a Different Voice*. Cambridge, Mass.: Harvard University Press.

Gordon, L. 1988. *Heroes in Their Own Lives: The Politics and History of Family Violence*. New York: Viking Press.

Gough, I. 1979. *The Political Economy of the Welfare State*. London: Macmillan.

Graham, H. 1983. "Caring: A Labour of Love," in Finch and Groves, eds., *A Labour of Love*.

Guberman, N. 1988. "The Family, Women and Caring: Who Cares for the Carers?" *Resources for Feminist Research*, xvii, 2: 37–40.

Harding, S., ed. 1987. *Feminism and Methodology*. Bloomington: Indiana University Press.

Hawkesworth, M.E. 1989. "Knowers, Knowing, Known: Feminist Theory and Claims of Truth," *Signs: Journal of Women in Culture and Society*, XIV, 3: 535–57.

Holter, H. 1984. "Women's Research and Social Theory," in Holter, ed., *Patriarchy in a Welfare Society*. Oslo: Universitetsforlaget.

Hooyman, N. 1990. "Women as Caregivers of the Elderly: Implications for Social Welfare Policy and Practice," in D. Biegel and A. Blum, eds., *Aging and Caregiving: Theory, Research, and Policy*. Newbury Park, Calif.: Sage Publications.

Jaggar, A., and S. Bordo, eds. 1989. *Gender/Body/Knowledge: Feminist Reconstructions of Being and Knowing*. New Brunswick, N.J.: Rutgers University Press.

Keller, E. 1985. *Reflections on Gender and Science*. New Haven: Yale University Press.

Land, H., and H. Rose. 1985. "Compulsory Altruism for Some or an Altruistic Society for All?" in P. Bean, J. Ferris, and D. Whynes, eds., *In Defence of Welfare*. London: Tavistock.

Lawton, M.P., E. Brody, A. Saperstein. 1989. "A Controlled Study of Respite Service for Caregivers of Alzheimer's Patients," *Gerontologist*, XXIX, 1: 8–16.

LeGrand, J. 1982. *The Strategy of Equality: Redistribution and the Social Services*. London: George Allen and Unwin.

Lerner, G. 1986. *The Creation of Patriarchy*. New York: Oxford University Press.

Lewis, J. 1986. "Feminism and Welfare," in J. Mitchell and A. Oakley, eds., *What is Feminism? A Re-examination*. New York: Pantheon Press.

Lewis, J., and B. Meredith. 1988. *Daughters Who Care*. London and New York: Routledge.

Mandell, N. 1988. "The Child Question: Links Between Women and Children in the Family," in N. Mandell and A. Duffy, eds., *Reconstructing the Canadian Family: Feminist Perspectives*. Toronto: Butterworths.

Mishra, R. 1984. *The Welfare State in Crisis: Social Thought and Social Change*. Brighton, England: The Harvester Press.

Morycz, R. 1985. "Caregiver Strain and the Desire to Institutionalize Family Members with Alzheimer's Disease," *Research on Aging*, VII, 3: 329–61.

Moscovitch, A., and G. Drover, eds. 1981. *Inequality: Essays on the Political Economy of Social Welfare*. Toronto: University of Toronto Press.

Noddings, N. 1984. *Caring: A Feminine Approach to Ethics*. Berkeley: University of California Press.

Pascall, G. 1986. *Social Policy: A Feminist Analysis*. London: Tavistock.

Pruchno, R., and N. Resch. 1989. "Husbands and Wives as Caregivers: Antecedents of Depression and Burden," *Gerontologist*, xxix, 2: 159–65.

Quayhagen, M., and M. Quayhagen. 1988. "Alzheimer's Stress: Coping with the Caregiving Role," *Gerontologist*, xxviii, 3: 291–96.

Qureshi, H., and A. Walker. 1986. "Caring for Elderly People: The Family and the State," in C. Phillipson and A. Walker, eds., *Aging and Social Policy: A Critical Assessment*. Brookfield, Vermont: Gower.

Rose, H. 1986. "Women and the Restructuring of the Welfare State," in E. Oyen, ed., *Comparing Welfare States and Their Futures*. Brookfield, Vermont: Gower.

Sayers, J. 1982. *Biological Politics: Feminist and Anti-Feminist Perspectives*. London: Tavistock.

Strong-Boag, V. 1979. "Canada's Women Doctors: Feminism Constrained," in L. Kealey, ed., *A Not Unreasonable Claim: Women and Reform in Canada, 1880's-1920's*. Toronto: Women's Press.

Tronto, J. 1989. "Women and Caring: What Can Feminists Learn About Morality from Caring," in Jaggar and Bordo, eds., *Gender/Body/Knowledge*.

Ungerson, C. 1987. *Policy is Personal: Sex, Gender and Informal Care*. London: Tavistock.

Ve, H. 1984. "Women's Mutual Alliances: Altruism as a Premise for Interaction," in Holter, ed., *Patriarchy in a Welfare Society*.

Waerness, K. 1984. "Caring as Women's Work in the Welfare State," in Holter, ed., *Patriarchy in a Welfare Society*.

Walker, A. 1983. "Social Policy, Social Administration, and the Social Construction of Welfare," in M. Loney, D. Boswell, and J. Clarke, eds., *Social Policy and Social Welfare*. Milton Keynes, England: Open University Press.

Walker, A. 1984. *Social Planning: A Strategy for Socialist Welfare*. London: Routledge and Kegan Paul.

Wilson, E. 1983. "Feminism and Social Policy," in Loney, Boswell, and Clarke, eds., *Social Policy and Social Welfare*.

CHAPTER II

The Professions and
an Ethic of Care

Carol T. Baines

INTRODUCTION

One of the major contradictions facing women who enter the
so-called women's professions of nursing, social work, and
teaching is, according to Barbara Finklestein, that they need
to be "saints, fools or sentimental idealists" (Finklestein, 1989:
94). In the 1990s, these professions are for the first time facing
competition as women flock to the more prestigious "male"
professions of law, medicine, and engineering.[1] While the
increased options may signal greater equality, part of the
explanation for this change can be found in the way the
women-dominated professions have been undervalued and

under-rewarded. The reality may be that women have begun to believe that the work they do in these fields has little value (Daniels, 1987; Finklestein, 1989). The high turnover in these professions suggests that this may well be the case.

Through an historical perspective, this chapter analyses the influence of an ethic of care on the evolution of social work, nursing, and teaching. Unlike other chapters in this book, it is focused on an examination of women's caring in the public sphere. It emphasizes the ways in which caring has shaped the public role of women and the division of labour in these occupations. Two main themes emerge: first, the relationship between maternal feminism and caring; second, the tension women have experienced in combining caring and professionalism.

In the last two decades, historians of women have identified maternal feminism as the underlying ideology that spurred the movement of women into the public sphere during the first wave of feminism. Determined to play a useful role in a society in flux, women transferred the values and caring functions they had learned and practised within the home and the community to new fields of work. The paradox was that, although maternal feminism provided women with a rationale to work outside the home and served to unite women, it also reinforced the traditional role of women as caregivers. Women today continue to struggle with reconciling the contradictions in exercising their right to autonomy and equality without abandoning an ethic of care.

The second theme examines the experiences of women in social work, teaching, and nursing as they began to model their work on the male professions of medicine and law. Professionalization, as it materialized in the late nineteenth century, was a process in which white, middle-class males carved out new roles and ultimately obtained a monopoly for their services. Critiques of professionalization suggest that although special knowledge and expertise are characteristics attributed to the professions, the key element is social power (Melosh, 1989). In contrast, the women who entered the women-dominated professions were primarily motivated by an ethic of service or care. Glazer and Slater (1987) suggest that for the most part this was true for the few women who penetrated the ranks of medicine. A commitment to provide service to marginal populations became the grounds for women's efforts to gain social power. Yet this was not explicitly acknowledged or understood. Service to society and an ethic of care constrained women in the professions who had assumed that meritocracy and new fields of work would provide women with equal opportunities.

A review of the literature, which examines the movement of women from the private world of the home to the public sphere, reveals a range of different interpretations. Cott (1977) has argued that, initially, interpretations focused on women as victims oppressed by the rigid definition of women's domestic status. A subsequent perspective suggested that women took advantage of participating in the public sphere and increased their satisfaction as well as their opportunities. A third interpretation argues that women developed a subculture, a sisterhood and a solidarity that was attributed to women's own motivations as much as impositions of male society.

The argument I wish to make follows the latter interpretation. As women moved into the public sphere to engage in caring activities, they were, as Carrol Smith-Rosenberg (1985) has articulated, more than actors in a male play. They seized the opportunities society presented, carved out a place for themselves, and developed a collective consciousness of themselves as women, different and separate from men. Some women worked in separate female organizations and gained collective strength; some accepted their subordinate status; others attempted to be the modern-day equivalent of the superwoman.

What follows is only a brief examination of the history of women in nursing, social work, and teaching. It attempts to increase our understanding of the way a commitment to an ethic of care framed the experiences of women in these fields but also constrained their opportunities as the surge to professionalize took hold.

The chapter begins with a discussion of maternal feminism and social reform at the turn of the century. It is followed by an examination of the links between an ideology of caring and maternal feminism as it unfolded in social work, nursing, and teaching. The third section explores how professionalization based on a male ethos and a traditional division of labour clashed with a feminine ethos of caring. Women were expected to care about and for their clients, while men in these professions assumed authority for the management and leadership. The final section presents some possible resolutions to the issues of women's caring and professionalism.

MATERNAL FEMINISM, CARING, AND SOCIAL REFORM

In the late nineteenth century, a "new woman" graced the Canadian landscape. Determined to play a part in the changing society, middle- and upper-class women moved into the public sphere. Some women found positions as teachers in the newly emerging public school system, while other women became involved in voluntary charity work in the fledgling health and welfare services. The care of dependent children, the establishment of health services for poor women, the education of the young, and the abolition of alcohol were some of the issues women began to address (Kealey, 1979).

However, the public work women performed was not, in fact, new work. It was an extension of the work women previously had carried out in the home. In caring for the sick, the aged, and the young, women developed skills that they recognized were essential to transfer to the public sphere. As part of the reform movement women were determined to extend their caring roles to the larger society and male reformers were only too willing to utilize the labour of women to complete their vision of a new Canadian society. The "grand mission of mothering" articulated by Lady Aberdeen, the first president of the National Council of Women, revealed the extent to which women accepted the reality that they were responsible for caring about and for dependent groups (Roberts, 1979). For mothers, as Dalley (1988) has argued, this can be a very artificial distinction. If one cares *about* (has feelings for) another person, it is difficult not to care *for* them. The women who moved into the public sphere to extend their caring mission believed that if poor women and children were to be cared about, it was their duty to see that they were cared for.

Maternal feminism ensured the transformation of women's caring into public caring, as Linda Kealey's (1979: 7) definition of maternal feminism indicates:

> the conviction that woman's special role as mother gives her the duty and the right to participate in the public sphere. It is not her position as wife that qualifies her for the task of reform, but the special nurturing qualities which are common to all women, married or not.

While this provided women with a rationale to move into the public sphere, it was also reinforced by the complex set of forces that spawned a movement for social reform.

In the late nineteenth century, Canada was confronted with pressing political and social issues. Family and community life was also affected by such factors as: the integration of immigrants, the introduction of machine technology, factory labour and trade unions, and the availability of transportation. Ontario, in particular, was undergoing a transition from a rural to an urban society and families were experiencing its economic and social impacts. Accompanying these signs of a developing industrial society were the corresponding problems of city slums, delinquent children, child labour, infant mortality, unemployment, poor sanitation, public health concerns, and the evil effects of "drink" (Brown and Cook, 1974).

While these problems were facts of life for working-class families and impinged on all family members, women usually bore the brunt of these difficulties. Coping with illness and death, the care of their children, poor nutrition, unsanitary milk supplies, and, perhaps most of all, the need for women to supplement meagre family incomes took an incredible toll on women's lives.

In contrast, middle- and upper-class women were experiencing increased affluence and leisure time and a declining birth rate. These factors fostered the growth of women's organizations and clubs. It was not surprising that these women, well schooled in the importance of Christian stewardship, responded to the troubles of their working-class sisters. An urban and economic transformation, a demand for a response to the problems facing an industrial society, and a changing conception of what women were able to do all contributed to the shaping of new institutions and laid the groundwork for the welfare state.

The church, the most important institution in Canada at the turn of the century, played a critical role in shaping the movement for reform and the entry of women into the public sphere. Part of the explanation for the Protestant churches' interest in reform was the realization that individual salvation no longer seemed relevant in a society confronted with massive social problems. By the late nineteenth century, Darwin's theory of evolution, the ascent of science in general, and historical criticism of the Bible were seriously undermining the authority of the church (Cook, 1985). Many theologians came to conclude that no longer could Christianity be based on faith alone (Emery, 1977). The "social gospel" movement developed in response to this conundrum and reinforced the idea that Christianity was a social religion, concerned with the Kingdom of God in this world. By making the church more socially responsive and creating a new mission – social regeneration – liberal Protestants believed that the scientific and historical criticism of the Bible could be ignored and the significance of religion in people's lives maintained (Cook, 1985).

Implicit in the move toward regeneration was the recognition that the church needed the "agency of Christian women" if it were to embark on a program of social evangelism (Austin, 1890: 33). Given the reality that women, over time, have been the most active supporters of the church, this was hardly surprising. However, it is too simplistic to claim that women were conscripted to carry out a mission of reform created by male leaders. Women themselves recognized the need to put their vision of a more caring society in the creation of services for women and children.

Agnes Maule Machar, for instance, an active participant in the social gospel movement, was "one of the most gifted intellectuals and social critics of the late nineteenth century" (Cook, 1985: 186). The author of many works of fiction and poetry, Machar became a strong advocate of translating the ethical teachings of Christ into social reform. Concerned about the problems of alcohol as a social disease and the deplorable conditions of industrial labour, she urged middle-class women to respond to the needs of their poorer sisters. Her description of Christian social action, which epitomized a maternal approach to reform, was that it should be "earnest, active and practical" (Cook, 1985: 187). This approach became the hallmark of women's reform efforts in Canada as well as in the United States (Scott, 1984; McDowell, 1982).

In summary, the reform work of women had the following elements: (1) women enacted their caring mission not as individuals but as members of women's organizations – women were able to do in concert things that would be difficult to do alone (Scott, 1984: 266); (2) women instituted new services and careers for women; (3) the targets of their reform efforts were typically poor women and children; and (4) women accepted subordinate and traditional roles under the aegis of the clergy.

Although maternal feminism was in many respects a narrow, biological, and conservative view of women's caring role, it empowered women to work in hospitals, church-based social services, and schools and fostered a feminine consciousness and the solidarity of women (Mitchinson, 1977; Freedman, 1979). Not only did women refine their domestic skills, they learned and developed new skills that changed their view of themselves. They became more autonomous and independent and were exposed to social and educational opportunities that had previously been denied. Although women were often working in tandem and under the leadership of middle-class, Protestant, Anglo-Saxon business and professional men, this replication of the familial division of labour was, for the most part, not seen as problematic.

WOMEN AND CARING IN SOCIAL WELFARE

One of the dilemmas women working in social welfare have confronted has been that the origins of their work lay in the activities of upper middle-class volunteers, the foremothers of the twentieth-century social worker. Despite the considerable labour expended by the early volunteer, she has been represented in the history of social work by the disparaging image of the "Lady Bountiful." In this respect, class has been considered a more important dimension for analysis than gender, and the feminist concerns underpinning the work of women's organizations has only begun to be examined. Committed to moral reform and rescue work, women's organizations focused on the needs of women and children. As the following examination of five women's organizations reveals, women transferred their private caring into the public sphere. Caring involved both love – the emotional overtones associated with moral reform and labour – and work that did not entirely replicate women's traditional role.

The easiest avenue for women to enter the public sphere was through the Women's Missionary Societies (WMS). These organizations, regardless of religious denomination, enabled women to take responsibility for public caring without affecting their primary caring role within the family. Two points are significant here. First, the phenomenal growth in membership is an indication of its importance as an outlet for women's social and educational aspirations. In 1882, the Methodist WMS had 900 members and supported two missionaries; by 1916, its membership had soared to 44,135 supporting 120 missionaries (Mitchinson, 1977: 309). Second, the WMS depended on a sense of sisterhood and collectivism to foster its maternal feminist goals. The refusal of all but the Anglican WMS to become an auxiliary to male missionary societies attests to the value women placed on a separate female organization. And although part of their motivation was evangelization, the needs of poor women and children in Canada and abroad awakened the feminine consciousness of the WMS (Mitchinson, 1977). It also sparked their interest and frequently led to women's involvement in other social service organizations.

An example of a women's organization that became an offshoot of the WMS was the Wimodausis Club (Wives, Mothers, Daughters, Sisters) of Toronto, formally constituted in 1906. Here we find an example of an upper-class group of women who made volunteer charity work their career. Public caring was expected for this group of women, but it was also marginalized. Daniels (1988) has suggested that the complex functions of volunteer work are frequently obscured and a commitment of service is extolled as the essence of women's caring.

Like other women's charitable groups, the Wimodausis Club began by providing food, clothing, and health supplies, along with moral and financial support, to poor women and children in downtown Toronto. In 1915, they decided to concentrate on the welfare of children and formed a permanent partnership with the Earlscourt Children's Home, a Methodist Institution established as an emergency resource for single-parent families in 1913.

The goal of the Wimodausis women was to make the Earlscourt Children's Home one of the finest "professional" institutions in Canada serving the needs of poor children from fragmented families. From 1915 until 1948, they were responsible for fund-raising, a building campaign, and policy directions and assessments, as well as for assisting in the direct work of the Home. As such, their work entailed both the private (domestic) and public (funding) operations of the Home. But as expected of women, they formally deferred to a small group of Methodist men, and the assets and properties of the Home remained vested with the Church (Baines, 1990).

The survival of the Earlscourt Children's Home, until the late 1940s, as an entirely privately funded organization was due to the caring labour of unpaid Wimodausis members and a dedicated group of poorly paid workers under the direction of Hattie Inkpen, a Methodist deaconess. Mrs. Mason, the president of the Wimodausis Club in 1926, expressed their commitment to a maternal feminist mission in this way: "It is work that particularly appeals to women, for here we find something greater than individual motherhood, that sublimation of the Mother spirit that opens the heart to all little children" (Baines, 1988: 35).

An ideology of caring about and for poor children ensured the survival of the Wimodausis Club and the Earlscourt Children's Home. By entering the public sphere of charity work, this group of upper- and middle-class women gained an understanding of themselves as builders of a more caring community. Yet what was equally important, but not acknowledged, was the success they achieved in raising money, managing Earlscourt, building networks, and developing a sense of autonomy and an appreciation of their own abilities. The self-sacrifice implied in caring fostered their own humility and subordinate status.

One of the largest networks of women's organizations that reinforced traditional views about women and the family, and yet embarked on energetic policy initiatives to improve the lives of young women, was the work of the Young Women's Christian Association (YWCA).[2] From 1870 to 1894, fourteen YWCAs were formed across Canada, with a national association established in 1893 (Mitchinson, 1977: 282). The work of caring about and for young working women was based on an awareness that the social and economic environment was not a nurturing place for women. However, their approach to change was not directed at the workplace. Rather, it was a woman's need for a suitable home that captured the impulse of reform-minded YWCA women. The early programs the YWCA instituted emphasized the building of good character, a Christian lifestyle, and the teaching of domestic skills, all of which prepared women for their future caring roles in both the family and the public sphere.

Inevitably, the good intentions of the YWCA reformers were frequently patronizing and evoked sharp criticism from some of the young women. The concerns of upper- and middle-class women for their poorer working sisters were coloured by a limited understanding of how gender and class intersected in their lives. Nonetheless, they were successful in drawing public attention to the needs of young working women.

Gradually, reforms directed at promoting protective labour legislation, social hygiene measures, street patrols, and even trade unions for women found their way on the agenda of the Y (Pedersen, 1987). The vision of reform involved the building of a prototype all-purpose YWCA facility that provided residential accommodation, a library, a kitchen, a cafeteria, classrooms, and a gymnasium and swimming pool. It was to be a "woman's refuge from an inhospitable male environment and a base from which they could attempt to modify that environment in the interests of women" (Pedersen, 1987: 227). To gain public support for young women, the Y members appealed to other women's organizations. The YWCA became a meeting place for women's clubs, and in return women's groups like the Woman's Christian Temperance Union (WCTU), the WMS, the Wimodausis, and the Imperial Order of the Daughters of the Empire made financial contributions to the YWCA.

However, the networks of support that had furnished resources for the early YWCA activities proved insufficient to build a modern YWCA. Public caring and their vision of a women's centre depended on the financial support of the male business community. Influenced by the successful fund-raising campaigns mounted by the Young Men's Christian Association, the YWCA developed a strategy that ensured the co-operation of businessmen. Using slogans such as "Building Today for the Womanhood of Tomorrow," the YWCA capitalized on the thrust for efficiency, sound business management, and prevention, the buzz words of professional and business men (Pedersen, 1987: 234).

The dependence of a women's organization like the YWCA on male philanthropy had mixed results. It helped to legitimate the myth that a shared sense of community existed and that men cared about the needs of young working women (Pedersen, 1987). But the reliance of the YWCA on support from the business community reinforced a division in public caring – men's caring was manifested in providing financial support; women's caring continued to be linked with serving others and self-sacrifice – and YWCA workers have remained among the most lowly paid of social service workers.

A further example of a women's group demonstrating an ethic of care was the Big Sisters Association of Toronto and its attention to delinquent girls. With the passing of the Juvenile Delinquent Act in 1908 and the subsequent changes in the care and control of delinquent children, a Juvenile Court judge suggested that the Local Council of Women establish a Big Sister organization (Robinson, 1979). Motivated by maternal feminist goals, their conception of caring included both personal goals for the individual girls as well as a vision of a society that was to be more protective of young girls.

By providing supportive relationships, such an organization could guide young girls in trouble and protect them from further crime and imprisonment. The work of the Big Sisters expanded to include advocacy for improved housing, schooling and recreational services, decent wages, and a more protected home environment. An ethic of caring depended on changes in policy. The constant pull between the need to provide personal counselling services and more political reforms was exemplified in Mrs. Sydney Small's address to the annual meeting in 1920:

> Some day, society will realize the unwisdom and folly of allowing any children to be born and bred in conditions of poverty, ignorance and preventable disease. In the meantime, it is our privilege and duty to help adjust these little starved lives to a fuller measure of health and happiness which should have been their heritage, and which has been denied them. (Robinson, 1979: 46)

The Big Sisters, as the need for their service mushroomed, were also confronted with the necessity of compromising their caring activities in the interests of ensuring support from the male-dominated Federation of Community Services. Instructed by the Federation to refrain from endorsing women candidates in municipal elections who supported their reforms, the Big Sisters felt compelled to comply. However, they vehemently resisted the suggestion that they should amalgamate with the Big Brothers. The Big Sisters recognized that the interests of men were quite different and that their mission could be best achieved through a separate women's organization.

The women's organization that achieved the greatest success in the political field was the WCTU. It was founded in 1874 by Mrs. Letitia Youmans, a widowed school teacher from Picton, Ontario. The belief that the social problems facing Canada were linked to the evils of drink led to the conclusion that the cause of poverty was intemperance. J.J. Kelso's assertion that three-quarters of child neglect cases were the result of alcohol centred the work of the WCTU on "removing the cause, rather than remedying the evils" (Mitchinson, 1977: 153). This took the WCTU women along a path directed at legislative changes to promote prohibition and the introduction of a temperance education program in the public schools (Mitchinson, 1977). To this extent, the members of the WCTU were a more militant brand of maternal feminists, and women's issues remained central to their mission. In advocating for higher education for women, the employment of women as factory inspectors, doctors, and teachers, child protection legislation, reformatories for juveniles, a hospital for women, and the establishment of cottage homes for children rather than large barrack-style institutions, the key to their conception of reform was the need "to make the whole world more home-like than when we found it" (Mitchinson, 1977: 174). Or as Youmans opined: "Who would say it was unwomanly or unladylike to plead for our children?" (Mitchinson, 1977: 153). In sum, the reforms of the WCTU were couched in familiar themes: service and caring for others.

In this pre-professional period, the unpaid work of women as members of voluntary organizations, coupled with the poorly paid work of church deaconesses and social service workers, expedited the development of services for poor women and children through city missions and fledgling social service organizations (Baines, 1988; Mitchinson, 1987). These institutions assumed a range of social service roles as they attempted to put in place a feminine vision of a caring society. In promoting an ethic of care, women were fundraisers, managers, planners, and policy-makers as well as providers of concrete services to poor women and children. A maternal mission of service and a feminine consciousness united these women as they formed networks of support and alliances. But the contradiction was that it was viewed as women's natural work, relatively invisible and unvalued.

Social welfare concerns also included the health needs of the poor, as the founding of the Hospital for Sick Children in 1875 attests. Raising funds, managing the institution, and caring for the patients offered women the opportunity of playing a prominent role in health care (Morrison, 1971). However, the most significant role women occupied in the health field was nursing.

CARING AND THE HEALTH CARE SYSTEM

Nursing has also been confronted with the contradiction inherent in a field of work based on both labour and love. Prior to industrialization, women had been responsible for the caring and healing of sick members within their families. The first European settlements in Canada had included the immigration of members of French nursing sisterhoods who provided health care. Unlike their nursing counterparts in Great Britain, who were members of the servant class, the French nursing sisters came from all walks of life, were viewed as highly competent, and were given responsibility to provide for the medical needs of the community. A French nursing order founded the first Canadian hospital, the Hotel Dieu in Quebec City in 1639; the Grey Nuns, another order, have been credited with the introduction of district nursing to other parts of Canada (Coburn, 1974).

The training of nurses in Canada and the United States adopted the model established by Florence Nightingale in the 1860s in England. Nightingale's primary goals were to eliminate the menial nature of nursing and to increase its professional stature (Kerr and MacPhail, 1988). The training for nursing became not only preparation for an occupation, it was character training for life. Moral development, proper behaviour, loyalty, order and discipline, and hierarchical control by a nursing matron who considered the hospital a home all became a part of the culture of a nurse's training. Uniforms and badges exemplified the military nature of hospital life (Reverby, 1988).

Nightingale's vision of nurses as independent and confident women who would define a clear role for themselves in the hospital hierarchy was not without its contradictions. Just as opportunities for women had been strengthened by the establishment of separate women's colleges in the United States, nursing sought to create a culture that would enhance the competence and autonomy of women. However, others have argued that it was the place where "women learned to be girls" (Reverby, 1988: 57). Efficiency and the standardization of procedures limited initiative and independence, and reinforced the male-dominated medical hierarchy.

The advent of hospitals and the institutionalization of health services accentuated a division of labour that allocated the "curing" role to men, with women relegated to the maternal tradition of "caring" (Reverby, 1988). Nurses were responsible for aseptic conditions, good nutrition, and meticulous aftercare (Keddy, 1986). In the early years of modern health care, nurses carried out a range of tasks. Along with drudgery and cleaning, they were expected to be nurturing and caring to sick individuals. An ethic of service and altruism committed to the public good underpinned the work of nurses (Kerr and MacPhail, 1988). However, as Charles Rosenberg (1981) has pointed out, efficiency, centralized control over the work force, and scientific medicine were the ideological influences that shaped the American hospital, and physicians became the key players in health care. Yet the organization of the hospital depended on a cadre of disciplined nurses to uphold the authority and primacy of the physician.

Male domination was not only evident in the relationship between doctors and nurses; women who completed medical training were also expected to assume subordinate positions. Professionalization meant that medicine needed to be identified as a science, and hence were developed rigid criteria and accreditation standards to gain the prestige and credentials essential to ensure its authority. In effect, medicine needed to be seen as a masculine profession and distanced from the unorthodox female practice of home medicine. Creating a culture of like-minded educated men was crucial to the development of a medical monopoly.

As middle-class men tightened their control of health care, women such as Emily Stowe and Jennie Trout, who had been denied access to Canadian universities, were forced to go to the U.S. to obtain their medical training. Arguments against women pursuing university education were numerous – women lacked the academic background in Latin and science and were not strong enough to cope with rigorous study. Most importantly, women were expected to stick to their natural role – caring for children and the home. The barriers to medicine were even stronger as opponents to women's entry argued that women were too nervous and emotional. By 1906, despite the extraordinary discrimination faced by women, a total of 146 women had graduated from medical schools in Canada (Strong-Boag, 1979: 118). Although women doctors were active in the Canadian suffragist movement, which pressed for women's right to equal access to education and the professions, this movement did not open the doors for women in medicine. Women continued to represent only a small percentage of the profession. From 1911 to 1921, the number of women in medicine declined from 2.7 per cent to 1.8 per cent (Strong-Boag, 1979: 128).

Like other women reformers, Canada's early female doctors, often critical of male physicians' treatment of women, centred their attention on developing services for poor women and children. Others became medical missionaries and provided services to vulnerable groups in foreign lands. Reflecting a maternal feminist ideology as they confronted discrimination within the profession of medicine, women doctors reinforced "women's unique nurturing qualities," yet they failed to see how this philosophical approach constrained them and, ultimately, the women they served. As women doctors became more identified with "professionalism" they began to adopt a male orientation to the practice of medicine (Strong-Boag, 1979).

CARING AND TEACHING

Teaching, similar to social work and nursing, had its roots in a maternal caring ethic. Women teachers were to uphold the domestic virtues of the home and transmit these to the broader community through the education of the young (Graham, 1974). For most of the eighteenth and nineteenth centuries, most children in rural Canada were educated at home or in small private schools, and many of their teachers were women (Prentice, 1977). Given a rudimentary knowledge of the three R's, girls and boys were taught domestic and agricultural skills respectively.

Beginning with private institutions and followed by partially supported government schools, schooling as an institutional force began to take root in the mid-nineteenth century. In 1846, with the appointment of Egerton Ryerson as the

Superintendent of Schools in Ontario and the enactment of the Common Schools Act in 1848, free public schooling was gradually put in place. The passing of the Ontario School Act of 1871 made school attendance compulsory for children aged seven to twelve for four months of the year, and this greatly accelerated the feminization of teaching (Graham, 1974; Prentice, 1977).

Alison Prentice (1977) has attributed the involvement of women in public school teaching to three factors. First, the introduction of public schooling was accompanied by the desire to make education more efficient through consolidating schools and grouping pupils by age. This gave the more experienced teachers responsibility for the higher grades, and women could be employed at a much lower wage to handle the elementary levels. Second, advocates of public schooling, the "school promoters," came to believe that women were suitable for the job. In 1865, Ryerson reflected the essence of maternal feminism in his statement that women were "best adapted to teach small children, having, as a general rule, most heart, most tender feelings, most assiduity, and in the order of Providence, the qualities best suited for the care, instruction and government of infancy and childhood" (cited in Prentice, 1977: 54). The third factor that accelerated the feminization of teaching came from women themselves. The lack of alternative careers and the opportunity to work outside the home were motivating factors for women to become teachers. Teaching, although originally compared to work as a domestic servant, offered more status and higher wages than other women's work.

By the third quarter of the nineteenth century, women comprised the majority of elementary school teachers in Canada and a distinct division of labour was evident within the school system. Men taught in the higher grades and acted as principals and superintendents while women were relegated to a female ghetto of offering nurture and care to the youngest children. And not surprisingly, women teachers were paid considerably less. In 1861, the average salary for a male teacher in Ontario was $429 compared to $215 for a woman (Prentice, 1977). Despite the apparent widespread acceptance of their subordinate status, some women objected to the undervaluing of their work. However, for the most part, women teachers did not articulate the inequalities until the end of the nineteenth century.

PROFESSIONALIZATION AND CARING

The creation of social work, nursing, and teaching as new fields of work for women broadened the horizons of middle- and upper-class women and provided upwardly mobile working-class women an alternative to factory or domestic work. For some women, these career opportunities became an option to marriage. Although women were re-enacting their caring roles, which typified service to others, and despite the subordinate status of these jobs, such opportunities also provided women with a growing sense of power and competence. Women as social service workers, volunteers, nurses, teachers, and physicians collectively utilized the ideology of maternal feminism to participate in a new society. By adopting an argument that stressed the differences between men and women, a broadly based women's movement was created and was successful in gaining the vote in 1917. United by an ethic of caring that replicated their traditional work within the family, women could comfortably criticize masculine society without threatening the social order. However, the stress on male-female differences also reinforced a biological argument that would be difficult to overcome as women in these newly created occupations moved toward professionalization and the increased ghettoization within these professions that accompanied it.

The process of professionalization, which began in the late nineteenth century in Canada, greatly accelerated in the first two decades of the twentieth century. The new occupations of social work, nursing, and teaching must be understood within the context of the changing political and social environment. In the early twentieth century, Canada was faced with a burgeoning population, the settlement of the western provinces, immigration, urbanization, and industrial development. Yet mixed with the remnants of nineteenth-century idealism was the fear that Canada lacked a sense of purpose and direction for its economic and moral development as a nation (Owram, 1986).

Canada's involvement in World War One, reflecting both idealism and imperialism, was seized as an opportunity to bring the nation together. By the end of the war, however, Canadians were no longer sure the patriotic ideals that had united them during the war would live up to their promise. The carnage of the war and the loss of life, which touched the majority of English-speaking Canadian families, raised serious concerns about whether the survival of a British way of life was worth the means. Both the Wartime Elections Act, which disenfranchised recent foreign immigrants, and conscription were difficult to understand in light of the idealism so apparent in the pre-war period (Owram, 1986).

Given this tumultuous set of events, new solutions were required. Although the church and women had played an instrumental role in building new organizations to ameliorate the ills of society, the role of the state in legislating conscription and the granting of the vote to women appeared to open the door for a greater state involvement in social affairs. Yet the social and moral values that held society together had to be preserved (Owram, 1986). Bliss (1968) has argued that once the state used its influence to conscript wealth for the war effort, reformers came to believe that a stronger state would be able to mobilize wealth for the construction of a new social order. A combination of voluntary religious-based social services and government support would usher in the hope for a unified, socialist, and Christian society.

In the 1920s a new reform elite, made up of male middle-class social scientists, frequently educated at Chicago, Harvard, or Oxford, upheld the ideals of efficiency and social stability. A male ethos reflected the belief that a rational and scientific approach was essential for the eradication of social problems. Owram (1986) has suggested that professionalism and secularism, characteristic objectives of the new reformers, were intended to free these reformers from the moral reform movement. This altered the participation of women because maternal feminism was linked to moral reform. Although women would continue to form the majority of the direct workers in the health, education, and welfare sectors, their influence in policy and government agencies was marginal. Owram (1986) and Carol Bacchi (1983) have both argued that the women's movement was weakened by a loss of momentum after gaining the vote. In any event, the partnership forged between the social gospel movement and women's organizations was seriously eroded, as the new professional elite included few women and non-Anglo-Saxons in its ranks.

The recognition that professionalism has reflected a male ethos has been an argument made by a number of scholars who have examined the experience of women within the professions. Hearn (1985) has linked professionalization to patriarchy and traces the evolution of the "semi-professions" of nursing, teaching, and social work. He argues that men first gained a monopoly within the traditional professions and then gradually assumed control of the semi-professions. As men took over the management and leadership of these professions, a culture developed that affirmed male-centred values of order, efficiency, and a hierarchical division of labour.

Glazer and Slater (1987) have also argued that a male ethos has made women's entry and participation into the professions difficult. They suggested that "successful professionals were objective, competitive, individualistic and predictable: they were also scornful of nurturant, expressive and familial styles of personal interaction." One of the further differences identified by Glazer and Slater was that, for the most part, men in the professions first emphasized expertise and the creation of a monopoly for their work. Only after this was established were they concerned about the "greater social good" (Glazer and Slater, 1987: 229). Not only women in social work, nursing, and teaching emphasized an ethic of service; as well, women research scientists centred their work on marginal populations and issues such as lead poisoning in working men, birth control for poor women, and the quality of milk in babies' formulas (Glazer and Slater, 1987). Thus, the bases for women's special expertise and place within the professions continued to rest on an ideology of service that lionized caring as a virtue particular to women.

Those women who were successful in breaking the barriers of entry into the professions expected that, by emulating a male ethos of professionalism, meritocracy would prevail. However, the gaining of professional credentials did not establish a level playing field. Glazer and Slater (1987) have pointed out that even when women were aware of the limitations inherent in a service ethic, they continued to place this above professional power. Not surprisingly, compared to their working-class sisters, women professionals considered themselves fortunate and had little choice but to accept their roles as token women in a man's world. In addition, women in the professions also failed to understand how the success of their foremothers had been enhanced by the cultivation of close personal relationships that supported sisterhood and feminine consciousness, a reality recognized by modern feminism. Strong social and personal networks were instrumental in building female institutions, perhaps best exemplified by women in the settlement movement (Cook, 1979; Freedman, 1979; Smith-Rosenberg, 1985).

Social work, nursing, and teaching all laid down their roots during the nineteenth-century urban reform movement and were based on a maternal ethic of care and duty. In the post-World War One period, these professions attracted the majority of women pursuing post-secondary education (Prentice *et al.*, 1988). However, this was too often viewed as a stepping stone to women's main career: marriage. As a result, the development of a strong core of career women in these fields was limited. Yet each of the three professions sought to replicate a male ethos of professionalization as they began to formalize their training programs. The tensions between caring and professionalization increased and succeeding generations of women social workers, nurses, and teachers have had to struggle with this.

PROFESSIONALIZATION AND SOCIAL WORK

Social work's pursuit of professional status and its emphasis on a male ethos were evident in the division of labour created within the field. This was reflected in its search for a "scientific" body of knowledge and its attempt to distance itself from its historical roots as an occupation of women helping poor women and children.

The developing interest in adopting more scientific solutions to social problems fostered the growth of social work education. When the first class enrolled at the University of Toronto Social Services Department in 1914, the director of the school and the professors who provided the academic content were all respected male faculty members from the departments of philosophy, psychology, and political economy and all the students were women members of the Protestant churches. The practice and skills component, generally regarded as less important, was taught by prominent Toronto practitioners such as Miss Sara L. Carson, Miss J. Grant, and Miss E. Neufield (Hurl, 1983).

Closely affiliated with social agencies, the Toronto program adopted an approach to social work education similar to that of its American counterparts. In 1915, when Abraham Flexner addressed the U.S. National Conference on Charities and Corrections, the thrust to professionalize social work was under way. Flexner, who had a profound effect on medical education, argued that social work collaborated with other professions but had no specific area of expertise or knowledge and therefore lacked the necessary attributes for a profession. In the subsequent decades of the twentieth century, social work has earnestly and consistently pursued professionalization (Struthers, 1987a; Ehrenreich, 1985).

The professionalization to which social work aspired involved the adoption of a male "medical model" and casework as the cornerstone of the profession (Struthers, 1987b; Lubove, 1977). Investigation, co-ordination, and efficiency became the hallmarks of casework practice. The belief that clients needed "objective scientific treatment" infused social work with psychiatric knowledge and began a process that would change social work's commitment from providing care and support to poor women and children to a more middle-class clientele (Katz, 1986). The extent to which social work was successful in its objective of providing treatment has certainly been challenged. What was successful, though, was the illusion given the social worker that she had a distinct body of knowledge and thus met one of the objectives of professionalism. Research into social work practice in the 1930s concluded, however, that although social work touted psychoanalytical knowledge, social workers continued to rely on "practice wisdom" in their day-to-day work with clients (Ehrenreich, 1985).

The biggest challenge facing social work in its pursuit of professionalization was its identification with the image of the "Lady Bountiful" dispensing charity to poor clients. As early as 1927, Dr. Helen Reid, a Montreal social work educator, reflected the importance of identifying with a male scientific model. In her address to the Canadian Conference on Social Work, Reid categorized two groups of women in social work: female philanthropists and volunteers, whom she described as tradionalists, obstructionists, and sentimentalists, and the "new scientific women," the expert social workers committed to economy and efficiency (Rooke and Schnell, 1982). This was the beginning of an attack on the unpaid labour of women in social work. Volunteers have continued to be perceived in a sentimental, patronizing, and trivial way and not well understood. Daniels (1988), in a recent study of outstanding women volunteers in the United States, has pinpointed the invisible nature of volunteer labour and our inability to conceptualize it because it is considered caring and not work.

However, despite the conscious attempt to distance social work from its maternal and volunteer heritage, it continued to be viewed as women's work linked to "social motherhood," with low status and low pay (Ehrenreich, 1985). For women social workers, the paradox was that they were viewed as nurturers and emotional beings confined to the caring for others. Since women were perceived to be ideally suited to offering direct services, then, as Struthers (1987a) has pointed out, men were needed to fill the more elite administrative positions. Social work, a profession, largely made up of women, became a profession under the control of men.

Nonetheless, there is some evidence to suggest that some women resisted their subordinate status. The lack of historical research on social work in Canada limits our knowledge about the extent of the resistance. Charlotte Whitton exemplified a woman who openly confronted the subordination of women in social work. Whitton, however, did not articulate her feminist concerns until the 1940s when her career in social work was ended abruptly with her dismissal from the Canadian Council on Child Welfare. As she examined the salary inequities for women in occupations such as teaching, nursing, and social work, Whitton concluded that social work was the most discriminatory (Struthers, 1987b). Regarding her own professional career as one of service, Whitton was aware of the self-sacrifice this entailed.

Whitton's comment, that "the boys have discovered it [social work] now," symbolized a deliberate strategy that had begun in the 1930s and continued in the post-World War Two period, as schools of social work turned their attention to recruiting men into the profession and to lengthening professional training. Many women, including Whitton and Ethel Dodds Parker, had advocated the importance of attracting capable men to assume administrative roles. The sex-segregation within social work was also directed at fields of practice. Women were deemed more suitable to work in the fields of child and family welfare and medical social work, while men were more likely to be working in welfare councils, corrections, and social policy.

A similar pattern emerged in the United States. Although a number of outstanding women, such as Jane Addams, Grace and Edith Abbott, Florence Kelly, and Julia Lathrop, played a significant role during the progressive movement, the coalition of men and women that shaped the origins of American social work collapsed in the 1920s. According to Clarke Chambers (1986), a professionalism rooted in Western, white patriarchy set the stage for the subordination of women in social work.

Women social workers in the 1920s and 1930s, unlike the first generation of women leaders in social work, did not have the same network of support from unpaid women workers or colleagues from other disciplines. At the turn of the century, leaders in nursing, education, and social work, both paid and unpaid, co-operated to establish programs at institutions such as Hull House in Chicago and St. Christopher House in Toronto. However, professionalization was accompanied by

specialization and social workers wanted to distance themselves from the volunteers, district nurses, and deaconesses
who had provided many of the early social services in Canada. Without the support network that had accompanied the
creation of separate female institutions, women in social work
were particularly dependent on the approval of male
superiors.

This became an issue for Bertha Reynolds, the associate
director of the Smith College School of Social Work and a
leading American social work educator. Reynolds tried to
develop a theoretical and practical approach to social work
education that stressed a commitment to service and a concern for social justice integrated with the casework method.
Disturbed by the overwhelming economic problems that
impinged on family life in the 1930s, Reynolds supported left-
wing causes and the efforts of young radicals intent on organizing the poor. But the merging of Marxism with Freudianism
was not part of Smith College's grand plan for social work
education and Reynolds's activism placed her in a vulnerable
position. She was not prepared to compromise her principles
and in 1938, when she was forced to resign from Smith,
Annette Garrett, her successor and a leading casework
teacher, suggested to Reynolds that she should have been
more willing to subordinate herself to the male director –
"The politic thing would have been to ask for his advice and
to cultivate him much more" (Glazer and Slater, 1987: 198).
The tragedy of Reynolds's departure from Smith was more
than a personal one. She conceptualized social work practice
in a holistic way and she recognized the importance of forming coalitions with the poor to effect social change. From her
perspective the cared-for should be partners in social work's
mission.

The dominance of men in the more lucrative administrative
positions of leadership, so well documented by Struthers, has
continued to characterize social work. Although approximately 70 per cent of the profession are women, they are
concentrated in the lower-paying direct service positions
committed to an ethic of caring about and for marginal populations (Struthers, 1987a).

PROFESSIONALIZATION AND NURSING

A brief look at the history of nursing also reflects the tensions that developed as nursing educators advocated professionalization as a means to achieve both status and autonomy (Baumgart and Larsen, 1988). A commitment to service, coupled with a nurse's subordinate status to a physician in an increasingly complex hierarchical division of labour, presented severe obstacles to nurses who were interested in professionalization.

Nursing as a career was greatly enhanced by the influenza epidemic in 1918 in which 50,000 Canadians died (Prentice *et al.*, 1988). As hospital nursing began to replace private duty and public health nursing as the principal field of employment, nurses began to wrestle with a problem that continues to challenge them – the lack of autonomy in their work. Home and private duty nursing had produced a "Jill of all trades" who experienced considerable satisfaction and independence in her work despite the long hours and hard work. However, by the 1920s, the entrepreneurial role of nurses declined as pressures to staff hospitals increased, and physicians' criticisms of public health and private duty nurses intensified (Keddy, 1986).

As hospitals became the principal employer of nurses, onsite programs for nursing training were initiated. Like early social work education, most of the classes for nurses were taught by men, in this case, male physicians. The real training for nurses, however, occurred on the job. The apprenticeship model provided hospitals with the free labour of student nurses who spent twelve to fourteen hours a day caring for patients. In return, nurses received room and board and a small stipend, approximately $8 to $10 per month.

A culture of nursing education emphasized service, dedication, and self-sacrifice, the traditional attributes of caring women (Baumgart and Larsen, 1988). Fear of the erosion of this service commitment became the strongest argument made by the "traditionalist" nurses as advocates for professionalization surfaced. As "angels of mercy," the voices of tradition argued, "Nursing is not merely a profession – it is a vocation; not merely a gainful occupation, but a ministry" (Melosh, 1989: 673). According to this view, technical skills and the acquisition of knowledge were secondary to the skills of intuition and empathy that were crucial to its caring mission. In contrast, those in favour of professionalism emphasized objectivity, technique, and efficiency and, moreover, attempted to eradicate the image of the self-sacrificing nurse. With this, it was thought, higher status and wages would follow.

The ensuing conflict between traditionalists and professionalists was largely played out through different conceptions of nursing education. Proponents of professionalism pushed for an academic program for nursing education centred in the universities. In 1920, the first degree program was established at the University of British Columbia, followed in the 1920s by McGill and the University of Toronto (Coburn, 1974). However, university training in nursing accentuated the internal tension within the field. In Canada in 1932, the Weir Report recommended that responsibility for nursing education should be transferred to educational institutions (Baumgart and Larsen, 1988). This and subsequent reports on nursing education failed to change the hospital-based training model until the 1960s, when community colleges across Canada began to assume responsibility for nursing education.

Melosh (1982), in her study of American nursing, has contended that hospital-trained nurses considered a degree program as a direct devaluation of the basic skills associated with nursing on the job and detrimental to the cultural milieu that was essential for the socialization of a nurse. Despite different perspectives, the reality was that many working-class women entering nursing could not afford a five-year university program. As well, physicians were not interested in the elevation of nursing training and generally supported the continuation of the three-year hospital apprenticeship model for nurses.

As health care became more specialized, the forms and levels of personnel increased and exacerbated the development of a rigid and hierarchical division of labour within nursing. The internal dissension created by competition between different fields of practice and types of training proved to be formidable barriers to unifying and strengthening a nursing mandate (Coburn, 1974). By creating its own hierarchy within nursing, a hierarchy committed to efficiency and organizational goals, a sense of sisterhood or an analysis of their subordination was difficult to achieve. Unfortunately, as Melosh (1982) has suggested, advocates of the university model failed to identify ways to bridge the gap between hospital- and university-trained nurses.

The nurses who wished to buy into "professionalism" failed to recognize its essence reflected a male culture that was different from women's. In replicating the elitism associated with male professions, the fight for nurses to become "professional" was centred on licensing and registration. Theoretical knowledge and technical skills and the "naturalness" of women's caring were seen as opposites and the complexities involved in melding the two were not understood (Reverby, 1988).

The mission of service and caring that had shaped the formation of nursing as a field became a source of both strength and oppression. Baumgart and Larsen (1988) have argued that, as with other women's work, caring as part of a nursing mandate has been constrained by understaffing and by the priority given to more technical aspects of medical care. Concurring with this view, Susan Reverby (1988) has concluded that nurses lacked the power to implement their vision of an ethic of care. Nurses have also failed to see how caring was shaped not simply by women's psychological identity but by the social and political context in which nursing developed. It was a duty to care directed by a male medical hierarchy, not an ethic of care in which nurses would be able to make more autonomous judgements about the kind of care patients should receive.

In the last decade, issues of nursing autonomy and rights have intensified. The unionization of nurses has promoted a greater consciousness and may well prove to be a stronger force in ensuring that nurses have a greater say in the delivery of health care (Melosh, 1982).[3] However, Baumgart and Larsen (1988) have pointed out that unions have not confronted the structural inequalities within the health care system or issues of gender.

PROFESSIONALIZATION AND TEACHING

In a recent look at teaching as a profession, Finklestein (1989) presents a rather discouraging perspective on teaching as a field of women's work in the United States. She is saddened by the reality that her daughter's commitment to children "has led her to the courthouse rather than to the schoolhouse door." Questioning why young women are choosing law over teaching, Finklestein examines the way in which teaching as a women's career has been undervalued in the last 100 years. As she traces the evolution of teacher training in the normal school, Finklestein demonstrates how the emphasis shifted from the preparation of rural elementary teachers to the preparation of secondary school teachers, principals, and the teachers of teachers.

Women teachers, like nurses and social workers, were also limited in their ability to control the profession or to achieve equality. According to Finklestein, the explanation for this is found in efforts to professionalize teaching and gradual acceptance of the male university research model. Despite the ways in which training for teaching had opened the doors and minds of women, they continued to be regarded as intellectually inferior. Elementary school teaching was undertaken by women and rooted in practice. In contrast, the men who made up the ranks of the secondary schools and administration were expected to wrestle with a formal academic program of educational theory. Learning through classroom practice teaching continued to be downgraded in the twentieth century as teacher training programs were lodged within the university. Thus, the experiences of women gained from the day-to-day world of practice were gradually devalued.

Differences over the way teachers should be prepared for their role were also evident in Canada. Ryerson had advocated training for teachers in the middle of the nineteenth century, but this was not easily attained. By 1875, a quarter of the teachers in Ontario were graduates of the Toronto Normal School, which first offered a training program for teachers in 1847. Ryerson's interest in upgrading teaching through the development of the Normal School was a direct attack on the county model schools, an alternate form of teaching preparation for candidates who had one or two years of high school. Given three months of training under the supervision of a qualified teacher, graduates received a third-class teaching certificate enabling them to teach in their own county. The issue of what constituted appropriate training for teaching in Ontario was not resolved until 1971, when all teachers, including those in the elementary system, were required to have a degree.

Women teachers, like social workers and nurses, despite the opportunities these occupations provided for women, have also been marginalized. In 1981, less than 10 per cent of women in teaching were employed at the secondary level while over 80 per cent were in the elementary schools (Prentice *et al.*, 1988: 372). Denied the status that Ryerson envisioned, teachers' organizations have turned to the trade union movement to achieve solidarity and to work toward collective rights.

This has been a strategy women teachers entertained much earlier. In 1918, for instance, the Saskatoon Women's Teachers Association was established to develop their own strategies to speak for their constituency. Aware that women teachers received less pay, had lower status, and were generally regarded as intellectually inferior, less adept at using discipline, and not administratively prepared, Saskatoon women teachers realized that their interests would not be represented by men's teaching associations. The SWTA, as one of the largest teaching organizations in Saskatchewan, went on to become a strong political organization that fought for higher wages for women and objected to the policy prohibiting married women from teaching. It was also successful in encouraging the employment of women as principals (Kojder, 1986).

A less militant women's organization existed in Ontario with the establishment, in 1918, of the Federation of Women Teacher Associations of Ontario, which fought for the rights of women teachers. However, perspectives that favoured the identification of teaching with the trade union movement were in conflict with the middle-class aspirations of professionalism. The FWTAO was also faced with the contradiction experienced by women trained to assume self-sacrificing roles yet determined to enhance and gain greater autonomy over their work. Despite the difficulties experienced, the FWTAO did succeed in giving some women teachers a forum to develop the political and social skills of negotiating and public-speaking (Graham, 1974).

CONCLUSION

There is no easy way for women to resolve the contradiction of maintaining an ethic of care at the same time as they seek to have more autonomy and equality within the caring professions. The answer does not lie in either a glorification of caring or a repudiation of professionalism. Rather, we must begin with an understanding of how caring and professionalism have defined the work of women in these fields of work. Both have reinforced a gendered division of labour and both must be re-examined.

A beginning point in achieving change is recognizing women's caring as work. What needs to be emphasized is that caring has been "natural" for women because they have learned and developed these skills and continue to practice them in both the private and public spheres. As Daniels (1987) points out, when men begin to provide interpersonal and communication skills within business, they are highly valued. In contrast, when women emphasize an ethic of care, it is trivialized, viewed as sentimental and unscientific. The challenge is to identify the knowledge and skills derived from women's caring and value these in the same way as knowledge gained from more traditional modes of inquiry.

Similarly, it is important to acknowledge that professionalism, as it has been implemented, has not and will not be the panacea advocated by leaders in the fields of nursing, social work, and teaching. The expectation that equality and increased status will gradually prevail as men enter fields traditionally filled by women has proven to be false; nor have efforts to professionalize along the male model created gender-free systems of meritocracy. As this journey into the past reveals, women's experiences in the professions have been different from men's. Some women have resisted complete domination and developed strategies to ensure more influence. Both Reverby (1988) and Melosh (1989) argue that women's experience in nursing made them aware of the limits to their autonomy, one of the first requirements for change. In the last decade, nurses have made a strong case for more input into the health care system. The reality that nurses can shut down the system is a sobering thought for most physicians. Women teachers, through separate unions, have continued to see their interests as different from men.

For the most part, women in social work have been more conservative than their sisters in nursing and teaching, and they have tended to work toward equality in a more individualistic way. However, feminist critiques in social work are beginning to uncover the experiences of women as professionals and clients and these critiques provide a starting point for collaboration and consciousness-raising. Greater attention has been paid in social work to the development of a knowledge base that incorporates a more holistic view of private and public worlds, and of practice and theory.

A further major consideration is the relationship between the caring professions and the cared-for, a point that has received little attention in this chapter. Professionalization has been accompanied by an attempt to objectify the cared-for and has led to blaming the victims, i.e., the clientele. An argument can be made that the distance has increased between women teachers, nurses, and social workers and those they serve. As Reverby (1988) reminds us, an order now has to be made for nurses to provide TLC! Maternal feminism and an ethic of caring promoted a feminine consciousness and concern for their poorer and less fortunate sisters. In contrast, the expert professional frequently mystifies her work and places the recipient in an infantile role. A feminist ethos of professionalism needs to be based on an ideology that integrates an ethic of care and forms a more equal partnership with the cared-for.

Yet, an expectation that women in the professions will achieve equality without changing the ideology of the separate spheres seems unfounded. As Daniels (1987) has argued, the invisible work that women do as homemakers, mothers, and volunteers needs to become visible, not only for its economic value but for its worth in the formation of a caring community. The danger is that women themselves have begun to devalue their unpaid work in the home and the community. And when it becomes paid work, as evident in the above review, its value is only marginally higher. For those women in the professions who attempt to carry two careers, the price is often very high. Women may model and emulate successful men, but as superwomen they do not produce change.

A final point presents a formidable barrier to change in nursing, social work, and teaching: the presence of these occupations in large bureaucratic organizations. Women, as direct service professionals in these organizations, have had limited autonomy, control over their work, and influence in policy and resource allocation. Hierarchical divisions – whether between men and women, the caregiver and the cared-for, the administrator and the direct service worker, the professional and the volunteer, the principal and the teacher, the doctor and the nurse, the theoretician and the practitioner – all reflect differences in power, esteem, and autonomy. Dichotomies of this nature ensure rigid role definitions and organizational structures that fail to uncover the complexities and solutions involved in arriving at a collective responsibility for caring.

NOTES

1. From 1971 to 1987, the number of women in engineering increased from 1.2 per cent of the total graduates to 12.2 per cent; in law, from 9.4 per cent to 46.7 per cent; and in medicine, from 12.8 per cent to 41.7 per cent. See Statistics Canada, *Women in Canada: A Statistical Report*, Second Edition, Cat. 89-503E (Ottawa: Ministry of Supply and Services, February, 1990), p. 55.

2. For a history of the YWCA, see Josephine Harshaw, *When Women Work Together* (Toronto: The YWCA, 1966); Mary Quayle Innis, *Unfold the Years: A History of the YWCA in Canada* (Toronto: McCelland and Stewart, 1949).

3. It is estimated that 80 per cent of nurses working in hospitals and

two-thirds of all nurses employed in Canada are unionized. See Alice J. Baumgart and Jennifer Larsen, eds., *Canadian Nursing Faces the Future: Development and Change* (Toronto: C.V. Mosby, 1988), p. 11.

REFERENCES

Austin, B.F., ed. 1890. *Woman: Her Character, Culture and Calling*. Brantford, Ont.

Bacchi, Carol Lee, 1983. *Liberation Deferred: The Ideas of the English-Canadian Suffragists, 1877-1918*. Toronto: University of Toronto Press.

Baines, Carol T. 1988. *Women's Reform Organizations in Canada 1870-1930: A Historical Perspective*. Working Papers on Social Welfare in Canada #26, Faculty of Social Work, University of Toronto.

Baines, Carol T. 1990. "From Women's Benevolence to Professional Social Work: The Case of the Wimodausis Club and The Earlscourt Children's Home, 1902-1971," Ph.D. thesis, Faculty of Social Work, University of Toronto.

Baumgart, Alice J., and Jennifer Larsen, eds. 1988. *Canadian Nursing Faces the Future: Development and Change*. Toronto: C.V. Mosby.

Bliss, Michael. 1968. "The Methodist Church and World War I," *Canadian Historical Review*, XLIX (September).

Brown, Robert Craig, and Ramsay Cook. 1976. *Canada 1896-1921: A Nation Transformed*. Toronto: McClelland and Stewart.

Chambers, Clarke. 1986. "Women in the Creation of the Profession of Social Work," *Social Service Review* (March).

Coburn, Judy. 1974. "'I See and am Silent': A Short History of Nursing in Ontario," in Janice Acton, Penny Goldsmith, and Bonnie Shepard, eds., *Women at Work 1850-1930*. Toronto: Canadian Women's Educational Press.

Cook, Blanche Wiessen. 1979. "Female Support Networks and Political Activism," in Nancy F. Cott and Elizabeth H. Pleck, eds., *A Heritage of Her Own*. New York: Simon and Schuster.

Cook, Ramsay. 1985. *The Regenerators: Social Criticism in Late Victorian English Canada*. Toronto: University of Toronto Press.

Cott, N. 1977. *The Bonds of Womanhood*. New Haven: Yale University Press.

Dalley, G. 1988. *Ideologies of Caring: Rethinking Community and Collectivism*. London: Macmillan.

Daniels, Arlene Kaplan. 1987. "Invisible Work," *Social Problems*, 34, (December).

Daniels, Arlene Kaplan. 1988. *Invisible Careers: Women Civic Leaders from the Volunteer World*. Chicago: University of Chicago Press.

Ehrenreich, John H. 1985. *The Altruistic Imagination: A History of Social Work and Social Policy in the United States*. Ithaca, N.Y.: Cornell University Press.

Emery, George N. 1977. "The Origins of Canadian Methodist Involvement in the Social Gospel Movement 1890-1914," *The Bulletin Journal of the Canadian Historical Society*, XIX, 1-2 (March-June).

Finklestein, Barbara. 1989. "Conveying Messages to Women: Higher Education and the Teaching Profession in Historical Perspective," *American Behavioral Scientist*, 32, 6 (July-August).

Freedman, Estelle. 1979. "Separation as Strategy: Female Institution Building as American Feminism 1870-1930." *Feminist Studies*, 5, 3.

Glazer, Penima Migdal, and Miriam Slater. 1987. *Unequal Colleagues: The Entrance of Women into the Professions, 1890-1945*. New Brunswick, N.J.: Rutgers University Press.

Graham, Elizabeth. 1974. "School Marms and Early Teaching in Ontario," in Acton, Goldsmith, and Shepard, eds., *Women at Work*.

Harshaw, Josephine. 1966. *When Women Work Together: A History of the YWCA in Canada*. Toronto: The YWCA.

Hearn, Jeff. 1985. "Patriarchy, Professionalisation and the Semi-Professions," in Clare Ungerson, ed., *Women and Social Policy*. London: Macmillan.

Hurl, Lorna. 1983. "Building a Profession: The Origin and Development of the Department of Social Service in the University of Toronto 1914-1928," *Occasional Papers* (Faculty of Social Work, University of Toronto).

Innis, Mary Quayle. 1949. *Unfold the Years: A History of the YWCA in Canada*. Toronto: McClelland and Stewart.

Katz, Michael. 1986. *In the Shadow of the Poor House*. New York: Basic Books.

Kealey, Linda, ed. 1979. *A Not Unreasonable Claim: Women and Reform in Canada, 1880's-1920's*. Toronto: Women's Educational Press.

Keddy, B. 1986. "Private Duty Nursing Days of the 1920's and 1930's in Canada," *Canadian Women Studies*, 7, 3: 99-103.

Kerr, Janice, and Janetta MacPhail. 1988. *Canadian Nursing Issues and Perspectives*. Toronto: McGraw Hill-Ryerson.

Kojder, Apolonja Maria. 1986. "In Union There Is Strength: The Saskatoon Women's Teachers Association," *Canadian Women Studies*, 7, 3 (Fall).

Lubove, Roy. 1977. *The Professional Altruist: The Emergence of Social Work as a Career, 1880-1930*. New York: Atheneum.

McDowell, John P. 1982. *The Social Gospel in the South: The Woman's*

Home Mission Movement in the Methodist Episcopal Church, 1886-1939. Baton Rouge: Louisiana State University Press.

Melosh, Barbara. 1982. *'The Physician's Hand': Work, Culture and Conflict in American Nursing*. Philadelphia: Temple University Press.

Melosh, Barbara. 1989. " 'Not Merely a Profession': Nurses and Resistance to Professionalization," *American Behavioral Scientist*, 32, 6 (July-August).

Mitchinson, Wendy. 1977. "Aspects of Reform: Four Women's Organizations in 19th Century Canada," Ph.D. thesis, York University.

Mitchinson, Wendy. 1987. "Early Women's Organizations and Social Reform: Prelude to the Welfare State," in Allan Moscovitch and Jim Albert, eds., *The "Benevolent" State: The Growth of Welfare in Canada*. Toronto: Garamond Press.

Morrison, T.R. 1971. "Child-Centered Urban Social Reform in Late 19th Century Ontario," Ph.D. thesis, University of Toronto.

Owram, Doug. 1986. *The Government Generation: Canadian Intellectuals and the State, 1900-1945*. Toronto: University of Toronto Press.

Pedersen, Diana. 1987. " 'Building Today for the Womanhood of Tomorrow': Businessmen, Boosters and the YWCA, 1890-1930," *Urban History Review*, xv, 3 (February).

Prentice, Alison. 1977. "The Feminization of Teaching," in Susan Mann Trofimenkoff and Alison Prentice, eds., *The Neglected Majority*. Toronto: McClelland and Stewart.

Prentice, Alison, *et al*. 1988. *Canadian Women: A History*. Toronto: Harcourt Brace Jovanovich.

Reverby, Susan. 1988. *Ordered to Care: The Dilemma of American Nursing 1850-1945*. Cambridge: Cambridge University Press.

Roberts, Wayne. 1979. " 'Rocking the Cradle for the World': The New Woman and Maternal Feminism, Toronto, 1877-1914," in Linda Kealey, ed., *A Not Unreasonable Claim: Women and Reform in Canada, 1880's-1920's*. Toronto: Women's Educational Press.

Robinson, Helen C. 1979. *Decades of Caring (The Big Sister Story)*. Toronto: Dundurn Press.

Rooke, Patricia T., and R.L. Schnell. 1982. "Rise and Decline of North America's Protestant Orphanage as Woman's Domain, 1850-1930," *Atlantis* (Spring).

Rooke, Patricia T., and R.L. Schnell. 1987. *No Bleeding Heart: Charlotte Whitton, A Feminist on the Right*. Vancouver: University of British Columbia Press.

Rosenberg, Charles. 1981. "Inward Vision and Outward Glance: The Shaping of the American Hospital 1890-1914," in David J. Rothman and Stanton Wheeler, eds., *Social History and Social Policy*. New York: Academic Press.

Scott, Anne Firor. 1984. *Making the Invisible Woman Visible*. Urbana: University of Illinois Press.

Smith-Rosenberg, Carrol. 1985. *Disorderly Conduct*. New York: Alfred A. Knopf.

Strong-Boag, Veronica. 1979. "Canada's Women Doctors: Feminism Constrained," in Kealey, ed., *A Not Unreasonable Claim*.

Strong-Boag, Veronica. 1982. "Intruders in the Nursery: Childcare Professionals Reshape the Years One to Five, 1920–1940," in Joy Parr, ed., *Childhood and Family in Canadian History*. Toronto: McClelland and Stewart.

Struthers, James. 1987a. " 'Lord Give us Men': Women and Social Work in English Canada, 1918–1953," in Moscovitch and Albert, eds., *The "Benevolent" State*.

Struthers, James. 1987b. "A Profession in Crisis: Charlotte Whitton and Canadian Social Work in the 1930s," in Moscovitch and Albert, eds., *The "Benevolent" State*.

CHAPTER III

The Child-Care Crisis: Realities of Women's Caring

Evelyn Ferguson

INTRODUCTION

The Task Force believes that the present state of affairs with regard to the care of our children must not be allowed to continue. In fact, we believe that the child care situation is in a state of crisis, and that serious consequences will result if steps are not taken immediately to rectify the situation. (Status of Women, 1986: 279)

The current child-care crisis is directly related to women's caring. As women have swelled the paid labour force during the past two decades, our traditional "mother at home" model of child care has ceased to meet the needs of most Canadian families (Eichler, 1988; Status of Women, 1986). Parents are scrambling to create acceptable child-care arrangements from every available resource: formal licensed day-care services, informal unlicensed paid care such as "sitters" and "nannies," and unpaid services usually provided by family members.[1] The need to improve child-care services has spawned two federal task forces in the 1980s (Status of Women, 1986; House of Commons, 1987), numerous provincial government policy papers, and countless academic and professional research studies. Parents, child-care professionals, service providers, and women's groups have sought solutions ranging from more government intervention for licensed non-profit services (Status of Women, 1986) to appeals to women to stay at home with their children (Maynard, 1985: Fraiberg, 1977; Finlayson, 1987; REAL Women, n.d.).

However, most of the issues surrounding the child-care question have centred on controversies over profit or non-profit care, licensed or unlicensed care, and the acceptable degree of government involvement. Missing from the debate has been a theoretical perspective that highlights the centrality of the work of caring in all of these child-care situations. This chapter explores some of the common realities underlying pre-school child care and the implications for women, whether they are mothers, grandmothers, babysitters, nannies, or day-care workers. While many of these issues affect children of all ages, the particular dependency of pre-schoolers and women's primary responsibility in caring for them are the reasons why this chapter focuses on the care for this age level. By examining the similarities in the child-care work carried out in different settings we gain an understanding of how an ideology of caring underpins the undervaluing and the invisible nature of this work. It also enables us to formulate possible options that would benefit all women and acknowledge the critical importance of all child care.

Three issues provide the cornerstone of the present analysis. The first is that whatever the setting, it is women, not men, who care for dependent children and this work is not adequately recognized or remunerated. Second, the conception of children as a private responsibility has an important influence on the way we organize child care. Social policies reinforce the assumption that child care is women's work in both the private and public spheres. Finally, while there are differences in child-care work, this analysis also recognizes that whatever the setting, they are all based on an ideology of women's caring. By stressing the differences, public discourse has divided women, diminishing their opportunities to work together to change our social organization of child care.

The care of very young children is demanding but rewarding work that women in all settings describe with conflicting and contradictory feelings. In a recent article Marni Jackson (1989: 34), a journalist and mother, states that "interruption, contradiction, and ambivalence are the soul of motherhood." In a letter to the Task Force on day care a family home caregiver graphically describes the tasks and the feelings associated with her work:

> The job involves being a maid, a cook, a child psychologist, a teacher, and a mother to these children – from getting a baby onto solid foods, to toilet training, to teaching him to walk, talk, do's and don'ts, to the basics of the alphabet, counting, colours, body health and body grooming, to the day to day trivia and hassle of learning to be – what a deal . . . With such enormous output and so little recognition or recompense, you'd have to be a lunatic to want to be a Day Care mother. But I do. . . . (Status of Women, 1986: 108)

The chapter begins by describing the settings in which women care for pre-school children, emphasizing, in particular, the monetary value accorded to child care in each setting. Second, some realities shaping the context in which women care for children are explored. Finally, principles for restructuring our child-care system are discussed.

CHILD-CARE SETTINGS

Pre-school Canadian children receive care under a variety of conditions. These range from informal settings with family, neighbours, and friends, where there is no outside support or monitoring, to formal "licensed" care regulated by provincial governments. The latter form meets only a small percentage of the need for child care. A recent report for the federal government estimated that the informal sector provides 88 per cent of all Canadian child care (Baker, 1987: 13). All settings reflect the assumption that the primary responsibility for pre-school children rests with parents. These settings provide care for a specific number of hours per day and assume parents, usually mothers, will provide the balance of care.

The most common formal care is the group day-care centre, which employs trained day-care workers and is licensed to care for from ten children in some centres to over 100 children in others. The sponsorship of these centres incudes municipal governments, private non-profit groups such as churches, service clubs, and parent co-ops, and independent and franchised businesses. Licensed forms of care also include individual women, usually referred to as family home caregivers, who care for a small number of children in their homes. Although they represent only a very small share of licensed child care, family homes can be licensed in all provinces and territories except New Brunswick, Newfoundland, and the Northwest Territories (Status of Women, 1986).

Numbers of children, staff, and quality of facilities are some of the factors regulated by provincial statute in all licensed settings. The mandate of all child-care services is to provide care, rather than education, for pre-school children for all or part of their parents' working day. These settings provide supervision, meals, snacks, places for the children to nap, toys, and various kinds of activities. Licensed centres are typically open only during normal working hours, from 8 a.m. to 6 p.m., Monday to Friday.

A final category of licensed care is the nursery school or kindergarten, mandated to provide education for pre-school children. These use trained pre-school teachers and the programs are focused on the educational needs of children rather than the "care" needs of working parents. They are usually available only a few hours per day and working parents employed full-time must make additional arrangements. Local boards of education as well as private organizations offer kindergarten and junior kindergarten programs in a number of provinces.

However, by far the largest amount of the care provided to our pre-school children is by parents at home and by others in informal settings. These include unlicensed family home caregivers who "babysit" in their own homes and relatives, nannies, and other paid caregivers providing care in the child's home. Services are similar to those found in licensed settings, but the hours of care may be more flexible, and those providing care may do additional housekeeping work for the family. The nature and quality of the care provided in these settings is not known because they are not formally regulated (Status of Women, 1986: 125).

Many of these care providers are foreign domestic workers and/or women of colour who, while theoretically guaranteed certain minimal working conditions through Employment and Immigration Canada, are frequently subject to exploitation (Arat-Koç, 1990). Financial remuneration varies among these settings, but in almost all cases it is abysmally low (Status of Women, 1986). The report of the Canadian Commission for the International Year of the Child (1979) argued that child-care workers and other caregivers are chronically underpaid because they replace parents, particularly mothers, who are paid nothing for their work as caregivers. At the opposite end of the continuum are teachers working in nursery schools and kindergartens, who are the most highly paid. Unlike child care, teachers' salaries, particularly in the public sector, suggest that society is more prepared to recognize education as a child's right and an important form of public labour, although the age at which this begins is arbitrary. The differences, however, are substantial. Teachers' salaries are a function of a universal education system, strengthened by professional organizations and unions fighting for better wages and working conditions. Because these services are not primarily designed to meet the needs of working parents they are often excluded in discussions of child care. Lero and Kyle (1989) remind us, however, that the historical divisions between pre-school education and child care are disappearing as the educational components and qualifications of child-care workers increase.

Those caring for young children in licensed group child-care centres earn far less than their counterparts in education. Considered child care, not education, their services are not universally available and state financed, and as a result their funding arrangements are less secure. Provincial and federal governments partially subsidize low-income parents and provide start-up funds, maintenance, and salary enhancement grants, but child care is substantially financed through parent fees and some private contributions (Blain, 1985; Townson, 1985).

The type of centre, the nature of its sponsorship, and the presence or absence of unionization are important influences on the wages and working conditions offered by licensed centres. It is not surprising that the most poorly paid are the workers in family day-care homes who received in 1984 an average net wage of $2.26 per hour (Schom-Moffat, 1985: 131). Municipal government day-care services are all unionized, as are some private non-profit organizations, such as parent co-ops, churches, and service organizations. For-profit child care is rarely unionized, and figures for 1984 reported that only 8 per cent of all Canadian child-care workers were union members (Schom-Moffat, 1985: 101). The poorest wages and benefit packages are in the commercial centres, which usually receive fewer government subsidies and private donations than the non-profit sector. The highest wages and most favourable benefits are in the unionized government-run centres, confined almost exclusively to Ontario and Quebec (Schom-Moffat, 1985; National Day Care Information Centre, 1987). Figures for 1984, the latest available for comparison, indicate that the average hourly wage in municipal centres was $10.58 per hour compared to $7.46 in non-profit centres and $5.47 in commercial centres. The hourly wage in unionized settings was $9.90 while the comparable figure for non-unionized centres was $6.63 (Schom-Moffat, 1985: 117). The profit sector has provided the majority of day-care spaces in Alberta and Newfoundland, while in Ontario they comprise close to 50 per cent (National Day Care Information Centre, 1987).

The most commonly utilized but lowest-paid caregivers are in the informal sector (Status of Women, 1986). Nannies and other caregivers in the child's home usually earn more per child, while babysitters in their own homes earn proportionally less per child but often care for a larger number of children. Not surprisingly, studies indicate that the latter form of care is the most accessible and least expensive form of child care (Status of Women, 1986). Parents, child-care professionals, journalists, and day-care lobby groups have expressed concerns about the quality of care in this sector (Status of Women, 1986; Johnson and Dineen, 1981). Due to their unregulated nature, specific figures about wages and working conditions are not available, but the Status of Women Task Force concluded that their earnings are similar to those of licensed family home caregivers, but their per diem rates tend to be lower.

Informal care settings, unlike licensed centres, do not receive tax subsidies. Parents, however, may claim some child-care deductions on their income tax if the caregiver provides receipts. In 1989, parents could claim up to $4,000 for a child age six or under or for a child over six with "a severe and prolonged mental and physical impairment," and $2,000 for each eligible child from seven to fourteen years of age (Revenue Canada Taxation, 1989). However, many informal caregivers do not declare this income or provide tax receipts, so many parents are unable to take advantage of this deduction (Power and Brown, 1985). The child-care deduction will therefore tend to benefit those families who have access to licensed care. Higher-income families who can afford to pay higher child-care fees will benefit most from these subsidies, while middle-income families who cannot afford licensed care and lower-income families who receive subsidies will benefit least. In addition, these deductions only apply to families who purchase child care, not to families in which a mother provides full-time care for the children. Tax deductions, because they reduce the amount of tax an individual is required to pay, are worth more at higher levels of income. As a result, they have a regressive impact and will be of least benefit to lower-income families.

The lowest-paid but generally the least controversial form of pre-school child care is parental care, which is almost always provided by the mother. Historically, the only direct remuneration Canada has provided to recognize the costs of children are a nominal Family Allowance benefit and a Child Tax Credit that assists low- and middle-income families. In 1989, the Child Tax Credit was supplemented by $200 a year for each child, provided that no child-care expenses are claimed (Revenue Canada Taxation, 1989). Unlike tax deductions and exemptions, a tax credit has a progressive impact because it is worth more at lower levels of income. This recent supplement was designed to give some financial remuneration to low- and middle-income mothers caring for their children on a full-time basis, and is the first public acknowledgement of in-home child-care work. Unfortunately, the level of the benefit illustrates the low value placed on a mother's caring, particularly in comparison to the deductions allowed for "other than mother" child care. However, the changes in the tax system are significant if one remembers that Family Allowances were presented to Canadians as helping to defray the cost of raising children and maintaining purchasing power in the post-war economy, but not as explicit payments to mothers for caring for their children (Guest, 1980).

In addition to Family Allowances and the Child Tax Credit, low-income single mothers have received financial benefits to enable them to care for their children; Manitoba became the first province to usher in this legislation in 1916. These means-tested and stigmatizing benefits are variously referred to as "mothers allowances," "family benefits," or "public welfare." As Patricia Evans discusses in Chapter VI, public acknowledgement of this as socially useful labour was eroded as single mothers were pressured to become financially independent from the state. Subsidized child care for working single mothers only benefits women who are in the labour market. The shortage of affordable child care and the lack of decent paying jobs frequently mean that women are confronted with the unpalatable choice of struggling on a low income from work or a minimal benefit from welfare. Both of these alternatives pay little attention to the value of child-care work or to the importance of children.

REALITIES SHAPING THE CONTEXT
OF CARE

Feminist theorists who focus on the centrality of caring in women's lives have argued that we must make the realities about caring for young children explicit before we can seriously challenge the dilemmas inherent in our child-care structure (Pascall, 1986). This section explores four important realities that shape the context within which women care for pre-school children.

Many realities surrounding the care of pre-school children similarly shape the care of other vulnerable groups. For example, women's care of the frail elderly and the disabled is also invisible and undervalued (Pascall, 1986). Some factors, however, are unique: the degree to which the expectation of "mothering" defines many Canadian women's lives (Hutter and Williams, 1981); the temporary nature of this care as children grow and become more independent; the political nature of caring as women instil norms and values in our future Canadian citizens (Waerness, 1984); and the recent public debate about child care during election campaigns (House of Commons, 1987). An exploration of the dilemmas and contradictions inherent in current models of child care should suggest changes that will be more supportive to women and children.

Reality 1: Caring for children is a very important part of the work Canadian women do, but it is invisible and undervalued.

The first reality to be made explicit is the invisibility and low value attached to the work of caring for pre-school children. These characteristics have an important influence on the women who care and on the organization of child-care services. The most obvious reason for the invisibility of women's caring of children is the reality that much of it occurs in the private domestic sphere[2] or in the informal market where it is not recognized as an occupation (Graham, 1983; Johnson, 1987; Status of Women, 1986). Even when acknowledged, caring in the domestic sphere is frequently subsumed under "housework," which incorporates many other tasks (Eichler, 1988). Child care is considered an occupation only in the labour market, which comprises a small percentage of the child-care labour in Canadian society (Schom-Moffat, 1985).

A second aspect of this reality is that caring for children is only part of the work women do. In 1988, 58 per cent of mothers with children under the age of three were in the labour force, while 65 per cent of women whose youngest child was aged three to five were labour force participants (Statistics Canada, 1990). Since caring for children is considered women's work, the reality that women have at least two jobs is not acknowledged. For many women, child care is their "hidden" work while their paid occupation defines their public profile. In addition, this "invisible" work constitutes a very demanding twenty-four-hour responsibility. Women who work in the paid labour force are also confronted with arguments from some child development specialists who suggest that child care should be a mother's only occupation (White, 1980: Maynard, 1985). While this position is extremely controversial and typically argued in relation to the developmental needs of children, it does highlight the importance of and demands made by this work. Failing to acknowledge the significance of this work not only distorts the reality of many women's lives and vastly underestimates their working hours and conditions, but it also undervalues the importance of the child-care component of their work.

Another facet of this reality is that women, not men, are the primary caregivers for most very young children. Most professional child-care workers and informal care providers are women, and in families in which one parent works in the home caring for children it is very rare for the father to be that parent (Schom-Moffat, 1985; Eichler, 1988). In single-parent families, custody of children is overwhelmingly the mother's responsibility (Foote, 1988), and it is almost always mothers who collect social assistance while caring for children at home (Gorlick, 1988; Report of the Ontario Social Assistance Review Committee, 1988). Any research exploring the gender breakdown of work within the home shows that women assume most domestic responsibilities regardless of paid outside employment (Eichler, 1988). While some fathers are now more involved in rearing their children, there is as yet no indication of a broad-based gender restructuring of child care.

The devaluing of women's child-care work in the private sphere influences the structure of our public child-care services. As we compare the value of the labour across all types of child care, several factors emerge. First, all child care is undervalued. The most highly valued is that which is labelled as education and lodged within the public schools. However, the "educational" component in "child-care" settings is not acknowledged, nor is the "child-care" component in "educational" settings recognized. As the differences in mandate and purpose of these two major service streams diminish, the wage gap between them becomes more apparent and pressure is likely to grow to improve wages and working conditions in the child-care sector (Lero and Kyle, 1989). This pressure is already mounting in Ontario and Alberta, where day-care centres receive direct government grants to supplement wages (Lero and Kyle, 1989; Bagley, 1986), and in Manitoba, where day-care workers struck for a day in 1989 to back their demands for higher wages (Canadian Day Care Advocacy Association, 1990). However, as child-care workers seek to improve the status of their work through an emphasis on its educational component, there is a real risk that the "care" component may be devalued, and the distinctions between education and care will increase rather than diminish. As Carol Baines illustrates in Chapter II, models of professionalization have sometimes served to render more invisible the significance of women's caring.

Second, divisions in the delivery of child care and the differing monetary values attached to caring for children fail to provide women with a common understanding of women's caring. Resentment and hostility often emerge between different groups of women: between mothers in the paid labour force and caretakers who care for their children; between mothers who are employed and those whose work is confined to the home; and between licensed and unlicensed, trained and untrained caregivers. Child-care workers, for example,

may resent mothers, whom they perceive as spending insufficient time with their children; mothers working at home are
angry about the public money subsidizing employed mothers
using child-care centres; and untrained workers take offence
at the implication that they have limited skills when compared to a worker with a professional degree. These divisions
also reinforce competition between settings and their supporters, which undermines efforts to provide a united front for
developing mutual help and support and for negotiating and
advocating solutions together. Thus, we have advocacy
groups appearing to support licensed care over unlicensed,
non-profit care over profit, and mother-at-home care over day
care (Ontario Coalition for Better Day Care, 1985; REAL
Women, n.d.). These divisions make it easier for the issue of
the underfunding and undervaluing of all child-care labour to
be avoided in the political arena.

Third, this undervaluing of the work of child care has
psychological implications. "Mothers go through so much,
every day, that is never acknowledged" (Jackson, 1989: 36).
Mothers and other caregivers experience the contradictory
messages accorded to their work. They receive society's moral
message that caring for young children is a virtuous activity,
and neglecting it is a grave sin (Hutter and Williams, 1981).
Financially, they derive little monetary reward, making many
women dependent and vulnerable to both men and the state.
Dependent on men, they and their children risk physical and
emotional abuse, and dependent on the state, they risk the
stigma of charity or welfare. Whether caring for her own
children full or part time, or looking after someone else's
child, each woman is likely to experience the undervaluing of
an important part of her life.

Finally, and on a more optimistic note, the boundaries of
child care are being pushed from the private sphere of the
home into the public sphere, which suggests that changes
may be under way for women in a variety of care-taking roles.
Battles fought over child care now will not only benefit
women performing child care, but also those women engaged
in less visible forms of caring – relatives caring for the frail
elderly, the chronically ill, and other vulnerable members of
society. The now highly public and political nature of the

child-care dilemma, with its attendant task force reports and studies, prominence in party leaders' debates, and its contradictory messages, can be seen as an important development in that it has moved the caring debate into the political arena.

In summary, the invisibility and undervaluing of child-care work poses a dilemma for women. They experience financial and physical vulnerability to men and the state. At the same time women's commitment to caring is reinforced by love and the moral importance accorded this work. This commitment is also supported by a belief system, another reality of women's lives.

Reality 2: Women's caregiving is supported by the belief that it is "normal" and "natural."

A second reality about women's caring for young children is the belief that it is "normal" and "natural." As New and David (1985: 13) put it: "Women are given caring work on the grounds that they are mothers, or may become mothers, or should have been mothers." Hutter and Williams (1981) conclude that women who, through choice or necessity, do not bear children are considered deviant.

Reinforced by this belief, the public has remained relatively unconcerned about the gender imbalance so apparent in our child-care structure. Studies concerned about mother-child attachment have dominated the child development literature, but there is a striking lack of concern about paternal bonding (Rutter, 1981). A different form of caring is expected from fathers than from mothers. While mothers must demonstrate their love for their children by providing physical caregiving, fathers are expected to care by earning money and providing material resources. This breadwinner model of the family dictates that women provide physical and emotional care for children while they and their children depend materially on spouses or the state.

These expectations translate into Canadian social policies. Fathers who wish to look after their children receive far less state support than mothers. Only very recently has eligibility for maternity benefits under Unemployment Insurance been extended to some fathers to enable them to care for their newborn infants. Traditionally, it has been more difficult for single fathers to receive social assistance to care for their children at home (Eichler, 1988).

At the same time a double standard has been established for different groups of women. Mothers' dependent status is still an acceptable norm for those with breadwinner spouses, but recent family law and public welfare changes are pushing single mothers to be independent and provide both physical and material care for their children (Hurl, 1989; Foote, 1988). These changes most affect the poorest mothers on social assistance and those who are separated and divorced.

The belief that it is normal and natural for women to be mothers has important implications for men as well as women in that it limits choices available to both sexes. But it is single and poor women who possess the least control and have the fewest child-care options. With our present undervaluing of the caring work, these women and their children pay most dearly for the current organization of our child care.

Reality 3: Care for pre-school children is primarily a private responsibility of those parents who bear or raise those children.

Parents must plan, provide, and pay for child-care services unless their inability to do so is demonstrated and they are deemed to be financially "in need" or their children emotionally or physically "neglected." If parents are in financial need, the provincial and federal governments subsidize care through the Federal Canada Assistance Plan for parents using licensed day-care facilities (Townson, 1985). If mothers are deemed neglect-ful, child welfare authorities may recommend substitute care to counteract what they have identified as poor parenting. This rationale for government child-care subsidy is often described as the compensatory orientation to child care and gained popularity during the 1960s with the American War on Poverty and the Head Start Project (Roby, 1973).

"Normal" families not deemed to be in financial or emotional need receive minimal government help; what there is occurs primarily through tax deductions. As discussed earlier in the chapter, these deductions provide a larger benefit to higher-income Canadians and are therefore regressive in their impact. The token tax credit available to low- and middle-income families where the mother is at home caring for children only highlights the minimal value we attach to her labour and reinforces the privacy of the child-care responsibility.

The implications of the privacy of child care can be contrasted to the public responsibility assumed for education. Child care is supposed to be available through a child's family, typically provided by the mother, whereas education is universally provided in the public domain once a child reaches the age of four or five. Each begins with different perceptions of the child. Child care assumes that the child belongs to a parent, while education assumes that the child is a citizen in his or her own right.

The welfare state, therefore, is not totally absent from our system of child care. The support it provides "normal" families, however, is minimal and is regressive in impact, giving greater support to high-income families and those who purchase care in the child-care market. This, however, is not the only role the welfare state plays in our organization of child care. As Wilson (1977) has emphasized in her analysis of women and the welfare state, the state also controls the lives of women and children.

Reality 4: While women provide the daily care of pre-school children, the state intervenes by controlling important aspects of this care.

Caring for young children means socializing and preparing them to assume productive roles. This is ultimately political, and partially explains the protective or compensatory perspective that pervades the literature on child care (Pascall, 1986). For instance, if a young native mother is perceived as neglecting her pre-school child, the state, through its child welfare agents, may recommend that the child be enrolled in a licensed day-care centre. Control by the state is also manifested in the provincial regulations imposed on licensed child-care centres establishing the numbers and qualifications of the caregivers and the standards of care.

Feminists raise concerns about the sources of this control, including the professionalization of child care. Some argue that the state's interest in socialization has resulted in mothers and other caregivers losing control over children's care while they continue to do most of the labour (Maroney, 1985). While child-care workers' wages have increased as they expanded into the public sphere, concomitantly child-care experts, many of them men or women not providing daily care, have established the standards of care. The danger is that women's authority and respect have subsequently been eroded. Not only does this risk undermining women's confidence in their caring abilities, but by focusing state action on educating mothers and regulating caregivers, it diverts attention and resources from economic supports and public services offering relief and practical support (Waerness, 1984).

The state's control and the professionalization of child care have divided women. Professionals too often judge young, low-income, and/or single mothers as neglectful (Saraceno, 1984) and expect mothers to be educated child-care service consumers (Browne, 1984). "It is usually other women – health visitors, social workers, teachers, relatives – who approve or disapprove of the way mothers manage their children. In this way divisions form between mothers and women who look after children in different ways" (New and David, 1985: 22).

Whether from a feminist or traditional perspective, these political implications lend a moral and ideological tone to the child-care debate, often delivering contradictory messages. Pascall notes the "ludicrous outcome" of some of our social policies, for example, in the sudden shift in what is considered best for our four- and five-year-old children: four-year-olds are believed best cared for at home by mother, but "woe betide any parent who decides thereafter that she would prefer to keep her child at home" (Pascall, 1986: 84).

POSSIBLE SOLUTIONS TO THE
CHILD-CARE PROBLEM

The challenge we face in exploring alternatives to the present child-care system is how to respect the integral aspects of care while acknowledging and enhancing the value of this labour. Pascall states that those bearing the child-care burden are not clamouring to give others this work. Yet women and their children remain vulnerable, dependent, and poor, at least partly as a result of our present system.

To face this challenge, it is critical to examine how the private and public worlds intersect. Our view of the family places responsibility for child care within the private sphere of the home. This does not limit care exclusively to the home, but it does mean that the family, and usually the mother, has ultimate responsibility for care. She plans and organizes the care she does not personally provide, and when these plans break down the responsibility for caring generally reverts to her.

The public nature of the debate, however, suggests that the individual contradictions and conflicts confronting mothers are pushing the boundaries of child care increasingly into the public sphere. Children are cared for in the formal market; the government has started to provide tax deductions for the purchase of child care; and mothers at home now receive tax credits that acknowledge their child care. The outcomes of these changes are contradictory and the impacts at times unjust, but they portend movement from child care being seen as a private responsibility to the recognition that the well-being of children is a public issue.

A similar trend occurred when day nurseries were established during World War Two, but the direction was reversed after the war. Contemporary changes, fortunately, do not appear so transitory. The steady increase of mothers with pre-school children moving into the paid labour force over the last two decades, the increasing professionalization of child-care workers, two federal task forces on child care in the 1980s, and the high profile of the child-care debate during recent provincial and federal elections all suggest that this issue will no longer be pushed back into the privacy of the home and women's lives.

Nevertheless, we must not be lulled into believing that these changes will necessarily move quickly or in a manner that equally benefits all women. Our recent history suggests otherwise. Changes to date have benefited upper-income women at the expense of poor and middle-income women. Higher-income women have the resources to purchase child care and they have the most to gain from tax deductions that partially offset these costs. It is clearly the education, experience, and skills of these women to the paid labour force that are valued, not their caring labour within the home. Their gains, it can be argued, have been made at the expense of lower-income women, including those who care for children.

The challenge is to change our child-care system in ways that will benefit all women. The following principles for doing this acknowledge the centrality of caring in women's lives. These principles outline major issues to be addressed in altering our structure of pre-school child care. The discussion of each principle suggests a variety of concrete systemic changes as well as some of the difficulties and dynamics working against such changes.

Fundamental to each of these principles is one imperative: the need to acknowledge and enhance the labour value of child care in all settings. This means that we must recognize all child care, whether it occurs in the formal market, the informal market, or the private sphere of the home. Dividing our support to neglect any one sector undermines the long-term goal of change that would benefit all women. Wages and working conditions of child-care staff must remain priorities, even when policy-makers and politicians offer a choice between more spaces to meet need or improvements in staff salaries. At the same time we cannot ignore the abysmal working conditions found in the informal market. This labour must be brought into the public sphere for evaluation and financial reward. Finally, we must directly confront the difficulties of defining women's child-care work in the private sphere of the home as public labour. This is a long-term task, but steps need to be taken now to move our child-care system in this direction. Defining what is integral to caring is critical to ensuring that we protect it. We can begin by examining our conceptualization of caring.

Principle 1: The conceptualization of caring underlying our system of child care needs to integrate both physical and emotional dimensions.

This principle is based on the recognition that caring has two separate but interconnected dimensions: caring "for" children – the physical dimension – and caring "about" children – the emotional or affective dimension (Graham, 1983; Pascall, 1986). This conceptualization highlights a critical but often ignored distinction in our current arrangements for child care.

All types of caregiving contain an aspect of the physical dimension of care, what is often called custodial care – for example, feeding, supervising, and changing diapers. Regulations of licensed centres usually deal with these factors, making sure that children are in buildings with a sufficient number of caretakers to ensure they are safe and well cared for. However, the emotional or affective dimension – the idea that one's child is loved and cared "about" – is not always present or regulated.

Parents grapple with this issue when examining their child-care options. Arguments differentiating strengths and weaknesses of various child-care settings often focus on the affective component and debate the greater benefits of "mother care" or "substitute mother care." In a recent study of parents' preferences for child care the second most influential factor, after availability and reliability, was satisfaction with the amount of affection and attention for the child in care (Lero *et al.*, 1985). Other studies have found that parents preferring family home and informal care valued most highly the individualized affection given to their children (Johnson, 1977; Lero, 1981; Stevens, 1984). This concern is not limited to those who prefer "mother" or "mother substitute" care. In another study of parents' preferences for licensed group care, parents ranked low staff turnover as the most important of thirty-three factors affecting the quality of care (Ferguson, 1989).

Ironically, settings that provide the most individualized affection also provide the lowest remuneration to staff (Schom-Moffat, 1985). This appears to mirror the lack of value we attach to child care provided by mothers. We need to legitimate the affective dimension of caregiving, make it more visible, and include it in monetary assessments along with such other factors as professional qualifications and experience.

This principle implies the importance of connecting the caring "for" to the caring "about" in all settings. It requires an emphasis on low worker-child ratios, reduced turnover, and the fostering of close child-carer relationships in any child-care setting. It would include supportive training in child development and increased remuneration for family home caregivers. The result would be increased value and visibility for child-care work. Such an orientation would weaken a persistent argument against publicly provided child care, which suggests that "the impersonal and fragmental character of the public health and social services means that they lose the very qualities of personal commitment which transform a service into caring" (Waerness, 1984: 74). As long as the affectional component in child care is believed to be exclusively the domain of the unpaid mother or poorly paid mother substitute, parents will undermine public calls for universal child care and women's labour will be exploited in the name of love.

Assigning monetary value to the affectional dimension of caring is neither an easy nor a straightforward task. One of the factors working against such an evaluation is the trend toward professionalization. The professionalization of child care in the public sphere is producing highly educated experts who enjoy high status in the child-care community and are considerably better paid for their labour than child-care workers. As well, the organizational structure of publicly funded child care has produced managers, supervisors, and other administrative support workers, who receive higher wages than direct service workers. The contradiction is that the professionalization of child care has been largely responsible for the greater recognition and pay it receives. This has been made possible, however, because child care has been increasingly perceived as a form of pre-school education and caregivers have received professional degrees and diplomas.

Any solution to the child-care problem must combine the benefits of professionalization with a recognition of the value of the affective dimension of caring across the child-care spectrum. To assume child care is simply another form of education ignores one of caring's critical dimensions. We need, therefore, to integrate the affective dimension into our professional expectations while offsetting those aspects of professionalization that devalue daily child-care delivery. This will necessitate conscious efforts to protect the value of child care by paying workers good salaries commensurate with experts and administrators. It may also include assessing skills and knowledge gained from child-care experience as well as from formal training.

A critical role can be played by unions in this situation. Unionized workers already have the highest wages and best working conditions in the child-care field, yet only a small proportion of workers in the formal market are unionized. Unions, too, must understand the importance of the affective dimension in assessing the value of child care. It should be integrated into classification systems re-evaluating women's work as governments and unions attempt to implement programs of equal pay for work of equal value mandated by a number of provinces (Edgecombe-Dobb, 1987; OPSEU, 1987).

Government and workplaces need to be encouraged to implement more generous maternity and paternity leave policies to facilitate parental care of newborn infants. Canadian policies are not nearly as well developed as those found in other industrialized nations. In most European countries the duration of the leave is longer, the income replacement is higher, and a greater proportion of the population is eligible for benefits (Status of Women, 1986: 239).

Finally, changes are long overdue in the way we conceptualize our research. Pascall (1986) notes that the disciplines fragment and obscure the meaning and importance of caring. Our child-care studies are conducted by academics who historically have divided the material care and emotional care of children into separate disciplines. For instance, social policy analysts and economists have focused on the physical aspects of care, "emphasizing the material constraints within which women make choices about caring and the material effects on women's lives flowing from these responsibilities" (Pascall, 1986: 71). The psychological and clinical literature, on the other hand, has stressed the emotional and affective dimensions of caring. Few studies cross these boundaries and explore the interconnectedness of the physical and affective dimensions of caring.

Principle 2: Changes in the child-care system should be directed toward integrating men into the primary care-taking roles and shifting the system's present gender imbalance.

The second principle is directed toward sharing the demands and rewards of caring for children more equitably between men and women in both the private and the public spheres. Motivating men's participation in child care would likely be easier if the financial rewards attached to the work increased. If our organization of child care respected both women and men as carers and rewarded them adequately, the inherent fascination and joy that has motivated women for centuries in this work should attract a proportion of our male work force.

Feminists emphasize the importance of the child-care system for influencing society's gender structure (Chodorow, 1978; O'Brien, 1981). Currently, socialization encourages young girls to see themselves as potential paid workers as well as caregivers, but there is no converse for our young boys, whose socialization continues to dictate their future roles as task-oriented work force participants. Unlike our socialization of young girls, the importance of co-operative relationships and honouring the affective dimensions of people's lives remain secondary for boys (Gilligan, 1982). The present gender imbalance in our child-care arrangements reinforces and perpetuates these socialization patterns. If men began to participate in the child-care system, both girls and boys could see a broader range of role models, thus expanding the life choices of all children.

Without an increase in the value we attach to caring for children, it is unlikely that men will ever participate in significant numbers as primary carers of young children. People rarely change in a way that threatens their own self-interest. As women's vulnerability in their homes and their poverty are more publicly linked to their devalued work, men's incentive for giving up the status and rewards associated with male models of paid labour will be no stronger than it has ever been. We can expose them in our school system to a greater variety of work options and attempt to model greater gender equality in our homes and workplaces, but the likelihood of major changes occurring will remain slim.

An inherent risk in increasing the value of child care and encouraging men to participate more equitably is that they may eventually control and dominate it. Feminists have already demonstrated how the movement of child care into the public sphere has been accompanied by a weakening of women's control over the practices and the establishment of standards of care. While women have remained undervalued carers, they have remained responsible for the day-to-day work of child care. Any significant movement by men into the field risks a further erosion of women's power and influence. Any change in the gender structure of child care must therefore mitigate against this.

Principle 3: Changes in the child-care system should build on the strengths of the child-care arrangements already established by women.

While we need to recognize the extent to which parents' preferences for child care are constrained by the options available to them, we should not ignore some of the strengths of the current system. Parents use the informal market because of its low cost and availability as well as for the emotional care that children may receive. In addition, such arrangements are usually accessible and can be flexible, for example, about hours of service and the care of mildly ill children (Status of Women, 1986).

Studies of parental preferences in child-care arrangements indicate that parents' wishes vary for their children. Some prefer group care with more structure and professionalized input, others value the family home model's personal attention and flexibility, and still others choose to provide most of the care themselves. Factors such as age, health, and personality of the child also influence preferences. For example, parents may prefer mother care or family home care for infants while preferring group care for a toddler (Lero *et al.*, 1985; Stevens, 1984; Lero, 1981).

In private homes, however, and in settings modeling family homes, women are particularly exploited over wages and working conditions. Children are most at risk in some informal settings because the system offers no regulation or supports to carers. Parents express a preference for regulated care if available and affordable (Status of Women, 1986). This suggests that informal market care should be integrated into the formal market through licensing, which would more effectively protect children, promote good wages and working conditions, and potentially provide training and concrete physical supports such as back-up staff. It would respect many of the strengths in these settings while minimizing some risks.

Changes would also focus on the expansion of group centre care. Long waiting lists indicate that many parents now using informal care actually prefer group centre care. Government, non-profit agencies, and small and large businesses currently sponsor these centres. The low wages and poor working conditions so prevalent in the commercial sector need to be addressed. In addition, a variety of studies and task force reports have found that a substantial proportion of parents and Canadians, generally, seriously question the involvement of the profit sector in child care (Status of Women, 1986; Ferguson, 1989; Friendly, Mathien, and Willis, 1987; National Council of Welfare, 1988). Expansion of both government and non-profit sectors is the position taken by the major national lobbying group, the Canadian Day Care Advocacy Association (1990).

The organization of child care should acknowledge that mothers are caring for children in private homes. One of the challenges facing us is the development of some system to compensate them. This process should first separate the care of young children and other dependent populations from what we now call "housework" (Eichler, 1988). While some theorists have advocated private arrangements within families to compensate mothers, others realize the limitations of leaving this issue to the private sphere of the family (Scott, 1978; Riley, 1983). Giving serious consideration to some form of payment to mothers caring for children at home necessitates a greater acceptance of an active role by the state in the delivery of child care. Specifically, it requires greater involvement from the welfare state, the topic discussed below.

Principle 4: The responsibility for child care must be shared more collectively by the families and the welfare state.

The value of child-care work can only be enhanced if the responsibility for care is shared more collectively between families and the welfare state. The state's current residual role, in which help is provided only if parents are deemed in need or inadequate, does not ensure support for "normal" families and reinforces the perception that child care is the primary responsibility of women who work in the private sphere of the home. While tax deductions and tax credits are steps toward the state sharing in child care, the amount of money is minimal and the impact regressive, with the effects of greater benefit to higher-income families. Subsidies for low-income families through the Canada Assistance Plan are stigmatizing and limited to those most in need. Middle-income families are left with very little help with the cost of child care.

It is important that the state take a more active institutional role in the delivery of child-care services by providing more direct funding toward a system and/or providing more direct financial support to families/women who provide or buy that care. This funding would be provided for the care of every child regardless of financial need. It would bring child care more fully into the public sphere. Only then will women's undervalued labour be made public and its worth re-evaluated. In the process, children would be seen as citizens with a right to quality care, not left poor and vulnerable because society does not financially value their mothers' work.

Collectively sharing the responsibility for child care between families and the state facilitates a greater integration of the public and private spheres. The state would have a much clearer mandate than it does now to use public money to subsidize the system. This is what the Status of Women Task Force (1986) and various lobby groups, such as the Canadian Day Care Advocacy Association, mean when they recommend movement toward provision of a universal child-care system.

This would ease the problem of financially rewarding all those doing child care, including mothers in the home. There are a number of options. One is to increase direct grants to child-care centres for maintenance or directly to increase workers' salaries. A second option is to use the tax system, either through tax deductions that lower taxable income and benefit higher-income Canadians, or through refundable tax credits available to anyone who files an income tax form, whether or not they owe any tax, which are designed to benefit lower-income Canadians. A third option is a demo-grant, a universal payment like Family Allowances, sent directly to a mother or father providing or purchasing care. A final option is the provision of a state-provided voucher, the value of which would be comparable to the cost of child care for one child.

The last three options, which involve paying parents of children using child care rather than directly subsidizing the system itself, have the advantage of maximizing parental choice. However, if direct payment to parents is the only method of subsidy, this assumes that the private market will provide adequate and accessible child care for parents to purchase. Any of those methods could be used to pay moth-ers who care in the home.

The first option, directly subsidizing the system, has been supported by day-care lobby groups to ensure that a high-quality accessible system is available to parents (Canadian Day Care Advocacy Association, 1990). Direct payments to parents do not ensure a licensed system or reasonable wages to workers. On their own, such payments are likely to re-inforce the use of an informal system in which parents use their payments or vouchers to support it. In addition, it is difficult to provide direct subsidies to the informal system or mothers at home unless they can be formally integrated into a child-care system.

Many possible strategies could be developed by combining a number of these options or by using one or more along with a licensing system. The level of financial support attached to any of these options is a critical issue and would influence the usefulness of any one or combination of strategies. For exam-ple, our current system combines direct subsidy to day-care workers and child-care centres, tax deductions, tax credits, and a licensing system. However, the tax credit is minimal and the bulk of support to parents is through tax deductions. Subsidies to day-care centres and workers vary by province but none provide a licensed system that comes close to meeting need. The result is a very large and active informal system, an inadequate licensed system with poor wages for workers, and insulting payments to women at home, while the bulk of direct subsidies are delivered to parents with the highest incomes.

Any single strategy must be assessed in the context of a total package of changes. Organizations such as the Status of Women Task Force (1986), the Parliamentary Task Force on Child Care (House of Commons, 1987), and the National Council of Welfare (1988) have all recommended different combinations of these options for enhancing government involvement. Establishing criteria for assessing such proposals has been part of the purpose in developing these principles. The final principle presents one further essential criterion.

Principle 5: Reforms should always be assessed in terms of their implications for women of all classes, races, and geographical locations.

Although reforms should be considered in light of all the foregoing principles, it is particularly important that this final principle be made explicit. Changes in the 1980s have been of more benefit to higher-income women, who are usually white and urban. Licensed child-care facilities are in scarce supply all over Canada, but are particularly limited in rural areas and on native Indian reserves.

The child-care concerns of native women have much in common with those of other women, but they also require an understanding of unique cultural concerns. Several jurisdictions have instituted native control over child welfare; control over their child-care system would be an appropriate parallel service. The interests of immigrant and rural women must also receive special consideration. Our "nannies" and informal caregivers are often immigrant women who may be exploited. As well, immigrant parents frequently have special child-care needs.

To assess changes as they impact on different groups of

women, as providers and mothers, the particular effects of different options must be examined. For example, native mothers are among the poorest groups in Canadian society, so tax deductions are of limited benefit to them. A system utilizing tax credits would give them more support. These tax credits would be particularly useful if they were available to all mothers of pre-school children and were not dependent on a particular form of child care. These mothers would also benefit from a licensed system directly funded by government if it was available to them, and if there were some options, such as a tax credit or demogrant program, for subsidizing mothers caring for children at home.

In contrast, the option offering the greatest support to a double-income family with a professional mother using a "nanny" is an unlimited tax deduction, allowing the family to choose high-priced care in the informal sector and to be subsidized in the process. Such a family would not benefit from a tax credit program and a licensed day-care system would be of limited help if they specifically wanted a care provider to come to their home.

From the point of view of carers, reasonable salaries, benefits, and protected working conditions are available only in the licensed formal sector. Direct grants to a licensed system would, therefore, provide the best form of support if the informal sector were to be integrated into this system. If mothers at home are not included in a licensed system, however, direct payments in the form of a demogrant would be more supportive. For lower-income mothers at home a refundable tax credit system would be at least as helpful as a demogrant.

These examples illustrate how particular strategies benefit specific groups of women. By placing emphasis on the utilization of tax deductions, the federal government's recent child-care strategy supports upper-income families and reinforces the use of the informal system. Mothers at home receive token recognition but no direct benefit. Improvement in the wages and working conditions of child-care workers is not given explicit priority. In contrast, the strategy put forward by the National Council of Welfare (1988) recommends much greater support for the licensed child-care system and the conversion of the child-care tax deduction into an increase in the refundable tax credit. These recommendations, therefore, support lower-income over high-income mothers and support the formal system over the informal. While workers' salaries and working conditions are not directly mentioned in their recommendations, support for licensed workers is implied through increased support for the formal system. In addition, consideration is given to supporting mothers caring for their children full-time at home through the tax credit program.

CONCLUSIONS

These principles suggest guidelines for examining and reorganizing our present child-care system, and each emphasizes the critical importance of caring in women's lives. While this discussion focuses on child care, a number of principles apply equally to the reorganization of society's care of other vulnerable persons. The importance of protecting the affective dimension in caring as our services become professionalized, of bringing private caring into the public sphere, and, most critically, of acknowledging and enhancing the economic value of caring labour applies also to those caring for persons with disabilities and for the frail elderly.

We must not lose sight of the similarities of much of our caring work, despite our tendency to divide socially dependent groups by factors such as age, income, and the degree and nature of their dependency. Women, with their devalued labour, meet most of their needs. As we struggle to formulate options and convince politicians and other Canadians that change must occur, we should not forget that political will can make possible any alternative.

NOTES

1. The term, "formal market" refers to all the varieties of care licensed by government or a mandated agency. This includes group day-care centres in neighbourhoods, schools, and workplaces as well

as family home child-care centres. "Informal market" refers to unlicensed nonparental child-care arrangements. These include paid and unpaid "babysitting" in the homes of parents as well as other relatives, friends, neighbours, and strangers.
2. See Chapter I of this book, Graham (1983), and Waerness (1984), for discussions of the "private" and "public" spheres. This definition of private refers to labour by a parent, usually the mother, in her home. If the care is provided by anyone else it is usually referred to as child care in the "informal market."

REFERENCES

Arat-Koç, F. 1990. "Importing Housewives: Non-Citizen Domestic Workers and the Crisis of the Domestic Sphere in Canada," in Meg Luxton, Harriet Rosenberg, and Fedef Arat-Koç, *Through the Kitchen Window: The Politics of Home and Family*. Toronto: Garamond.

Bagley, C. 1986. "Day Care in Alberta: A Review with National Implications," paper prepared for the Sharing Our Future Conference, Calgary (March).

Baker, Maureen. 1987. *Child Care Services in Canada*. Ottawa: Library of Parliament.

Blain, C. 1985. *Government Spending on Child Care in Canada*. Report prepared for the Task Force on Child Care, Series 1. Ottawa: Canadian Government Publishing Centre.

Browne, A. 1984. "The Mixed Economy of Day Care: Consumer Versus Professional Assessments," *Journal of Social Policy*, 13, 3: 321–31.

Canadian Commission for the International Year of the Child. 1979. *For Canada's Children*. Ottawa.

Canadian Day Care Advocacy Association. 1990. *Vision*. Ottawa (March).

Chodorow, N. 1978. *Mothering: Psychoanalysis and the Sociology of Gender*. Berkeley: University of California Press.

Edgecombe-Dobb, R. 1987. "Equal Pay for Work of Equal Value: Issues and Policies," *Canadian Public Policy*, 4.

Eichler, M. 1988. *Families in Canada Today: Recent Changes and Their Policy Consequences*, Second Edition. Toronto: Gage

Ferguson, E. 1989. "Private or Public? Profit or Non-Profit? The Preferences of a Sample of Day-Care Consumers in Ontario," paper prepared for the 4th National Conference on Social Welfare Policy, Toronto (October).

Finlayson, A. 1987. "A New Emphasis on the Family," *Maclean's*

(January 5): 71–72.

Foote, C. 1988. "Recent State Responses to Separation and Divorce in Canada," *Canadian Social Work Review*, 5: 28–43.

Fraiberg, S. 1977. *Every Child's Birthright: In Defense of Mothering*. New York: Basic Books.

Friendly, M., J. Mathien, and T. Willis. 1987. *Childcare – What the Public Said: An analysis of the transcripts of hearings held across Canada by the parliamentary Special Committee on Child Care (March–June, 1986)*. Ottawa: Canadian Day Care Advocacy Association.

Gilligan, C. 1982. *In a Different Voice: psychological theory and women's development*. Cambridge, Mass.: Harvard University Press.

Gorlick, C. 1988. "Economic Stress, Social Support, and Female Single Parents," *Canadian Social Work Review*, 5: 194–205.

Graham, H. 1983. "Caring: A Labour of Love," in J. Finch and D. Groves, eds., *A Labour of Love: Women, Work, and Caring*. London: Routledge and Kegan Paul.

Guest, D. 1980. *The Emergence of Social Security in Canada*. Vancouver: University of British Columbia Press.

House of Commons. 1987. *Sharing the responsibility*. Ottawa: Special Committee on Child Care.

Hurl, L. 1989. "The Value of Policy Dynamics: Pattern of Change and Stability in a Social Assistance Program," paper prepared for the 4th National Conference on Social Welfare Policy, Toronto (October).

Hutter, B., and G. Williams, eds. 1981. *Controlling Women: The Normal and the Deviant*. London: Croom Helm.

Jackson, M. 1989. "Bringing Up Baby," *Saturday Night* (December): 36.

Johnson, L. 1977. *Who Cares? A Report of the Project Child Care Survey of Parents and Their Child Care Arrangements*. Toronto: Social Planning Council of Metro Toronto.

Johnson, L., and J. Dineen. 1981. *The kin trade: The day care crisis in Canada*. Toronto: McGraw Hill-Ryerson.

Johnson, N. 1987. *The Welfare State in Transition*. Amherst: University of Massachusetts Press.

Lero, D. 1981. *Factors Influencing Parents' Preferences For, and Use of Alternative Child Care Arrangements for Preschool Age Children*. Guelph, Ont.: University of Guelph College of Family and Consumer Studies.

Lero, D., et al. 1985. *Parents' Needs, Preferences and Concerns about Child Care: Case Studies of 336 Canadian Families*. A report prepared for the Task Force on Child Care, Series 5. Ottawa: Canadian Government Publishing Centre.

Lero, D., and I. Kyle. 1989. *Families and Children in Ontario: Supporting the Parenting Role*. Toronto: Child, Youth and Family Policy Research Centre.

Maroney, H. 1985. "Embracing Motherhood: New Feminist Theory," *Canadian Journal of Political and Social Theory*, 9, 1/2: 40-64.

Maynard, F. 1985. *The Child Care Crisis: The real costs of day care for you and your child*. Markham, Ont.: Penguin.

National Council of Welfare. 1988. *Child care: A better alternative*. Ottawa: National Council on Welfare.

National Day Care Information Centre. 1987. *Status of Day Care in Canada*. Ottawa: Health and Welfare Canada.

New, C., and M. David. 1985. *For the Children's Sake: Making childcare more than women's business*. Markham, Ont.: Penguin.

O'Brien, M. 1981. *The Politics of Reproduction*. London: Routledge and Kegan Paul.

Ontario Coalition for Better Day Care. 1985. *Time for a Change, A brief to the Government of Ontario*. Toronto.

Ontario Public Service Employees Union (OPSEU). 1987. *Equity at Work: A Pay Equity Manual for Practitioners*. Toronto.

Pascall, G. 1986. *Social Policy: A Feminist Analysis*. London: Tavistock.

Power, D., and M. Brown. 1985. *Child Care and Taxation in Canada: Who Pays?* A report prepared for the Task Force on Child Care, Series 1. Ottawa: Canadian Government Publishing Centre.

REAL Women. n.d. "Universal Day Care" (pamphlet).

Report of the Ontario Social Assistance Review Committee. 1988. *Transitions*. Prepared for the Ontario Ministry of Community and Social Services. Toronto: Queen's Printer for Ontario.

Revenue Canada Taxation. 1989. *General Tax Guide*. Ottawa: Canada Government Publishing Centre.

Riley, D. 1983. "The Serious Burdens of Love? Some Questions on Childcare, Feminism, and Socialism," in L. Segal, ed., *What is to be done about the Family?* Harmondsworth: Penguin.

Roby, P. 1973. *Child Care, Who Cares?* New York: Basic Books.

Rutter, M. 1981. *Maternal Deprivation Reassessed*. Harmondsworth: Penguin.

Saraceno, C. 1984. "Shifts in Public and Private Boundaries: Women As Mothers and Service Workers in Italian Day Care," *Feminist Studies*, 10, 1: 7-29.

Schom-Moffat, P. 1985. *The Bottom Line: Wages and Working Conditions of Workers in the Formal Day Care Market*. Report prepared for the Task Force on Child Care, Series 1. Ottawa.

Scott, A.C. 1978. "The Value of Housework," in A. Jaggar and P. Struhl, eds., *Feminist Frameworks: Alternative Theoretical Accounts of the Relations between Women and Men*. New York: McGraw Hill.

Statistics Canada. 1990. *Women in Canada*. Cat. 89-503E. Ottawa: Minister of Supply and Services (February).

Status of Women Canada. 1986. *Report of the Task Force on Child Care*. Ottawa: Canada Government Publishing Centre.

Stevens, H. 1984. *Child Care Needs and Realities in Winnipeg - 1984*. Winnipeg: Social Planning Council of Winnipeg.

Townson, M. 1985. *Financing Child Care Through the Canada Assistance Plan*. Report prepared for the Task Force on Child Care, Series 1. Ottawa: Canada Government Publishing Centre.

Waerness, K. 1984. "Caring as Women's Work in the Welfare State," in H. Holter, ed., *Patriarchy in a Welfare Society*. Oslo: Universitetsforlaget.

White, B. 1980. *A Parent's Guide to the First Three Years*. Englewood Cliffs, N.J.: Prentice-Hall.

Wilson, E. 1977. *Women and the Welfare State*. London: Tavistock.

CHAPTER IV

Girls Learn to Care;
Girls Policed to Care

Marge Reitsma-Street

INTRODUCTION

When Dell was eighteen, she participated in a survey on the development of delinquency and conformity in siblings. Dell admired her grandmother for being a doctor. But she wondered why her grandmother told her "to put everyone ahead of yourself" while her grandfather stressed that Dell should "try to do what I wanted to do" (Reitsma-Street, 1988).[1]

Dell's puzzlement about these two different messages illustrates troublesome questions about caring for others and caring for oneself in today's world (Gilligan *et al.*, 1990; Wilson, 1988). What does it mean "to put everyone ahead"?

While putting others ahead, how can girls pay serious attention to trying "to do what they want to do"? What influences the balance between putting others ahead and doing what you want to do? What costs are there, and to whom, if girls focus on putting others ahead? What is the price they pay if they try to do what they want to do? For instance, Mies (1989: 54) questions what will happen to the "re-creation of living relations" among males and females when females pursue the type of autonomy idealized in our culture as self-determination.

Each chapter in this book wrestles with these questions, using different data, areas of interest, and groups of women. This chapter focuses on adolescent girls. The chapter begins with a description of a study of delinquent and non-delinquent sister pairs. The data from this study provide one major source of ideas for the development of caring in adolescents in this chapter; the second source includes historical and contemporary research on delinquent and non-delinquent girls in the Western industrialized world, in particular in Canada.

Using information generated in part from delinquent girls may appear an odd source for understanding the development of caring in ordinary adolescent girls. Very few girls report they commit or are convicted of crimes, especially serious ones. For example, in each year of the last decade fewer than 2 per cent of Canadian girls were charged in youth court for crimes against federal, provincial, or municipal laws; also, only 10 per cent of charges in youth court are against girls (Reitsma-Street, 1990b; Canadian Centre for Justice Statistics, 1989: Table 3).

The conventional wisdom is that those few girls who are convicted are quite different from non-delinquents in their relationships, personality, attitudes, life experiences, educational pursuits, and behaviours (Tanner, 1988: 354; Cowie *et al.*, 1968; Felice and Offord, 1975; Konopka, 1966; Konopka, 1976; Widom *et al.*, 1983). This concept of difference is challenged in this chapter. Despite definite differences in delinquent behaviour, evidence supports the concept of commonalities in samples of delinquent and non-delinquent girls. The data from the sister study solidly ground several commonalities in the development of caring in girls. The commonalities refer to what is occurring often in the daily lives of the girls, especially the familiar events and pressures affecting the girls, as well as the essential similarity in their feelings, choices, and behaviours. Three common lessons about caring shared by delinquent and non-delinquent girls are presented in this chapter: (1) women are the primary providers of emotional and physical care; (2) adolescent females learn a very restrictive notion of what self-care means; and (3) boyfriends become the primary recipients or objects of care. Thus, ideas about the development of caring in adolescence are strengthened by evidence from various samples of girls, including convicted delinquents.

Feminist scholarship and practice take the varieties of women's experience seriously. One particular contribution of Canadian feminist criminology is to bring female offenders out of the backwaters of scholarship and practice, to look at their experiences, and to hear their voices. Feminist criminology also aims to examine the indifferent, or discriminatory, sexist practices toward girls in criminal, correctional, and mental health organizations (Bertrand, 1979; Berzins and Cooper, 1982: 405; Langelier-Biron, 1983: 70; Geller, 1987). For instance, most of the infrequent delinquencies by girls were ignored and the personal needs of convicted female delinquents were responded to indifferently with minimal services – unless a girl's behaviour violated standards of femininity or no male in her household took responsibility for her care and behaviour. Although probation, fines, and community service orders are the common sentences for girls now and before, up to 60 per cent of girls admitted to Canadian correctional institutions before the 1980s were admitted for status offences (Bertrand, 1979: 142; Weiler, 1978; Nease, 1966; Hatch and Faith, 1989–90: 443, 449). Status offences, such as running away, incorrigibility, truancy, prostitution, or other sexual immoralities, were not considered offences if committed by boys.

One aim of the Canadian federal Young Offenders Act (Revised Statutes of Canada, c. y-1, 1985) was to decrease discriminatory, inadequate, and unfair treatment against delinquent girls purportedly spawned by interpretations of the previous Juvenile Delinquents Act (Statutes of Canada, 1908). In the Young Offenders Act age ranges for youth courts were made common across the provinces. Status offences could not be used as reasons to charge a girl. Determinate and minimal sentences were to replace indeterminate sentences. A litany of rights in the Young Offenders Act aimed to ensure fair, due process for boys and girls alike. Also, youth were now held accountable in part for their actions and were not considered by the courts as misdirected or in need of protection.

The reduction in discrimination of the YOA toward girls is currently under study. It is known, however, that charges and convictions have not dropped from before to after the YOA for either boys or girls, despite the absolute decrease in Canadian young people under eighteen years of age; that pre-trial detention has increased quite dramatically for both sexes; that the use of lawyers and time between charge and conviction has increased substantially; and that intrusive custodial sentences have not decreased as hoped for, although the stay in custody may be shorter than before introduction of the YOA in 1984 (Caputo and Bracken, 1988; Corrado and Markwart, 1988; Reitsma-Street, 1990a; Trepanier, 1986). Informal reports from the field and more formal studies elsewhere (Chesney-Lind, 1988; Schwartz *et al.*, 1989; Lerman, 1984) suggest that girls still endure various forms of discrimination and inappropriate services. A recent tragic example is that in January, 1990, two of the four girls who died in a fire in a Montreal secure locked custody facility were only charged with truancy. The girls were in the secure custody facility because alternatives were not available (Collister and Scott, 1990: A5).

Besides exposing discrimination toward female delinquents, feminist criminologists made another important contribution that is particularly relevant to this chapter. They argue that definitions and control of deviance in females are pervasive in all aspects of life, with criminal justice and correctional processes on the end of a continuum of controlling devices (Smart, 1976; Morris, 1987). The study of formally convicted delinquents can unmask the starker aspects of these processes of definition and control over the daily lives of females (Schur, 1984; Schwendinger and Schwendinger, 1985; Cain, 1989). Using samples that include delinquent girls reveals more clearly the range of costs borne by girls as they grow up and learn their lessons of caring, and the costs of challenging those lessons.

Three types of costs are borne by delinquent and non-delinquent girls for the lessons they learn about caring. Girls not only learn to care and to bear the costs of caring, they are also *policed to care and to bear the costs*. Although girls may want to develop a range of ways to care, they are pressured subtly and forcibly to care for others in certain ways, especially for boyfriends, fathers, and children, *more than* for themselves. The evidence is clearest in the lives of girls who more obviously challenge the prescribed expectations, in word and especially in deed. The more a girl fights against how she is expected to care for others and for herself, the greater the costs she is likely to bear. Sadly, the most serious cost is in the constriction of her already limited opportunities to care for herself and her loved ones. Because caring is so important to delinquent and non-delinquent girls alike, the risk of losing limited opportunities to care effectively constrains the development of alternative ways to care for self and others.

The chapter concludes with a discussion of several avenues girls explore to resist prescriptive pressures to care and to create the necessary space to develop new, more varied, and liberating ways to care for others and themselves.

THE SISTER STUDY

The sister study was part of a larger research project on the development of delinquency and conformity in pairs of siblings. Between 1978 and 1981 the files of 638 mostly Caucasian girls and 1,292 boys who were referred to Ontario correctional, mental health, and social service agencies were reviewed to identify sibling pairs who met the criteria of minimal age differences, shared early upbringing, and definite differences in delinquency and agency contact. In each pair, one of the siblings had been convicted in youth court for delinquent activities and had used social services extensively, while the other sibling was free of judicial convictions and had minimal service contacts.

Twenty-six sister and forty-five brother pairs who met the criteria agreed to engage in: (1) a four-hour semi-structured life history interview focused on their experiences in and perceptions of health, home, school, work, and relationship interactions; (2) short parental telephone interviews of the youths' early life; (3) birth, school, and agency record reviews; and (4) two standard instruments to estimate educational achievement and cognitive abilities (Reitsma-Street *et al.*, 1985).

The parent sibling study used the logic and procedures of a quantitative hypothesis testing survey, including univariate and multivariate matched-paired statistical analyses of over 250 variables (Reitsma-Street *et al.*, 1985). The analysis of the quantified variables, however, did not adequately help in understanding the development of delinquency and conformity in girls. Furthermore, much of the data, especially the semi-structured questions and the interviewers' rich field notes, had not been analysed. Thus, in 1985 I received permission to use the data for a doctoral thesis on the sister pairs. This time the logic and procedures of a qualitative multi-case study were used, including purposive sampling, examination of themes, the constant comparative analysis of the themes in depth, and the search for negative cases (Reitsma-Street, 1988).

The theme of commonality, rather than difference, emerged from this study of sisters. Of most relevance to women and caring were the core commonalities, which revolved around how the sisters learned to care for themselves and for others, the costs they bore for caring, and how they were policed to conform to expectations about caring. These commonalities, or "the similarities that tie us together" (Hubbard, 1981: 219), are developed in the subsequent sections. The fictitious names for the sisters have been chosen to help readers remember the distinction that originally divided the sisters and to illustrate that commonalities are grounded in the experiences of both delinquents and non-delinquents. Thus, those names beginning with a "D," like Dell whose words opened this chapter, are the delinquent siblings; those with an "N" are the non-delinquent sisters. Direct quotes from the comprehensive record compiling all observations from interviews, records, and tests will be indicated by the initials "OR," standing for "Observation Record."

LEARNING TO CARE: THE THREE LESSONS

(1) *Females as care providers*. The sisters learned early that females, young and old, are the major providers of care. Spontaneously, repeatedly, and specifically the sisters reported that they received far more care from females than they did from males. The sisters said they had lunch, sang, lived, and shopped with females; they learned about money and getting along with others from females; and they looked for help from and, above all, spent time with and talked with females. While peers primarily consisted of sisters and close friends, adult females included aunts, babysitters, neighbours, mothers of friends, a homeroom teacher, a guidance teacher, and several social workers. Despite dissatisfaction with some mothers who did not act like "a *real* mother who is quiet, caring and understanding" (OR: 253), the sisters saw mothers, stepmothers, or grandmothers as the most important sources for companionship, advice, learning, and a home.

The sisters certainly did things, ranging from fishing to planning burglaries, with fathers and other males. Some of the sisters appreciated fathers "putting a roof over our heads and giving us food" (OR: 66), or as Nasya said, "my father helped me overcome shyness" (OR: 124). But the sisters spoke far more of the indifference from males who were not around or too busy, of the absence of affection and conversation, and of the physical and sexual violence they experienced from males inside and outside the home.

The caring received by the sisters can be categorized into two dimensions identified in the literature as: (1) *love and affection about others*, that is, the emotional work needed to create, enrich, and maintain human relationships; and (2) *labour and help for others*, which includes the daily domestic work to meet the basic necessities of life (Tronto, 1989; Finch and Groves, 1983).

Caring, as expressed in love and affection, was emphasized more in the sisters' comments. That is, they were more conscious of wanting to give and to receive this element of caring. All the sisters spoke of talking as an important activity – all wanted to understand others and to be understood. They seemed to understand that communication is essential to achieving a sense of intimacy, well-being, a foundation for making decisions about what is important in life. For instance, Nola felt that the school social worker listened and wanted to help her: "She understood me like a friend; she wanted to find out what I wanted, and to help me; turn me on to good things" (OR: 34).

The labour of caring was evident in frequent references to the concrete forms of aid they received – a good meal, a safe place to live – especially if a girl could not stay in the parental home. At the same time the girls showed care for others by performing such tasks as child care and housework, helping mothers tend to a sick husband, and assisting in the store. From other women the sisters learned the skills of housekeeping as well as the more joyous skills such as singing, "the gift of gab, communicating with people in public, enjoying jewelry" (OR: 259). Although the sisters frequently reported that these types of caring activities were routinely done by the women in their lives, they were not aware of their importance or the energy that went into the labour aspect of caring.

Not only did the girls report that the females in their lives were the primary providers of affection and help, but they also saw themselves as giving affection and help to others. As early as late childhood, and definitely by adolescence, both delinquent and non-delinquent sisters reported their responsibilities for supervising children, doing housework, and, when able, providing money and a place to stay to those who needed it. The most important people they cared for included their own or other people's children, boyfriends, then parents and siblings, and to a lesser extent other relatives, peers, and at times strangers. For example, Nasya earned money by babysitting regularly and stayed at home after her mother's suicide to take care of the household for her father. Dolly ran away from the physical abuse of her father and then kept house for an older boyfriend with whom she committed many burglaries. Natalie also spent much energy in caring, as the following paraphrase of her words illustrates: "I took care of myself as of age eight; I also tried to take care of my brother and sister, because mom had lost interest. I just feel responsible for Darcy; I don't want anything to happen to her" (OR: 271, 242).

(2) *Learning to look nice and to be nice.* The sisters first learned that women were the major providers of care for others and that they were expected to do likewise. But they also learned not to provide such care to themselves, except in a very restricted sense. The goal of self-care was not directed at meeting present personal needs or planning for their future welfare. Rather, the sisters reported that they learned primarily to care for their physical appearance in order to look nice and to avoid actions that prompted labels, such as "tomboy" or especially "tramp" or "prostitute." Thus, the focus in caring for themselves was on developing distinctive physical features and personality, conceptualized in the literature as the making of the Western *feminine* female (Sharpe, 1976; Oakley, 1982; Broverman *et al.*, 1972). Education, individual interests, or job opportunities can be developed as long as they enhance, or at least do not seriously impede, the pursuit of femininity.

Nicci, for example, reported that she learned very early "to dress nice, cook a lot, be a lady, be petite" (OR: 91). Darcy tried to be more like her grandmother, who was "sweet, mellow, there when needed" (OR: 239), and less like her mother or herself, that is, "hyper, lying, irritable, and tricky, trying to evade everything" (OR: 237). Nasya wanted to be like her mother and her babysitter Cleo. Both were very nice, as she summed up in these remarks:

Mom is able to get along with people. She makes friends easily. Basically she is soft spoken, and gives any help that is wanted. She's there whenever I needed her. Cleo, my babysitter, was soft-spoken and understanding. She takes me out for supper. We get along together and talk. From Cleo I learned to get along with others. (OR: 123, 124)

The sisters still tried to put energy into activities that attended to their own needs and aspirations and reflected a broader understanding of caring for themselves. All the sisters reported repeated attempts to pursue their schooling despite disruptions, failures, and boredom. Many spoke of extensive participation, enjoyment, and skill in sports or recreational interests – whether pruning trees, earning a black belt in martial arts or Grade 8 piano certificate, going to parties and travelling to new cities, singing musicals with an aunt, or writing for the school paper. Earning money and planning for a future job, sometimes even a non-traditional job such as a diesel mechanic or a cowhand, were also included in the sisters' attempts to pay attention to their needs.

The delinquent girls were more likely than their non-delinquent sisters to report that they fought against giving priority to looking nice and being nice. Sometimes they tried to dress "like a tomboy" and to avoid wearing dresses (OR: 308). Sometimes they swore and talked loudly, and explored physical fighting as a way to meet their needs. The delinquent sisters were far more likely than their conforming sisters to explore their own interests and sexuality without adult permission: for instance, they spoke of travelling, learning to use birth control, and experimenting with lesbian relationships. Also, the delinquent sisters pursued excitement and fun more frequently than their siblings and rebelled against abusive, unjust, or unpleasant situations because they wouldn't "take it" (OR: 249). Mothers, and a few fathers, were more likely to remember the delinquent girls as "pesty," boisterous, running everywhere, moving furniture at the age of two, and not wanting to go shopping. In contrast, the non-delinquent sisters, such as Naomi, were more often remembered by parents as "quiet, shy, and good" (OR: 298).

It is interesting that the non-delinquent siblings sometimes reported admiration, even envy, of the delinquent sisters' struggles to develop their own personalities, interests, and appearance beyond looking and being nice. For example, although Nola said her sister Dawn was stubborn, spoiled, and wanted everything, Nola also expressed admiration: "Dawn used to fight all the time with me and others. I like Dawn's guts and I know she had more guts than me" (OR: 25).

But, by late adolescence, both delinquent and the non-delinquent sisters had learned to restrict the care of themselves to primarily looking and being nice, and above all to not "making a fuss." For example, Deborah still loved fighting physically and verbally, but she said she was "learning from mom *to hold it all in, and to cry like her*" (OR: 302). The following words from Darcy poignantly capture how a girl learns to restrict her care of herself to looking and being nice. Darcy had finished her stay in a training school, returned to live at home, and had enrolled in college for upgrading. She stopped wearing boy clothes and learned that she could not do what boys do. Instead, she sums up the prescription of what looking after oneself means for girls: "I am learning to stop being selfish, and to think of others, and to like myself. I am learning to be passive, but also to get out of my shell. I am learning that if I stay at home, be good, all will be okay" (OR: 237, 253).

(3) *Boyfriends as the primary object of caring.* In their first lesson on caring, girls learn to see other females and themselves as the major providers of caring. The second lesson is to restrict the care of themselves to an emphasis on personal appearance and appropriate demeanour. Successfully learning these two lessons makes it possible to learn the third lesson: a singular focus on making and maintaining a relationship with a boyfriend.

By mid-adolescence, if not sooner, all the sisters had made or were systematically seeking a steady, encompassing relationship with a boy. With only one exception, the sisters made relationships with boys who were older. Before their twentieth birthdays, all the sisters had had sexual relations with males. Sexual activity rarely occurred outside the context of romantic love or the possibility of a committed relationship with a boyfriend.

A number of sisters, including Nicci, Dolores, Deborah, Nora, Nadine, and Natalie, clearly stated that they judged their happiness by their ability to attract boys. They worked to encourage a steady relationship with a boy, which might lead to an engagement. Spending time with boys was essential, even if this meant skipping school or not pursuing their own interests. For example, Natalie remembered that she first became interested in boys at age ten. She was pleased that losing weight brought her more boyfriends. By her twelfth birthday she was visiting boyfriends about once a week, and she went steady by age fifteen with a boy three years older. Natalie reported feeling "comfortable with guys but not without" (OR: 242). The break-up with her first boyfriend was accompanied by a clinically diagnosed depression and by leaving school.

There were some girls, such as Dawn and Darcy, who had less romantic views about making a boyfriend the primary object of their caring. Dawn's relationships were shadowed by "horrible" thoughts and feelings about her father, her brother, and other males from whom she suffered serious physical abuse, rape, and indifference. But she also wanted to live in a decent place and to provide a home for foster kids, which she thought she could do through getting a boyfriend. Her terse, angry story is replete with attempts to attract a boyfriend:

> I was engaged to two men whom I met in court. When I was in jail, I wrote to one who also was in jail. When I got out, I asked to marry him, but no answer. In London, I lived with and got engaged to another man. He tattooed my name on his body. But, don't know where he is now; he left me in the air. Now I stay with Paul; he works; I take care of the house. There is a chance I might be pregnant now. (OR: 12)

Caring for a boyfriend can mean a relationship that includes affection, friendship, and excitement. Unfortunately, learning to care for a boyfriend is likely to produce other outcomes and be at the expense of caring for herself in a broader way or for other females who provide care. These costs are explored in a subsequent section. Before doing so, however, the findings from this study are placed within a broader context. In brief, the lessons learned by the sisters, whether delinquent or not, are all too familiar when one examines the conditions of girls' lives in the past and in the present.

THE LESSONS OF CARING
IN OTHER RESEARCH

On the one hand, it appears trite to talk about females as the major providers of care. It is so obvious and commonplace (Finch and Groves, 1983; Dalley, 1988). On the other hand, the consciousness and implications of this phenomenon are much less obvious and need to be made explicit. Caring may be an assumption but it is not yet a dominant question in the literature on female development. It is almost embarrassing to admit that during the first year of analysis in the sister study I did not attach significance to the fact that it was women who primarily provided the love and labour of caring in the sisters' lives. Rather, I was following the more usual method of sorting through the sisters' separate relationships with their fathers versus their mothers, and then the relationships with their adult friends versus their peers. Besides being less connected to their fathers and more ambivalent about their mothers, I could not see strong patterns in the sisters' relationships that could be argued to contribute either to delinquency or conformity. Only when gender was introduced to categorize the relationships did I begin to see a clear and very strong pattern with a distinctive shape. Thus, females were the primary providers of care, and females were judged on their ability to care – through creating, enriching, and maintaining relationships, especially with one boyfriend.

Learning to restrict the care of oneself to looking nice and being nice is a lesson learned over and over by girls. The conception of feminine beauty and personality may be expanding somewhat in this century to include pluck and strength. But the standards of self-care for delinquent and non-delinquent girls emphasize physical appearance and attitude, according to the tastes of males, and are accorded more importance than health and psychological, material, and social needs (Brenzel, 1983; Clarricoates, 1980; Dyhouse, 1981; Jephcott, 1942; McRobbie, 1981; Sharpe, 1976; Kostash, 1987; Strong-Boag, 1988). As the Schwendingers (1985: 167) wrote in their review of two decades of empirical and theoretical work on California adolescent subcultures: "[Girls] are under great pressure to organize their personalities around themselves as objects that are valued as sexually attractive things."

The third caring lesson revealed in the sister study is that female adolescents learn to make a boyfriend their major object of caring. This lesson, if not inevitable, is pervasive and is apparent in the more general literature (Hudson, 1983). For example, in her study of 249 West Indian, Caucasian, and Asian girls in four working-class schools in England, Sharpe (1976: 302) comments that "The idea of finding true love with Mr. Right is always the primary goal and the key to everlasting happiness."

Finding Mr. Right is as common to delinquent girls (Campbell, 1981; Gagnon and Langelier-Biron, 1982; Konopka, 1966; Shacklady Smitt, 1978) as it is to non-delinquents (Hudson, 1983; Konopka, 1976; Kostash, 1987; McRobbie, 1981). For many, especially poorer girls, caring for a boyfriend who eventually will become a husband is the chief means of getting away from parents, becoming an adult, and establishing a home of one's own (Davies, 1984). This third lesson of caring is also strongly reflected in the world of literature and fantasy. After reviewing the adolescent female heroine in over 200 representative American novels of the last 100 years, Barbara White (1985) concludes that the heroine still focused her life around a man or caring for sick relatives. Despite the introduction of the themes of sexuality, women's liberation, and lesbianism, she suggests that the image of the trap caused by limited options continued to dominate realistic novels of the 1970s. Only older female heroines, who are almost past child-bearing or who are no longer especially attractive to a male, sometimes find strength and interest in lives not dominated by caring for or about a relationship with a male.

Three lessons of caring for girls have been presented, grounded in examples from a study of sister pairs and other literature: (1) women, whether young or old, are the major providers of the love and labour that is caring; (2) young women are expected to restrict caring for themselves to personal appearance and demeanour; and (3) boyfriends become the special objects of caring. Learning these lessons imposes high costs on girls, and girls do not simply learn to bear these costs; rather, they are policed or pressured to do so.

THE COSTS OF CARING

The first major cost is that in learning the skills and attitudes needed to care for others, girls seriously restrict the development of their own interests and independence. Daisy was aware of this, for though she valued the way her mother "showed me to care for someone," she did not want to dedicate her whole life to kids and a husband, only to find out that, like her mother, she would be "left out" (OR: 313).

To continue caring for a boyfriend meant that sisters not only restricted their own interests, but also gave less emphasis to their caring relationships with others, especially females. For instance, Dolores commented: "I used to like sports and movies. But now I act differently. I changed my friends from girlfriends to a boyfriend who does drugs. We just hang around, with his boyfriends and their girls" (OR: 277, 281).

Sisters reported changing their educational and recreational activities, or their preparation for future work, in order to spend time with their boyfriends, listen to them, admire them, and run errands for them. Dallas worked hard to get a driver's licence when she was just sixteen, to rent her own apartment, and to think "things out on my own" (OR: 165). But her boyfriend moved in and life began to revolve around his parties, drinking, and friends. The shift in caring was most prominent if a sister lived with a boyfriend or became pregnant. By her fourteenth birthday Naomi had narrowed her interests to focus on caring for her boyfriend, who later became her husband, and then extended her caring to the children she bore. At the time of the interview Naomi still lived with her parents, minded the children, and listened to the baseball and shop talk of her husband. In a final example from the sister study, a probation officer noted that Dee has "settled down," demonstrated by the fact that she had "no time for any actions, including antisocial ones, other than caring for her son" (OR: 228).

The costs girls learn to bear in caring for others more than themselves are also documented in historical studies of girls (Jephcott, 1942; Dyhouse, 1981) and other contemporary research (Oakley, 1982; Sharpe, 1976). The cost of negating their own interests means, for example, a reduction in time available for study and for play (Propper, 1979). It means that thinking of helping and caring for others comes before thinking of one's self (Gordon, 1988). McRobbie and McCabe (1981: 4) poignantly sum up the cost of emphasizing the care of others while restricting the care of self: "Growing up for girls is little more than preparation for growing old prematurely."

The second cost of female adolescent caring is inattention to her basic health needs. A girl learns to take care of her physical appearance and acquire the necessary social skills to look nice and be nice. If she learns this lesson well, she may attract and keep a boyfriend. But with this focus, a girl does not learn how to seriously care for and care about the needs of her body, especially in its capacity to experience pleasure or to produce children. In the sister study, Nicci loved to be treated like a lady and was adored by a boy who "made me feel good, made me happy, got on his knees to do anything for me" (OR: 95). But Nicci felt confused and betrayed by her experiences with boys: she endured forced sex at a party, was impregnated by her adoring boyfriend, and then had to deal with the pressure to either get an abortion or quit school. Surveys of adolescents indicate that as many as two-thirds do not use contraception, especially in the first few instances of sexual intercourse or if they are minimally exposed to sexual education. However, the girl is left to deal with the pregnancy (Herold, 1984; Orton and Rosenblatt, 1986; Taylor, 1985). With the lessons of caring concentrated on looking nice and being nice, girls too often find their bodies and spirits pay the price of sexual assault, unwanted pregnancy, inadequate birth control, as well as miscarriages and abortions (Messerschmidt, 1987; Smart, 1985). Kostash (1987: 175), in her study of a cross-section of fifty Canadian girls, captures the apprehension that accompanies this bodily cost:

Suddenly her body is no longer at her own disposal but has become a zone where others have competing interests –

parents and boyfriends and social workers and ad agencies – a territory liable to a whole series of catastrophes: diseases, pregnancy, rape, abortion.

In addition to the way girls restrict their interests and neglect their bodies, the third cost girls pay is the risk of poverty and dependence. Pat Evans explores this in detail as it affects adult women in Chapter VI, but for many women the seeds of their economic dependency are sown in adolescence. Despite attempts to advance their education and job skills, the sisters in the sibling study had trouble preparing for economic independence, or even for interesting work. The importance of caring for their appearance and demeanour, and the focus on the care for others, especially boys, too often interfered with or interrupted their schooling and job preparation. Moreover, surveys during the 1980s of young girls who wanted and expected to combine education, marriage, motherhood, and work showed that their aspirations were threatened by the harsh realities in which girls try to earn a living and care for themselves and others (Baker, 1985). Divorce, juggling home and paid work, pink ghettos, poor pay and poorer welfare and child care, and increasing unemployment, especially during times of recession, make girls even more vulnerable to poverty or dependence on others for food and shelter (Cain, 1989).

In the sister study, Nora revealed her desire to be both a mother and vice-president of her company, and not to be dominated like her mother. But to her dismay she found that her husband earned more on unemployment insurance than she did working (OR: 302). Linda Davies's (1984) two-year participant observation study of girls in a large comprehensive London school found that working-class girls saw the major route out of the parental home and into the adult world was through caring for a boyfriend and minding his house and children. Unfortunately, by turning marriage into a personal victory and by resisting the school curriculum, girls risk "deskilling themselves occupationally." Anne Campbell (1984: 266) concludes her study of New York girl gangs with a bleak picture of the economic price girls can pay for their lessons in caring: "But in the end, gang or no gang, the girls remained alone with their children, still trapped in poverty and in a cultural dictate of womanhood from which there was no escape."

This economic vulnerability reflects the tragic fact that by caring for others more than for self in their early years, girls risk not being able to care for themselves or those they love later. Without the skills, education, and time to find a job in an economy geared to hire males before females and pay males better, girls have a hard time earning enough money to help feed, clothe, and shelter themselves or their loved ones. Paradoxically, while focusing care on a boyfriend is a source of economic vulnerability, continuing such care is critical because a relationship with a male who earns a satisfactory income is the major hope girls have for minimizing the impact of that vulnerability.

POLICED TO CARE

If learning the lessons of caring is so costly for girls, why do they pay these costs of constricted independence and physical as well as economic vulnerability? Why are not other ways to care developed to decrease the costs, and to increase the capacity to care for self and others? Why is change so difficult? Under what conditions can caring and its costs change?

These questions have fueled some of the feminist scholarship of the past decade. There is one particularly helpful perspective from feminist criminologists who examine why laws and punishment in the criminal justice system are, on one hand, so harsh toward certain behaviours such as running away and prostitution but, on the other hand, indifferent to most of the deviant behaviour and needs of girls (Smart, 1976; Chesney-Lind, 1989). This contradiction is captured in the phrase "policed to grow up good" (Cain, 1989).

The concept of policing pulls together the evidence that girls are more than encouraged and socialized to learn their lessons of caring and to pay the attendant costs; rather, *they are policed to learn their lessons*. Policing, or what Donzelot (1979: 8) defines as the "techniques of regulation," includes the subtle, helpful pressuring and monitoring of behaviours and attitudes that are built into daily norms and interactions. Policing also includes, however, the stronger pressures of laws and sanctions inherent in policies and programs. Drawing from the literature, with illustrations from the sister study, three levels of policing are discussed here, beginning at the subtle, pervasive daily level and ending with the obvious, less frequent formal level of policing embodied in the criminal justice system. The three policing levels pressure girls to restrict their experimentation with alternative ways to care in order to avoid risking even further restrictions on their already limited opportunities to care for self and others.

The first level of policing is the most common, the most deadly, and the most effective. This is the judgement of a girl's reputation (Hudson,1983; Schur, 1984; Hutter and Williams, 1981). Every study on female adolescents speaks to the pervasive, daily assessment of whether a girl's clothes, appearance, personality, enthusiasms, speech, associations, and actual or imputed sexual activity are acceptable (Kostash, 1987; Davies, 1984; Shacklady Smitt, 1976; Sharpe, 1976; Smart, 1985; Wilson, 1978; McRobbie; 1981). The assessment examines whether a girl cares enough about herself in the right way to get and keep a boyfriend, and can then eventually acquire a decent husband and the associated status and economic rewards. For instance, in the many interviews Sue Lees (1989) conducted with 100 English girls from various backgrounds, she found that even in the 1980s the vague, fluid, but potent use of the term "slag" effectively policed girls to minimize any behaviours that may lead to this label – and to being dropped by a boy. No girl wanted to be called a slag, or a "slut," "wench," or "tramp," or to be described as "loose," terms used in other studies. Unfortunately, the only way to avoid being tagged is to become a loner or by having a steady relationship with a boy. As Lees (1989: 27) concludes:

> The result is that a girl either suppresses her sexual desire or channels it into a steady relationship that is based on an unwritten contract of inequality – that she will be the one to make compromises over where she works, lives and spends

her leisure. She will bear the main burden of domesticity and child care without pay and adjust herself, and indeed contribute, to her husband's work, life-style and demands.

The second level of policing is the extensive, albeit intermittent, use of physical force or the threat of force by males to vent frustration, to settle conflict, to get sex, and to maintain dominance over girls. The primary policers at this level are mostly the males that girls know well – fathers, brothers, relatives, teachers, neighbours, and spiritual advisers (Barrett and McIntosh, 1982; Committee on Sexual Offences, 1984; Russell, 1986). Although not a secret, this second level of policing remains powerful. Many of the girls in the sister study spoke of their fear and hatred of the sticks, screams, taunts, and wandering hands of fathers, grandfathers, uncles, boyfriends, and occasionally mothers. The extensiveness and impact of this level of policing is the focus of Chapter VII by Imogen Taylor.

Finally, numerous studies since 1970 have documented how public law and judicial interventions act as the third and most obvious level of policing to reinforce and to supplement the violence toward girls found within intimate relationships as well as in the daily assessments of female reputation. Girls risk complaints from parents, arrests and sentences from judicial representatives, and treatment in correctional centres (before the 1980s) or medical and private establishments (in the last decade). If caught committing a delinquency, however small or serious, girls learn that their behaviours and motivations will be measured primarily against a male standard of femininity. A girl may steal to get clothes, run away from sexual abuse, try drugs to escape boredom and find excitement, sell sex because prostitution pays more than selling donuts, or strangle an abusive partner. But these behaviours are not seen in the context of a society that limits the ways that girls can care for themselves and their loved ones, and restricts avenues of protest against these limitations. Instead, behaviours such as hanging around in the streets, running away, selling sex, truanting from school, breaking curfew, sleeping with more than one male, fighting and not getting along with their parents, or generally behaving in an unseemly or disorderly way are all interpreted by parents, teachers, and lawmakers as signs of disturbances in the girl's personality, especially her identity as a girl. *She needs help, protection, or correction to act more like a normal girl* (Felice and Offord, 1975; Byles, 1980; Chesney-Lind, 1989; Lerman, 1984; Morris, 1987; Petrie, 1986; Schwartz *et al.*, 1984; Smart, 1976; Parent, 1986).

In the sister study, Dolly and her boyfriend committed over twenty home burglaries. Burglary is a serious crime against property and invokes community sanctions. But, the judge argued, Dolly was simply following her boyfriend and thus was not really culpable for the burglaries. The judge, therefore, gave Dolly a light sentence – she was banned from living in British Columbia. However, when Dolly made her own decision to run away from a residential treatment centre and thus break one condition of her probation order, she was treated much more harshly and sent to a training school. In the sister study, the most serious judicial responses were reserved for running away from home and truancy from school, not for crimes against persons or property.

In the research literature, even when the severity of offence and criminal record is controlled, girls face earlier and harsher sentences if they are not "respectable" or strongly tied to a parental or marital home in which a male will take responsibility for restricting the girl's conduct (Eaton, 1986; Kruttschnitt, 1982; Morris, 1987). Also, with few exceptions, interventions for convicted female delinquents are minimal and inadequate, but not benign. Rather, the high referrals for home investigations and counselling, repeated gynecological examinations, the perusal of sexual history and emphasis on positive familial relationships, the focus on poorly paid service jobs in cosmetology and housekeeping, and the reinforcement for good mothering or volunteer services all forcefully constrain girls who are adjudicated as delinquent and warn others to stop exploring alternatives to being a girl and to caring, and to "curb the right of young women to defy patriarchy" (Chesney-Lind, 1989; Ackland, 1982; Brenzel, 1983; Davidson, 1982; Geller, 1987; Kersten, 1989; Strange, 1985).

In sum, girls bear the costs for the way they are expected to learn to care. These costs include limits in the available energy for personal development, minimal control over their bodies, and economic vulnerability. But it is not easy to explore other ways to care. The daily judgements made on their reputations, the intermittent violence experienced in intimate relationships, and infrequent coercive interventions by public agencies for unladylike behaviours are the three common levels of policing used to pressure girls to learn the three lessons of caring and to discourage learning alternative lessons.

If a girl deviates too far from what is expected, she risks losing her reputation, possibly a school year, and perhaps some liberty. But she also risks disruption in what she values a great deal: caring for and about others, and being cared for by others. Ostracism from a group of friends at school or disruption in contact with parents and children while in treatment is a high cost (Carlen, 1987; Llewellyn, 1980; Ve, 1984).

But most problematic is that the majority of girls still believe that "boys are girls' destiny because boys are girls' livelihood" (Cain, 1989: 9). *Thus, girls feel they cannot afford to not attract a boy.* The economic realities and the perspectives of most males about heterosexual relationships mean that girls must be "just girls" to get a man and thus have some chance of having a decent place to live, status, legitimate children, and some opportunities to get ahead. A girl learns quickly that to be different or bad is not to be more like a boy, with the attendant privileges, or to be regarded as a more rounded person, an individual, or maybe a new breed of girl. Rather, she learns that she risks not even being "just a girl," what Heidensohn (1987; see also Schur, 1984) calls the double jeopardy and double failure deviant girls face. Losing her gender, a girl may well miss the chance to sign up for the "unfair gender contract" (Worral, 1989: 79) in which she provides domestic, sexual, and personal caring for others, particularly a man, in return for some opportunities to be cared for by others. In brief, the very high costs of deviation police girls to continue paying the high costs for the way they care for others and themselves

Compliance, endurance, and resignation to the lessons, tasks, and costs of caring are common among girls of all classes and colours, yesterday and today (Cain, 1989). Protest is hidden (Cloward and Piven, 1979) and the struggle for change is often channelled into personal rituals, escapism, martyrdom, and anger (Connell *et al.*, 1982; Hall and Jefferson, 1975; Davies, 1984). Research on change that is rooted in the actual experiences of girls, their mothers, and grandmothers remains limited. But there are hints about the nature and directions for change.

Change starts with resistance. Resistance means the sustained use of routines, discourse, and actions to oppose and modify the "dailiness" or immediate circumstances in which a person or group lives. Resistance is not a unitary concept. Three aspects or approaches to resistance are considered here: "not taking it," building mutual support systems, and the active pursuit of power.

Darcy used the words "not taking it" to sum up her stance to the abuse, injustice, indifference, and confusion in her world, and her willingness to break rules to get something else. This type of resistance includes straightforward opposition to expectations, rules, and demands, and some form of gentle, rude, or violent refusal. Girls in the sister study exemplified this type of resistance in their attempts to have fun, to get away, to find the answer, and to search for a better life for themselves. In her study of three Boston child welfare agencies over an eighty-year period, Gordon (1986) also found examples of girls who tried to resist the repeated demands for sexual and domestic services from males in their homes by, for instance, refusing to do housework, running away to a religious order, or escaping to the streets and getting paid for their sexual services. From her study of two groups of Puerto Rican girls, Campbell (1987: 464) describes resistance as rejection of certain oppressive aspects of race, class, and gender: "She is Puerto Rican but neither provincial nor unamerican. She may be poor but her life is neither drab nor criminal. She enjoys her femininity but rejects passivity and suffering."

This approach to resistance emphasizes the need to take

better care of self – to put more value on one's own needs, interests, and desires. Cain (1989: 17) conceptualizes this approach to resistance as the "circuitous strategies for salvaging autonomy" (also see Gordon, 1988: 242).

Building supportive relationships is another approach to resistance, which minimizes the damage of problematic daily life and maximizes the protection of others. Girls try to take care of each other, like Natalie protecting her younger sister from their father's belt or running to her friend's mother for some loving and fun. Gordon (1988), for example, found that girls went to child welfare agencies for help when the father began to molest a younger sister.

Aptheker (1989) goes further in conceptualizing this second approach to resistance, based on an extensive review of the art, songs, life stories, and needlework of generations of women of all races. She speaks of the resilient and persistent efforts of women to refuse to tolerate oppressive situations and ugliness by salvaging, coping, building, putting up a struggle to celebrate, and strengthening "connections between people in the family, at work, and in the community" (Aptheker, 1989: 178–80). She argues that the attention women give to singing, celebrations and rituals, bake sales, pretty curtains, mutual aid, working at double jobs to keep their children in school and out of the mines, or making something out of nothing is a form of resistance – despite the appearance of compliance – *to what men define as important in life*. For instance, black author Alice Walker writes of the way her mother always found time for her flower garden, no matter how poor they were or how long she had to work. In *Revolutionary Petunias and Other Poems* Walker (1973: 70) captures the resistance in caring for beauty:

Rebellious. Living.
Against the Elemental Crush.
A Song of Color
Blooming Gloriously
For its Self.

A third aspect of resistance is the active search for power, or what Davies (1984) conceptualizes as the ability to alter the course of events and to create possibilities where none existed before. In the sister study Diane and Daphine, two girls convicted for many delinquencies, were the most articulate and conscious in their development of strength and power in order to do more things for themselves and others they cared about. Although they worried they were ugly and not lady-like, they also resisted the pressures to act just like a girl. Moreover, they valued strength and consciously pursued it in its physical, intellectual, and emotional dimensions. Diane was proud that "it took six men to hold me" in a fight, and she admired a female social worker because "she had the power to do things" (OR: 298). Daphine felt she could learn and do anything, and was very pleased she "beat fourteen guys when I wrote the test for the Armed Forces" (OR: 312).

In the vast majority of research studies and artistic literature, girls do not seem very clear about what they wish to create with this fledgling strength and power. What is clear is that girls are searching for the power to create the "space for change" (Brophy and Smart, 1985: 17), so they can learn to name, explore, enjoy, expand, and construct alternative ways to care for themselves and others. It is also clear that one important realm of resistance is in areas of intimacy, such as in relations with boyfriends, in the struggle against physical violence from loved ones, and in control over reproductivity. In the sister study, Deborah finally decided her boyfriend was making the important decisions about the use of drugs and school, and it was not good for her. Therefore, upon leaving training school she resisted building her life around one boy and resumed her earlier interests in the theatre, outrageous dressing, and caring for close female friends. A second arena for change is economic independence. Again, from the sister study, one-quarter of the girls aspired to non-traditional jobs. If they are successful, they may earn at least some money to support their struggle for a space to change.

Far more research is needed to understand the varieties of resistance and the conditions under which resistance best promotes alternative ways for girls to care for themselves and others at less cost than at present. Too often we learn about the acts of resistance that were built on a fuzzy analysis of what was wrong and what was necessary for change. Just as often resistance becomes sporadic, individualized, or neutralized. But the one promising condition for the promotion of resistance that needs close scrutiny is the development of caring for and about other females in our daily worlds as well as our political causes (Ve, 1984). Luxton (1980: 210) speaks to the importance of women discovering that their dreams and sorrows are not unique: "it wasn't just me – it was all of us." Although girls fight over boyfriends and unfeminine behaviours (Campbell, 1986; Shacklady Smitt, 1978), there are examples of "defensive solidarity" among girls in their bedroom subcultures (McRobbie and Garber, 1975: 221), the safety in numbers that Gordon's (1986) sex delinquents found on the streets, and the challenge of ideas and lifestyles from women's liberation and lesbianism (Aptheker, 1989; Baker, 1985; Kostash, 1987). The girls in the sister study understood that females were the major providers of caring. Those few sisters who tried to nourish their relationships with several important women seemed more likely to resist the costs of caring by learning to care better for themselves, to celebrate life, and to find some space for change. These suggest directions for finding alternative ways to care that enrich the tasks and love of caring for self and others, but decrease the costs.

NOTE

1. Thanks to Dr. David R. Offord for permission to use the sister data from the McMaster University "Comparison of Hard-to-Serve Adolescents and Their Siblings" study, and for years of insightful suggestions. The financial assistance of the Ontario Ministry of Community and Social Services, the Laidlaw Foundation, and the Social Sciences and Humanities Research Council helped in the collection of data and supported me while writing the findings.

For further information on the original sibling survey, see Reitsma-Street *et al.* (1985), and on the sister study, see Reitsma-Street (1988). All but one of the twenty-six sister pairs were Caucasian. The average age of the delinquents was 16.9 while the non-delinquent sisters averaged 19 – one-third of them firstborn. The questions and analysis took into account differences in age and birth order. Four-fifths of the parents were English-speaking, and 75 per cent of the families had more than three children. Names and identifying details about the girls from the study have been changed. Quotations are taken from the record made of all the interviews, records, tests, and summary data available on twelve of the twenty-six sister pairs (twenty-four girls), theoretically selected for intense qualitative analysis (Reitsma-Street, 1988). The quotes accurately reflect what the interviewers wrote to capture a girl's response to open-ended questions or her spontaneous comments to structured questions in the eighty-page interview schedule. Occasionally I changed syntax and grammar.

REFERENCES

Ackland, J.W. 1982. *Girls in Care: A Case Study of Residential Treatment*. Hampshire, England: Gower.

Aptheker, B. 1989. *Tapestries of Life: Women's Work, Women's Consciousness, and the Meaning of Daily Experience*. Amherst: University of Massachusetts Press.

Baker, M. 1985. *What Will Tomorrow Bring? A Study of the Aspirations of Adolescent Women*. Ottawa: Canadian Advisory Council on the Status of Women.

Barrett, Michele, and Mary McIntosh. 1982. *The Antisocial Family*. London: Verso.

Bertrand, Marie-Andrée. 1979. *La Femme et le Crime*. Montréal: L'Aurore.

Berzins, L., and S. Cooper. 1982. "The Political Economy of Correctional Planning for Women: The Case of the Bankrupt Bureaucracy," *Canadian Journal of Criminology*, 24, 4: 399–416.

Brenzel, B. 1983. *Daughters of the State: A Social Portrait of the First Reform School for Girls in North America, 1856-1905*. Cambridge, Mass.: MIT Press.

Brophy, J., and C. Smart, eds. 1985. *Women-in-Law: Explorations in Law, Family and Sexuality*. London: Routledge and Kegan Paul.

Broverman, I., S. Vogel, D. Broverman, F. Clarkson, and P. Rosenkrantz. 1972. "Sex-role Stereotypes: A Current Appraisal," *Journal of Social Issues*, 28, 2: 59–78.

Byles, J.A. 1980. "Adolescent girls in need of protection," *American Journal of Orthopsychiatry*, 50, 2: 264–78.

Cain, M. 1989. "Feminists transgress criminology," in M. Cain, ed., *Growing Up Good: Policing the Behaviour of Girls in Europe*. London: Sage.

Campbell, A. 1981. *Girl Delinquents*. Oxford: Basil Blackwell.

Campbell, A. 1984. *Girls in the Gang: A Report from New York City*.

Oxford: Basil Blackwell.

Campbell, A. 1986. "Self-report of fighting by females," *British Journal of Criminology*, 26, 1: 28–46.

Campbell, A. 1987. "Self definition by rejection: The case of gang girls," *Social Problems*, 34, 5: 451–66.

Canadian Centre for Justice Statistics. 1989. *Youth Court Statistics Preliminary Tables 1988-1989*. Ottawa: Statistics Canada, Department of Justice (revised April).

Caputo, Tullio, and Denis C. Bracken. 1988. "Custodial dispositions and the *Young Offenders Act*," in J. Hudson *et al.*, eds., *Justice and the Young Offender in Canada*. Toronto: Wall & Thompson.

Carlen, Pat. 1987. "Out of care, into custody: Dimensions and deconstruction of the state's regulation of twenty-two young working-class women," in P. Carlen and A. Worrall, eds., *Gender, Crime and Justice*. Milton Keynes, England: Open University Press.

Chesney-Lind, M. 1988. "Girls in jail," *Crime and Delinquency*, 34, 2: 150–68.

Chesney-Lind, M. 1989. "Girls' crime and women's place," *Crime and Delinquency*, 35, 1: 5–29.

Clarricoates, K. 1980. "The perception and categorization of gender conformity and gender deviation in primary schools," in R. Deem ed., *Schooling for Women's Work*. London: Routledge and Kegan Paul.

Cloward, Richard A., and Francis Fox Piven. 1979. "Hidden protest: The channeling of female innovation and resistance," *Signs: Journal of Women on Culture and Society*, 4, 4: 651–69.

Collister, E., and S. Scott. 1990. "Girls' parents demand inquest," *Montreal Gazette*, January 23: A5.

Committee on Sexual Offences against Children and Youths (Chairman R. F. Badgley). 1984. *Sexual Offences against Children*, Vols. I and II. Ottawa: Minister of Supply and Services.

Connell, R.W., D.J. Ashenden, S. Kessler, and G.W. Dowsett. 1982. *Schools, Families and Social Division*. Sydney: George Allen and Unwin.

Corrado, Raymond R., and Alan Markwart. 1988. "The prices of rights and responsibilities: An examination of the impacts of the *Young Offenders Act* in British Columbia," *Canadian Journal of Family Law*, 7, 1: 92–116.

Cowie, J., V. Cowie, and E. Slater. 1968. *Delinquency in Girls*. London: Heinemann.

Dalley, Gillian. 1988. *Ideologies of Caring: Rethinking Community and Collectivism*. Houndmills, Basingstoke, Hampshire: Macmillan.

Davidson, S., ed. 1982. *Justice for Young Women*. Seattle: New Directions for Young Women.

Davies, L. 1984. *Pupil Power*. London: The Falmer Press.

Donzelot, Jacques. 1979. *The Policing of Families* (trans. Robert Hurley). New York: Pantheon Books.

Dyhouse, C. 1981. *Girls Growing Up in Late Victorian and Edwardian England*. London: Routledge and Kegan Paul.

Eaton, Mary. 1986. *Justice for Women? Family, Court and Social Control*. Milton Keynes, England: Open University Press.

Felice, M., and D.R. Offord. 1975. "Girl delinquency," in R. Cavan, ed., *Readings in Juvenile Delinquency*, 3rd ed. Philadelphia: J.B. Lippincott.

Finch, J., and D. Groves, eds. 1983. *A Labour of Love: Women, Work and Caring*. London: Routledge and Kegan Paul.

Gagnon, R., and L. Langelier-Biron. 1982. *Les filles en marge*. Rapport No. 6, Groupe de Recherche sur L'Inadaptation Juvénile, Université de Montréal.

Geller, G.R. 1987. "Young women in conflict with the law," in E. Adelberg and C. Currie, eds., *Too Few To Count*. Vancouver: Press Gang Publishers.

Gilligan, C., N. Lyons, and T. Hammer, eds. 1990. *Making Connections: The Traditional Worlds of Adolescent Girls at Emma Willard School*. Cambridge, Mass.: Harvard University Press.

Gordon, L. 1986. "Incest and resistance: Patterns of father-daughter incest, 1880–1930," *Social Problems*, 33, 4: 253–67.

Gordon, L. 1988. *Heroes of Their Own Lives*. New York: Viking.

Hall, S., and T. Jefferson. 1975. *Resistance Through Rituals: Youth Subcultures in Post-War Britain*. New York: Holmes and Meier.

Hatch, Alison, and Karlene Faith. 1989–90. "The female offender in Canada: A statistical profile," *Canadian Journal of Women and the Law*, 3, 2: 432–56.

Heidensohn, Frances. 1987. "Women and crime: Questions for criminology," in Carlen and Worrall, eds., *Gender, Crime and Justice*.

Herold, E.S. 1984. *Sexual Behavior of Canadian Young People*. Markham, Ont.: Fitzhenry & Whiteside.

Hubbard, R. 1981. "The emperor doesn't wear any clothes: The impact of feminism on biology," in D. Spender, ed., *Men's Studies Modified. The Impact of Feminism on the Academic Disciplines*. New York: Pergamon Press.

Hudson, A. 1983. "The welfare state and adolescent femininity," *Youth and Policy*, 2, 1: 5–13.

Hutter, Bridget, and Gillian Williams. 1981. "Controlling women: The normal and the deviant," in B. Hutter and G. Williams, eds., *Controlling Women*. London: Croom Helm.

Jephcott, A.P. 1942. *Girls Growing Up*. London: Faber & Faber.

Kersten, Joachim. 1989. "The institutional control of girls and boys," in Cain, ed., *Growing Up Good*.

Konopka, G. 1966. *The Adolescent Girl in Conflict*. Englewood Cliffs, N.J.: Prentice-Hall.

Konopka, G. 1976. *Young Girls*. Englewood Cliffs, N.J.: Prentice-Hall.

Kostash, M. 1987. *No Kidding: Inside the World of Teenage Girls*. Toronto: McClelland and Stewart.

Kruttschnitt, C. 1982. "Respectable women and the law," *Sociological Quarterly*, 23 (Spring): 221–34.

Langelier-Biron, Louise. 1983. "The delinquent young girl: A nonentity?" in R.R. Corrado, M. LeBlanc, and J. Trepanier, eds., *Current Issues in Juvenile Justice*. Toronto: Butterworths.

Lees, Sue. 1989. "Learning to love: Sexual reputation, morality and the social control of girls," in Cain, ed., *Growing Up Good*.

Lerman, Paul. 1984. "Child welfare, the private sector and community-based corrections," *Crime and Delinquency*, 30, 1: 5–38.

Llewellyn, Mandy. 1980. "Studying girls at school: The implications of schooling," in Deem, ed., *Schooling for Women's Work*.

Luxton, M. 1980. *More than a labour of love*. Toronto: The Women's Press.

McRobbie, A. 1981. "Just like a Jackie story," in A. McRobbie and R. McCabe, eds., *Feminism for Girls: An Adventure Story*. London: Routledge and Kegan Paul.

McRobbie, A., and J. Garber. 1975. "Girls and subcultures," in S. Hall and T. Jefferson, eds., *Resistance through Rituals*. New York: Holmes and Meier.

McRobbie, A., and R. McCabe. 1981. "Introduction," in McRobbie and McCabe, eds., *Feminism for Girls*.

Messerschmidt, J.W. 1987. "Feminism, criminology and the rise of the female sex 'delinquent', 1880–1930," *Contemporary Crises*, 11: 243–63.

Mies, Maria. 1989. "Self-determination: The end of a utopia," *Resources for Feminist Research*, 18, 3: 51–56.

Morris, A. 1987. *Women, Crime and Criminal Justice*. Oxford: Basil Blackwell.

Nease, Barbara. 1966. "Measuring juvenile delinquency in Hamilton," *Canadian Journal of Criminology and Corrections*, 8, 2: 133–45.

Oakley, Ann. 1982. *Subject Women*. London: Fontana.

Orton, M., and E. Rosenblatt. 1986. *Adolescent Pregnancy in Ontario*. Hamilton: Planned Parenthood of Ontario and McMaster University.

Parent, C. 1986. "Actualités and bibliographics: La protection chevalresque ou les représentations masculines du traitement des femmes dans la justice pénale," *Déviance et Société*. 10, 2: 147-75.

Petrie, C. 1986. *The Nowhere Girls*. Aldershot, Hants, England: Gower.

Propper, Alice. 1979. "The relationship of maternal employment and sex to adolescent's parental relationship," in Ishwaran, ed., *Childhood and Adolescence in Canada*.

Reitsma-Street, M., D.R. Offord, and T. Finch. 1985. "Pairs of same-sexed siblings discordant for antisocial behavior," *British Journal of Psychiatry*, 146: 415-23.

Reitsma-Street, M. 1988. "Female Delinquency and Conformity in Adolescent Sisters," Ph.D. thesis, University of Toronto.

Reitsma-Street, M. 1990a. "Implementation of the *Young Offenders Act*: Five Years Later," *Canadian Social Work Review*, 7, 2.

Reitsma-Street, M. 1990b. "A review of female delinquency," in A. Leschied and P. Jaffe, eds., *The Young Offenders Act Revolution*. Toronto: University of Toronto Press.

Russell, D. 1986. *The Secret Trauma: Incest in the Lives of Girls and Women*. New York: Basic Books.

Schur, E.M. 1984. *Labeling Women Deviant*. New York: Random House.

Schwartz, Ira M., Martha W. Steketee, *et al*. 1989. "The incarceration of girls: Paternalism or juvenile crime control?" paper presented at the annual meeting of the Academy of Criminal Justice Sciences, Washington, D.C., March.

Schwartz, I.M., M. Jackson-Beeck, and R. Anderson. 1984. "The 'hidden' system of juvenile control," *Crime and Delinquency*, 30, 3: 371-85.

Schwendinger, H., and J. Schwendinger. 1985. *Adolescent Subcultures and Delinquency*, Research Edition. New York: Praeger.

Shacklady Smitt, L. 1978. "Sexist assumptions and female delinquency," in C. Smart and B. Smart, eds., *Women, Sexuality and Social Control*. London: Routledge and Kegan Paul.

Sharpe, S. 1976. *"Just like a girl."* Harmondsworth, Middlesex: Penguin.

Smart, Carol. 1976. *Women, Crime and Criminology*. London: Routledge.

Smart, C. 1985. "Legal subjects and sexual objects: Ideology, law and female sexuality," in Brophy and Smart, eds., *Women-in-Law*.

Statutes of Canada. 1908. *An Act Respecting Juvenile Delinquents*. 7-8 Edward VII, c.40.

Statutes of Canada, Revised. 1985. *An Act Respecting Young Offenders*. c. y-1.

Strange, Carolyn. 1985. " 'The criminal and fallen of their sex': The establishment of Canada's first women's prison, 1874-1901," *Canadian Journal of Women and the Law*, 1: 79-92.

Strong-Boag, Veronica. 1988. *The New Day Recalled: Lives of Girls and Women in English Canada, 1919-1939.* Toronto: Copp Pitman.

Tanner, J. 1988. "Youthful deviance," in V.F. Sacco, ed., *Deviance, Conformity and Control in Canadian Society.* Scarborough, Ont.: Prentice-Hall.

Taylor, D. 1985. "Women: An analysis," in *Women, a world report.* New York: Oxford University Press.

Trepanier, Jean. 1986. "La justice des mineurs au Québec: 25 ans de transformations (1960-1985)," *Criminologie,* xix, 1: 189-214.

Tronto, Joan C. 1989. "Women and caring: What can feminists learn about morality from caring?" in A. Jaggar and S. Bordo, eds., *Gender/Body/Knowledge: Feminist Reconstruction of Being and Knowing.* New Brunswick, N.J.: Rutgers University Press.

Ve, Hildur. 1984. "Women's mutual alliances: Altruism as a premise for interaction," in H. Holter, ed., *Patriarchy in a Welfare Society.* Oslo: Universitetsforlaget.

Walker, Alice. 1973. *Revolutionary Petunias and Other Poems.* New York: Harcourt Brace Jovanovich.

Weiler, K. 1978. "Unmanageable children in Ontario: A legal review," in H. Berkley *et al.,* eds., *Children's Rights.* Toronto: Ontario Institute for Studies in Education.

White, Barbara A. 1985. *Growing Up Female: Adolescent Girlhood in American Fiction.* Westport, Conn.: Greenwood Press.

Widom, Cathy Spatz, Faith S. Katkink, Abigail J. Stewart, and Mark Fondacaro. 1983. "Multivariate analysis of personality and motivation in female delinquents," *Journal of Research in Crime and Delinquency,* 21, 2: 277-90.

Wilson, Deidre. 1978. "Sexual codes and conduct: A study of teenage girls," in Smart and Smart, eds., *Women, Sexuality and Social Control.*

Wilson, Leslie. 1988. "Is a 'feminine' ethic enough?" *Atlantis* 13, 2: 15-23.

Worall, Anne. 1989. "Working with female offenders: Beyond 'alternatives to custody,' " *British Journal of Social Work,* 19: 77-93.

CHAPTER V

Dutiful Daughters and Undemanding Mothers: Constraining Images of Giving and Receiving Care in Middle and Later Life

Jane Aronson

In Canada, as in comparable Western economic systems, it is estimated that 85 to 90 per cent of the care of old people is provided informally, largely in the context of families (Chappell *et al.*, 1986). The rest, only 10 or 15 per cent, is supplied by the formal health and social services. In the world of informal care, women – most commonly wives, daughters, and daughters-in-law – are generally the care providers and, by virtue of women's longer life expectancy, it is predominantly women, especially in older age groups, who are the care receivers.

This chapter addresses the way in which this pattern of care actually unfolds in women's lives in contemporary Canada and with what consequences for their welfare. Drawing on the literature on societal responses to the elderly and on a qualitative study of women giving and receiving care, I will explore how women in middle and later life confront images of family ties, femininity, and old age that press them into relations of dependency and obligation. These relations come at high cost to women in that they limit their opportunities for self-enhancement and security over the life course. In the latter part of the chapter, I will consider the possibilities of changing this pattern of care and dependency, guided by a fundamental question posed by Lynne Segal (1987: 242) in her consideration of the project for feminism in the future: "How do we provide for the needs of all, and not at the expense of women?"

For several reasons, consideration of this question in relation to the needs of old people is an especially fruitful area for exploring women's caring. First, this area has received a lot of attention over the last decade. There is, therefore, a substantial amount of material to draw on and consider, as well as clearly identifiable patterns in the tone and content of government activity and public debate. Anticipation of the increased number and proportion of elderly people in the population in the years to come has prompted concern about the growing demands that will be made for health and social services (Crane, 1989; Health and Welfare Canada, 1986). While many people require little assistance as they age, a substantial proportion, especially among the growing numbers of the very old, are unable to care for themselves alone. These concerns have emerged during a gradually worsening climate of cuts in public expenditure and questioning of social welfare programs. Public debate has at times been couched in terms of alarm and we hear "the community" invoked as the source of better solutions to the needs of old people. As has now been well-documented – especially in the U.K., where these developments are more advanced – the rather slippery notion of "community care" tends to mean the unpaid care provided by female family members (Finch and Groves, 1983).

Second, population aging means that most people will have elderly relatives, at least some of whom will need support of

one kind or another. Most will not require very heavy physical care but what Lewis and Meredith (1988: 32) term "semi-
care" and Hasselkus (1988: 686) terms "anticipatory" and
"protective" caregiving – in other words, a mix of practical
support and invisible emotional work. Thus, while only a few
of us know what it means to have a disabled child or a
chronically ill spouse, many of us have an aging father or
mother. We therefore have direct experience of thinking
about our own or our families' relationships with and obligations toward them, their expectations or wishes in relation to
us, and the place of collective provision for their welfare.
Furthermore, we can now all reasonably expect to grow old
ourselves. Practices, ideas, and beliefs about meeting the
needs of old people therefore touch the lives of a great many
people.

Lastly, it is important to recognize that women are implicated in the care of old people in families as the majority of
both givers *and* receivers. As noted above, because of women's
greater life expectancy, they represent the majority of old
people, especially among those over eighty – a trend that will
continue in the coming decades. Thus, exploration of the care
of old people in families (daughters and daughters-in-law
assisting mothers and mothers-in-law being the most common
care relationships) provides an opportunity for understanding
women's experiences on both ends of care relationships. It
provides an opportunity, too, for thinking about ways of
meeting people's needs that value and enhance the interests
and welfare of both care providers and care receivers.

This chapter addresses the ways in which women's experiences of giving and receiving care are shaped by social
policies and penetrated by prevailing values concerning the
family, gender, and old age. To explore these processes, I will
link critical analyses of the present pattern of care of old
people with selected material drawn from a qualitative study
of women's caring done in Toronto in 1987–88 (Aronson,
1988). The thirty-two women who participated in in-depth
interviews ranged in age from thirty-five to eighty-five and
described themselves as either aging women who had adult
daughters and were concerned about the future or as daughters of such women. The thirty-two subjects' accounts of their

experiences constitute both descriptions of individual situations and life histories and "points of entry" into the wider social and ideological processes that frame them (Smith, 1986: 7).

In exploring dimensions of women's caring by building on these data, it is important to note that my observations about giving and receiving care are limited in several respects. They focus only on the context of the mother-daughter relationship – the most common but not the only intergenerational care relationship – and, thus, only on the experiences of older women with children. They are also confined to the experiences of a relatively privileged white middle-class group. All the subjects had worked outside the home as school teachers at some point in their lives and none were in economic hardship. Comparing the accounts of these women with other groups (e.g., women of different class and ethnic backgrounds; women without daughters or childless women) represents an important future research agenda.

Before turning to some aspects of the data generated in the study, a brief review follows of the present pattern of care of old people and of the underlying assumptions about women's realities within it.

ASSUMPTIONS UNDERLYING THE PRESENT PATTERN OF CARE OF OLD PEOPLE

Publicly provided services for old people include a range of health and social services: different types of congregate care (e.g., homes for the aged, nursing homes, chronic care facilities) and a mix of services and resources intended to support people in their own homes (e.g., homemakers, visiting nurses, meals-on-wheels). With the exception of specialized medical interventions, all these services can be provided informally – they have a high degree of what has been termed "substitutability" (Arber *et al.*, 1988). The boundary between formal and informal care is, thus, a very permeable phenomenon and, as noted earlier, the division is set in such a way that government services remain very much in the background. Allocation of these scarce resources is not a random process.

Research and the observations of service providers suggest consistently that government resources are distributed according to the availability of female kin and in the spirit of what has been termed "casualty intervention" – that is, when informal care arrangements have been so overtaxed as to break down, rather than on a truly shared or supportive basis (Walker, 1985).

Social policies and programs for the elderly rest heavily, then, on the informal sector, specifically on the care provided by women in families. This pattern of intervention and non-intervention is sustained and legitimated by the ideology of familism – by the assumption that "the family" is the proper locus of care for elderly relatives (and others deemed dependent). Policy documents and proposals are couched in language that implies the "naturalness" of family ties and obligations to older kin. For example, the Ontario Office for Senior Citizens' Affairs (1986: 10) has stated that, "Generally, family and friends provide the most effective support for older persons." Similarly, the National Advisory Council on Aging (1986: 5) has proclaimed: "We believe in the importance of the family and that it is desirable for family members to help one another when help is needed."

The "descriptive and prescriptive" (Finch, 1989: 236) elements in such assertions of familism extend, further, to the notion that the provision of more state support would actually erode or undermine family care. The political right and "pro-family" lobbies warn that increased government intervention heralds the demise of "proper" family life (Eichler, 1988). Research indicates, rather, that obligation does not lessen when formal services are introduced (Doty, 1986; Levin et al., 1983; Montgomery and Borgatta, 1989). This pattern has been identified consistently, beginning with analyses of historical material demonstrating that the original introduction of state pensions facilitated rather than strained supportive family ties (Anderson, 1977; Synge, 1980).

Critical analysis suggests that the interests of women – either as providers or receivers of care – are not a central concern of social policies regarding old people. Female family caregivers are the object of policy interest in the sense that their work is recognized as crucial to the present organization of care. Indeed, awareness of their shrinking numbers and availability (because of smaller family sizes and women's increased labour force participation) is articulated with increasing concern (Ontario Office for Senior Citizens' Affairs, 1986: 10; Canadian Medical Association, 1987: 1). Stemming from this concern, we see social programs intended to shore up their efforts and help them to carry on caring; for example: "Professional services should be used to enhance and supplement, not replace, family support services" (Ontario Ministry of Community and Social Services, 1988: 8).

Such programs as caregiver support groups and respite care thus provide minimal short-term relief, but with the intention of sustaining the present division of care rather than changing it or asking whether it is in women's best interests to be, effectively, pressed into caregiving.

Just as women carers are of policy interest as a critical labour supply rather than as complete persons with aspirations and needs of their own, so it seems that the welfare of old people themselves is not, either, at the centre of debate about the care of the elderly. It is taken for granted that family care is the best care. Inattention to old people's perspectives renders them passive participants in care arrangements – as if they were the objects rather than the subjects of the circumstances of their aging. Looking at elderly women in particular, the absence of choice in determining the conditions of their aging can be understood as one element of the systematic and lifelong disadvantage they experience in a culture that favours youth, independence, and masculinity. The small amount of existing research on elderly women's realities suggests, unsurprisingly, that the experience of needing assistance can often be tense and problematic (Evers, 1981, 1985).

In the emphases of public debate and academic and public policy attention, women giving care have received more visibility than old women receiving care. Feminist analyses are now beginning to focus on the social position of older women (Peace, 1986; Reinharz, 1986). Research in the social and health sciences has tended to segment the life course. Images of "intergenerational conflict" and the "old age dependency burden" are heard increasingly in public discourse

(Binney and Estes, 1988). In relation to women and care of old people, we see these divisive conceptualizations in the tendency to frame caregivers' and care receivers' interests in oppositional terms as givers or takers (Briar and Ryan, 1986). Predictably, more than half of the older women in my study had cared for their own elderly mothers at some point. Exploration of their realities as both caregivers and care receivers over time counters the tendency in the literature to focus on static life stages and underscores, rather, the continuity of gender identity and experience over the life course. The biographies of two of these women are presented below. Their experiences illustrate sharply the degree to which women's lives are shaped by their care for and overlapping commitments to others. Their accounts also suggest how their caregiving experiences influenced their thoughts and feelings about receiving care in later life. After briefly addressing the patterned realities of women's life course that their experiences typify, I will explore how the assumptions and values embedded in social policies and public debate, discussed above, unfold and translate into women's lives as mothers and daughters engaged in care relationships. From the case material, I will discuss aspects of this process of translation over the life course, elaborating key issues by introducing the accounts of other women who participated in the research.

THE LIFE COURSE VIEW:
MRS. C AND MRS. S

Mrs. C

Mrs. C is sixty-six, a widow who has a son and two daughters, all living in the Toronto area. She lives alone in the family home and has a number of chronic health problems: heart condition, post-cancer treatment complications, and impaired mobility. She continues to drive a car and is quite self-sufficient with some outside help: home care provides assistance with cleaning; she pays someone to do the heavy garden work; she attends a foot clinic and has a general practitioner whom she likes. She is in regular phone and visiting contact with her children, especially her daughters, whom she describes as supportive and helpful with "the incidentals." She "feels sorry" for an older friend who has no children.

Mrs. C went into teaching when her children were all in elementary school, prompted by her husband's unemployment. Her salary became crucial as he grew increasingly disabled as a result of diabetes. Shortly after Mrs. C finished her teacher training, her mother's health deteriorated; Mrs. C felt she was overprescribed tranquilizers and, as a result, became slow and confused. Mrs. C. contemplated having her mother come to live with her, but with a full-time job, a sick husband, and small children she decided it was too much. Instead, for a period of time she ran two households. She tried to limit the amount of time she gave to her mother, feeling torn and concerned to devote proper attention to her husband and children.

As her mother's condition worsened, she realized that she "couldn't handle everybody" and – very reluctantly – organized her mother's admission to a nursing home. She resented that her brother, her only sibling, was uninvolved in this, partly because he lived outside Toronto and partly because his wife kept her in-laws at a distance. Mrs. C recalled upsetting weekly visits to her mother and the poor care provided in the nursing home. She expressed guilt at the memories and reflected that "I should have sued them, but I didn't have enough energy to take it on."

Over the next few years, Mrs. C's husband had to give up work completely and her children married and left home. When she was in her late fifties, Mrs. C's mother died, and shortly afterwards she had to retire because her husband required constant care. She regretted retiring and, for a time, tutored children privately at home because it brought her so much satisfaction. However, her own health then deteriorated and, as a result, her husband was admitted to a chronic care hospital where he died three years before the time of the interview.

Talking of her current situation, Mrs. C was determined to stay in her own home and to be as independent as possible. While sometimes expressing a fierce independence and anger at the poor treatment meted out to old people, Mrs. C also expressed some fears and uncertainty about her future. She acknowledged that her children were helpful and supportive and described their lives as busy and successful. Recognizing their limitations, she recognized her own a generation before:

> As my son said to me at one point: "Mum, I'll come and help you as much as I can, but my first obligation's to my own family – you know, to my wife and children." And I thought that was kind of callous . . . and then I thought afterwards: I did the *same* thing, you know, with my mother.

She explained that she made a point of not asking her daughters for too much, trying to pace her requests so as not to exceed their capacities. They did not talk about the future and she did not want to share her anxieties with them. She likened herself to her mother, whom she described as "too proud" to say what she needed or was concerned about. Her mother's indirectness had irritated her, but now she felt she understood it. It was, thus, a matter of pride to Mrs. C to be as independent as possible and not to expose her needs or concerns.

Mrs. S

Mrs. S is a seventy-four-year-old divorced women who lives alone in an apartment in Toronto and has a daughter who lives about an hour's drive away. Mrs. S enjoyed the early years of her retirement. However, at seventy she had a heart attack followed by surgery and a caution from her doctor to be very careful. In the year or two before the interview, she had given up driving, hired someone to do housework, and no longer took the kinds of trips and vacations that she had enjoyed previously. She expressed anxiety about the future, concerned that she might be unable to manage alone in her apartment and frightened particularly at the prospect of dying alone. Her experiences of being hospitalized and of a local seniors' centre that she had "tried" once left her with a distaste for "being herded together."

Mrs. S left her husband when their daughter was an infant, taking her back to her parental home in northern Ontario where she began working as a teacher. When her daughter left home and moved to Toronto, Mrs. S followed some years later, found a teaching job, and established friendships and ties centred on her local church. When her daughter's first marriage ended, she and her small daughter lived with Mrs. S for a few years. After her daughter remarried and moved to the suburbs, Mrs. S's mother – by then a widow and becoming frail – sold her home and stayed with Mrs. S and her two sisters on a rotating basis for six months or a year at a time.

Mrs. S saw it as unremarkable that her mother would stay with her and remembered, gratefully, her helpfulness to her when she had left her husband. She also recalled, with some guilt at talking about it, the tensions that her mother's long visits introduced into her life – the lack of privacy at home, the constraints on her social life – and how she tried to put limits on their duration. When her mother's health deteriorated she went into a local home for the aged for a period, but she hated it because she so disliked "being ruled" by other people. She eventually became confused and spent her last years in a hospital near one of Mrs. S's sisters in another province. She had died only a few months before the interview.

Mrs. S spoke to her daughter several times a week and described her, her son-in-law, and granddaughter with great affection. After Mrs. S's heart attack, her daughter had raised the possibility of Mrs. S going to live with them, but the plan did not materialize because of her son-in-law's objections. Mrs. S noted: "we didn't make a big thing of it. You know, it's a good stand to take because they [parents] can cause trouble." She thought that her own mother's stays with her "could have changed my mind about things." Mrs. S and her daughter had not spoken of the future since that time. She described herself as "an ostrich," wanting to keep her head firmly in the sand and not to talk about the future. Recognizing her daughter's busy life, she asked for little help. She sometimes asked a friend favours of certain kinds, but hated to be "dragging on people" and would sooner go without whatever it was she wanted. Summing this up, she said:

> Once in a while, I get kind of depressed, low-spirited, and I miss them, not seeing them. I think: "Oh, grow up, will

you! You know, they can't be running over here at night to see me after their work." But I feel that they're doing all they *can* do. And I don't want to be one of these possessive mothers that just . . . will act the martyr or . . . play dependent, you know, at all. I like to be able to live my own life and see them in a nice social way.

Mrs. S said that she would not share her dark moods or sense of loneliness with her daughter because it would make her feel ashamed.

In Mrs. C's and Mrs. S's biographies, we can identify certain patterned forms that characterize the life course for women. Recalling herself as a young woman, Mrs. C represents the "woman in the middle" described by Brody (1981). She is set in the midst of competing commitments to her mother, her children, her sick husband, and her job. Evident in her account is the sheer hard work of juggling responsibilities and managing paid work, running two households, and responding to other people's needs – she is "swamped" by caring for and about those around her.

Mrs. S's biography introduces another reality of women's caring over the life course – that women are caring for elderly parents for much longer periods and at later times in life than ever before. Because of increased life expectancy, generations of women in families can expect to have longer overlapping biographies than ever before (Hagestad, 1986) and to experience care relationships of increased duration. Mrs. S's mother depended on staying with her for periods over a stretch of almost twenty years. She had died at the age of ninety-nine a few months before I met Mrs. S, who was then herself seventy-four.

The profile of "women in the middle" (Brody, 1981) has highlighted the complex commitments that characterize women's lives. The term has captured well the notion of women's activities in relation to others. However, it has tended not to include aspects of women's orientation to themselves – their own needs and aspirations. Remembering her mother's long visits, Mrs. S minded that her presence meant that she saw friends less. In discussing the years she had cared for her mother, her reluctant retirement, and the inability to devote more time to her work, Mrs. C communicated regret at opportunities for self-development and advancement that she had forgone. Both spoke of their guilty feelings at voicing these regrets. Because caring is understood as an other-directed activity and a central feature of female identity, raising such self-directed concerns as these is not easy for women. These self-directed issues are, nonetheless, part of the landscape of realities into which caregiving expectations fall in women's lives.

Women's reluctance to raise individual concerns accords with Allatt and Kiel's (1987) observations that ideas about the life course and the interrelationships of individual and family time have been very different for women and men. For women, there is a systematic entanglement or fusion of individual and family time – a pattern well illustrated by Mrs. C's and Mrs. S's life experiences. Men's life trajectories, on the other hand, are thought of in terms of the public domain and their life transitions are relatively unfettered by the concerns of family time, e.g., household organization, the care of children and dependants. The challenge, then, is "to unshackle our conceptualizations of women's life experiences from the family life cycle" (Allatt and Kiel, 1987: 1).

Turning to later life stages, Mrs. C and Mrs. S introduce characteristic features of older women's realities. Both experience significant chronic health problems that, in different ways, limit their activities and prevent them from looking after themselves alone. Both were in a position to purchase services they needed and, thus, could exercise a degree of choice and self-determination that is not the privilege of the majority of older women. Nonetheless, both felt apprehensive about how they would manage if their health worsened and alluded to fears about the future of which they seldom spoke. While feeling well connected in terms of friends and social ties, both mentioned a narrowing of horizons in terms of social activity that they expected to become even narrower with time.

These, then, were the realities of Mrs. C's and Mrs. S's lives: complex processes of juggling and balancing commitments in a very broadly defined "middle" period, and, in the later period they were just entering, a growing awareness of constraints on their activities and the possibility, if not the reality, of increased dependence. In the next section, I will move beyond this descriptive picture to consider the ways in which the prevailing beliefs and normative expectations of women, old age, family life, and public policy – discussed earlier – are reflected in women's experiences over the life course. The experiences of Mrs. C, Mrs. S, and the other women I interviewed suggest considerable tension between their everyday realities and received social expectations about the appropriate conduct of mothers and daughters in middle and late life.

SOCIAL EXPECTATIONS: DUTIFUL DAUGHTERS AND UNDEMANDING MOTHERS

Like most of the women interviewed, Mrs. S and Mrs. C took it for granted that, as a general rule, daughters should assist elderly parents in need of support. Assumptions were made at two levels: first, families were seen as an obvious support for elderly parents; and second, daughters were the logical caregivers within families. For example, two women in their fifties commented:

> I think it goes beyond a sense of duty. . . . I think I have a strong feeling that the world would be a better place if we had much stronger family relations, where it was expected and conformed to that parents lived with their daughters.

> I think it's our duty to do those things. . . . I think most people find it natural to do it . . . you have to do certain things at certain stages of life.

Older respondents also reflected these assumptions about family ties and gender. One noted her "good fortune" at having a daughter; others, like Mrs. C, felt sorry for elderly friends who did not or who, worse, had no children at all. Qureshi and Walker (1989) have identified the normative processes that designate female relatives as carers of choice, giving empirical support to the now well-developed analyses of the association of femininity with caring (Graham, 1983). Women who participated in my research found these patterns of caring so self-evident as to be unremarkable; as Qureshi and Walker observe: "Norms need no explaining" (1989: 132).

Several women, like Mrs. C, noted the absence of their brothers in the division of caring labour and were at pains to explain and justify their resentful feelings, which were, effectively, challenges to the normative ordering of responsibility. A few others voiced guilty feelings about brothers and sisters-in-law who, because of geographical proximity, were more involved with their mothers than they were themselves. Again, their discomfort suggested recognition of normative expectations about care and gender that were not being followed and therefore had to be accounted for.

The general social expectation of daughters, as understood by these women, was to be dutiful and responsive to elderly parents. The general social expectations of old women have been less explored in the literature. We know that they occupy a marginal and disadvantaged social position (Cohen, 1984) but know little of their experiences of needing support. Mrs. S, like other older women participating in the research, had an acute sense of how she should *not* behave. She was at pains to distance herself from old women who were "possessive," "dependent," or "martyrish." Another respondent referred with disdain to her daughter's mother-in-law, who was "fearful" and "demanding." Thus, older women's accounts revealed a strong imperative to be independent and self-sufficient – echoing the often-heard wish not to be a burden to anyone. The strength of this imperative to be independent motivated women not to "impose" on their daughters and to "let them live their own lives."

These normative images of dutiful daughters and undemanding mothers were further shaped and confirmed by encounters with formal health and social services. Speaking from the perspectives of daughters, many women referred to the lack of interest of their mothers' family doctors – people they rightly saw as pivotal in the formal care system. In the absence of interested and active general practitioners, women felt, as one said: "I'm 'it' then" – the only person feeling responsible for her mother's health and welfare and mindful of whatever future planning might be needed.

One woman described her frustrated efforts to make arrangements for her mother to get a homemaker when she was discharged home after a period in hospital. She noted how "grudgingly" the hospital responded to her request and how little information was made available: "I had to fight for it. I felt it should have been offered." This woman's description of the "fight" was accompanied by a long justification for her request for services – a justification she had felt obliged to impress on the hospital staff. It included a list of her commitments – to a demanding job, to three children and her husband – and her assertion of entitlement to public services:

> *We're* under pressure too . . . there really were limits. . . . It sounds really awful, but my mother's been a Canadian citizen for umpteen years and I pay a hell of a lot in income tax every year, my husband pays a hell of a lot every year, my sister and her husband pay . . . and now and then, when we need some short-term help, I don't think it should be difficult to find, I really don't.

Experiences like these reveal the way in which the division of care between formal and informal spheres, described above, actually shapes our ideas of "dutiful" behaviour. Janet Finch's work on the social construction of obligations draws attention to these patterned processes, underscoring how public policies and institutional practices "form part of the structure of constraints within which individuals conduct their own negotiations, restricting or expanding the range of alternatives available" (Finch, 1987: 162).

There has been less study of the way potential care recipients experience the restrictions imposed by social policies and programs. Just as grudgingly provided services communicate diminished entitlement for women in caregiving positions, so do they for older women. For example, many older respondents felt they had weak claims on public resources:

"We can't expect much"; "There are so many of us now"; "They just don't have the money, you see." Such comments suggest the effectiveness of political rhetoric that has cast the elderly as an expensive burden on society (Minkler, 1983). In addition to having an uncertain sense of entitlement to public services, women also had low expectations – even fears – about the quality of the services available. Mrs. C, for example, was apprehensive about the kind of care provided in institutions for old people – apprehensions informed by her observations of her mother's and friends' experiences.

To summarize, if we juxtapose these perceptions of entitlement and social expectation with the realities of women's situations at different life stages, we see some difficult tensions and contradictions. Women speaking of being caregiving daughters endorse, on the one hand, the general notion that daughters should help their aging parents, yet, on the other, they often find themselves in the midst of competing commitments, feeling over-extended and suppressed in terms of the pursuit of their own needs and objectives. Women speaking about the experience of growing older feel they should not be burdensome and should not impose on daughters, but they recognize their need and are motivated to achieve security and confidence. These dilemmas were reinforced among the women I interviewed by their perceptions of public services that – by virtue of being unavailable, hard to obtain, unwelcoming, or of poor quality – did little to expand their options. Smith (1979: 141) captures the tension between normative expectations and values and the everyday lived experience central to these dilemmas when she notes:

> . . . how ideas and social forms of consciousness may originate outside experience, coming from an external source and becoming a forced set of categories into which we must stuff the awkward and resistant actualities of our worlds.

In the next section, we will consider women's experiences of managing this tension, exploring how they "stuff" their realities into prevailing images of caregiving and receiving, and with what consequences for their welfare.

MANAGING THE CONTRADICTIONS OF
BEING DUTIFUL AND UNDEMANDING

The different dilemmas that characterize women's experiences of caregiving and receiving accord closely with developing analyses of women's psychological development, which underscore the degree to which concerns of personal integrity and identity change over the life course (Allatt *et al.*, 1987). Women's dilemmas were shaped by the combined impact of social expectations and predictable life events – in this instance, by images of family ties, gender, old age, public and private responsibility, and the health problems and losses associated with aging. The concerns of different life stages also evoke different strategies of negotiation – in Hanmer and Statham's terms, they call forth different "survival behaviors" (1989: 96).

For women speaking from the viewpoint of daughters, the central contradiction they confronted lay between normative expectations that they be caring and responsive to their aging mothers and their competing commitments to others, including themselves. While often wanting to be responsive and deriving satisfaction and pleasure from assisting their mothers, women's situations rested, nonetheless, on this underlying disjuncture. To manage the resulting tension, respondents spoke at length about the ways they tried to set limits on their supportive activities with their mothers – ways of "drawing the line." For example, Mrs. C described how she decided against bringing her mother to live with her because she felt it was not in her children's best interests. When her children were small, she also limited the time she devoted to her mother. In a sense, having her mother admitted to a nursing home, despite feeling torn and guilty about it, was a way of limiting what she did. Similarly, Mrs. S described how she took steps to limit the length of her mother's visits, encouraging or organizing her to move on to stay with one of her sisters, so that Mrs. S could "have some privacy" and "get back to normal."

Women articulated limits in terms of their time, space, competing commitments, energy, and emotion, sometimes offering complex justifications and explanations for their conduct. Whatever the form, this limit-setting consisted of efforts to preserve their integrity and self-determination, whether that meant securing some privacy, more time with husbands and children they felt they had neglected, the opportunity to see friends or become more engaged in work-related activity, or relief from tiredness. Several respondents spoke of the need to protect their own futures. For example, a divorced women in her mid-fifties reflected on how important it was to her that her very frail and confused mother either receive extensive community services at home or go into an institution:

> If they'd forced me into that [sharing her home with her mother] I would have had to stop my development of a second career, which is going to help me in my retirement. I would've had to stop, you know, a lot of things that interest me and it would have interfered with my job to some degree, as well, so . . . it would have closed my life down, I think.

This awareness of the consequences of assuming responsibility for very substantial care of her mother echoes Finch and Groves's observation that for women in their middle years, accommodating their work lives to the care of elderly relatives can be "a prelude to poverty in old age for the carer" (1980: 507).

The setting of limits emerged as a clear theme from older women's perspectives, too, though in rather different form. Their limits were expressed in terms of how much they would ask or accept from their daughters. Mrs. C, for instance, explained how her requests for assistance were "measured" in an effort not to lean too heavily on her daughters. Rather than ask too much of others, Mrs. S noted that it was easier simply to go without. Such limits seemed to serve the central purpose of lessening older women's sense of dependence and indebtedness. For example, to fend off diminishment one respondent explained to me how her daughter and son-in-law helped her each week with shopping and laundry, then added hastily: "And they don't make a big song and dance about it and I don't. I'm grateful and I let them know, but . . . you know, it's not 'poor granny' or any of that at all, you know."

Older respondents often set limits in terms of their daughters' interests, effectively containing their demands to protect their daughters. An elderly woman described her daughter's life – her work, her children, and her home life – and observed:

> I don't want to put any extra burdens on her. Because of her nature . . . she would assume responsibilities that perhaps she shouldn't . . . you know, take too much on herself and I don't want her to do that.

Like others, this woman enjoyed her daughter's attentiveness and warmth and was comforted by it, yet she remained watchful and alert to the impropriety of overstepping her own sense of its bounds.

In setting limits on the ways they gave or received care, respondents seemed to be trying to manage and contain the tensions, noted above, between the realities of their situations and what they felt they should do, that is, be dutiful daughters or undemanding mothers. The limits represented efforts to reconcile these valued images: for caregivers, with their busy, overcommitted lives and aspirations; for women needing care, with their real needs for assistance and a sense of confidence that they could manage their lives securely. Some of the resolutions achieved by the limits – for example, Mrs. C conserving some energy by admitting her mother to a nursing home, and Mrs. S maintaining her sense of integrity by doing without things rather than asking for help – may, indeed, have resolved some immediate tensions. However, such resolutions came at considerable costs and did not modify in any fundamental way the underlying tensions that women confronted in giving and receiving care.

THE COSTS OF CONFORMING TO EXPECTATIONS

The costs of trying to conform to expected images of caregiving daughters and cared-for mothers were revealed sharply in the feelings that characterized women's experiences. Speaking as caregiving daughters, women consistently said they felt guilty in relation to their mothers – a feeling well documented in the literature on parent care (Brody, 1985). Many, like Mrs. S, felt guilty at simply talking about the limits they set on the support they provided. Another respondent who was very involved with her frail widowed mother talked about her fatigue and the tension she felt at trying to mediate between her husband, children, and mother, then added: "I shouldn't be either complaining about her or talking about her as if she's a burden . . . there's a fair amount of guilt to that."

Women spoke also of their guilt at not doing enough for their mothers. The strength of their feeling seemed unrelated to how much care they actually provided or how affectionately they described their ties. Mrs. C, for instance, felt guilty at being unable to "cope" with the many demands on her and at admitting her mother to a nursing home. After describing her life – a full-time job, three children, and living an hour's drive from her mother – another respondent, a widow, talked at length about feeling guilty that she could only help her mother out at weekends.

We can understand guilt as what has been termed a "reflexive role-taking sentiment" (Shott, 1979: 1324). Such emotions are evoked by considering how one appears to others or to the generalized other. One regards and judges oneself as if through the eyes of an outside audience, generating an inner process of self-censorship; normative rules of conduct are internalized and levelled at the self. Shott (1979), Hochshild (1979), and others writing about the sociology of emotion reveal how feeling states signal this invisible process of social control. The account of a respondent who had once contemplated bringing her mother over from Holland to live with her illustrated this complex process of self-control and self-critical internal dialogue. She had recognized that – had her mother come to live with her – her mother's needs for substantial care and the lack of compatibility in their interests and lifestyles would have constrained her significantly. She spoke of her ambivalence tearfully:

So that's how I imagined it would be if I brought her over and yet I had such a *tremendous* guilt feeling . . . that it was a duty that I had to do. . . . someone pointed out to me how much one's life is ruled by "shoulds" and "oughts" and I began to see what happened . . . and I knew it would be a sacrifice to my mother . . . but that was so ingrained in me at the time. I thought that was what I *really* believed. It's something that's very hard to escape.

This woman crystallized her internal struggle in relation to her mother in her account of a women friend in a situation similar to her own. On the one hand, she noted with admiration that her friend was much better at setting limits on her support for her mother: "She is *so* strong, she's able to say: 'I do this much and no more. I have my own life to live and I have my duty to myself too.' " On the other, she judged her friend harshly, thinking to herself: "I'm surprised at your coldness, you know, you really ought to be more dutiful; you should understand your mother more."

This woman's internal struggle typifies the dilemma between self-enhancement and self-sacrifice that has been articulated in different ways over the last ten years in feminist analyses of women's psychological and moral development. It accords, too, with Mrs. C's and Mrs. S's difficulties in speaking of regrets about opportunities they had forgone for themselves when caught in a web of commitments to their mothers or their families. Gilligan (1982) notes that despite general public assertions that women are entitled to autonomy and self-direction, exercise of such choices often conflicts with powerfully internalized imperatives to be responsive and caring in relation to others. To be self-directed and autonomous is to risk being thought uncaring – a damning indictment in the context of the current construction of femininity (Graham, 1983).

We have seen that the central dilemma experienced by the older women studied lay in trying to resolve the tension between the cultural imperative to be independent and undemanding and their wishes to feel secure and confident. Resolving this tension by limiting the demands they made on others or exercising care in the ways they asked for or accepted help meant that they adhered to the strongly felt value of self-sufficiency but at the cost of suppressing their own needs and concerns. Again, the feelings associated with these limit-setting strategies reveal the power and the consequences of normative expectations placed on older women.

In their accounts of their situations, many of the older women recognized their precarious social status and their weak claims on both their families and public services. Mrs. C's and Mrs. S's biographies illustrate particularly acutely the interplay of these socially structured realities and states of feeling. Mrs. C noted that – as for her mother before her – pride motivated her not to let her daughters know the extent of her concerns for the future. Identifying this as another reflexive role-taking emotion, Shott (1979: 1326) suggests that pride derives from knowing one has behaved in accordance with normative expectations. Mrs. C and her mother thus preserved their pride at the expense of not revealing their needs and, in so doing, excluded the possibility of having their needs met and anxieties allayed.

When I asked Mrs. S what it would be like to tell her daughter about her anxieties and loneliness, she said she would feel ashamed. Shame represents the opposite of pride – a feeling provoked by recognizing that one's self is inadequate or disreputable. Mrs. S thus fends off shame – the humiliation of her daughter or others knowing that she does not feel independent or secure – by not sharing her real concerns. Like Mrs. C, there is, therefore, no possibility of her concerns being addressed or of her security being enhanced. Further to this, Mrs. S distances herself from older women who do not live up to the undemanding ideal and are, rather, "possessive" or "martyrish."

In summary, feelings of shame and guilt sustained women in their commitments to duty and to undemanding independence. For the women who participated in my research, these internalized processes of social control resulted in varying degrees of self-alienation (Mrs. S, for example, is a very harsh critic of her own experience) and in the stifling of their aspirations for self-enhancement and security. The costs of struggling to conform were high.

THE FUTURE: THE POSSIBILITY
OF MEETING NEEDS AND
ENHANCING WOMEN

With this appreciation of the costs to women of the present pattern of care of the elderly, we can now return to the question posed at the outset: "How do we provide for the needs of all, and not at the expense of women?" (Segal, 1987: 242). Applying this fundamental question to women's experiences of the current pattern of care of old people offers direction for thinking about change, specifically, change that could: relieve women of the privately borne pressure to be dutiful and undemanding and permit them, rather, to give and receive care by choice in keeping with the particular nature of their wishes and capacities; foster in older women a sense of entitlement and confidence in articulating their needs without shame; and, in younger women, foster a sense of entitlement to pursue their own interests and development without a sense of guilt and inadequacy in relation to others.

In this chapter we have seen that the present pattern of care of old people offers women little room to manoeuvre in regard to giving or receiving care. They are trapped in ties of dependency and obligation. Materially, they are trapped by the minimal provision of acceptable public services. Ideologically, they are ensnared by constraining images of family ties, old age, and femininity. Care relationships between generations of women may be, variously, acceptable, unremarkable, resented, or welcomed by different women in different situations. However, it is important to recognize that they are structured in a coercive fashion. They are not choices exercised among real alternatives and they come at high cost to women's self-enhancement and security. In considering ways in which these costs to women could be lessened and more equitably distributed, we must look at both the material and ideological dimensions of the current pattern of care and begin to appreciate the complex entanglement between them. To envision concrete, practical possibilities of reshaping the boundaries of care arrangements among families, the state, and the market and between women and men, it is necessary to consider, too, the values, ideas, and cultural meanings of care, dependence, and femininity that sustain the present divisions.

In regard to the material aspects of women's situations in giving and receiving care, one approach to expanding their possibilities and enhancing their welfare would be to work toward more generous provision of formal services. Features of formal care that would be important to incorporate are, increasingly, being explored and articulated. For example, we are hearing more of the need for flexible community care (Lewis and Meredith, 1988; Qureshi and Walker, 1989) and of qualities of congregate care that would enhance people's sense of control and self-direction (Dalley, 1988: Willcocks *et al.*, 1987).

It is suggested in some quarters that old people can exercise choice and achieve greater control over the circumstances of their aging in the private market. In some Canadian provinces, government policy has fostered the development of private care options (Patterson, 1987). The potential of this public policy direction to enhance women's welfare in old age is slim, however. Only those women with sufficient resources can choose to pay privately for services – a minority, given the large proportion of old women who are poor (National Council of Welfare, 1989). It is suggested, further, that even when private means are available, the notion of consumer sovereignty is an ill-fitting model to apply to old people's need-meeting experiences (Tarman, 1989). Indeed, among the relatively privileged women who participated in the research discussed here, the ability to pay for supportive services at home and the knowledge that relatively expensive institutional care would be affordable did not bring a sense of security or confidence. The structured disadvantage of being old and female and, actually or possibly, dependent appeared more determining of their experiences than did their ability to engage in the private market.

Just as simply having private care options available did not relieve the tensions experienced by older women, obtaining formal supports for their mothers was not an easy process for younger women. That Mrs. C, for example, sought formal care – a nursing home – for her mother left her with a painful sense that she had failed in her duty. The Association of Carers, a lobby and support group of family carers in the U.K., has identified the common reluctance of carers to seek or accept formal support (Briggs and Oliver, 1985). For many, the acceptance of outside help represents a failure to cope and to care. As noted before, the association of femininity with caring renders the inability to cope a personal inadequacy. As a logical corollary to this, in the few instances where subjects' brothers assumed a more than usually significant role in supporting their mothers, women felt guilty and uneasy.

It is evident, then, that there are profound ideological barriers to exercising options for obtaining or sharing care when, in simple material terms, they are available. Identifying and challenging these barriers is a crucial dimension of envisioning different ways of caring for old people that do not disadvantage women. Two particular facets of these ideological barriers emerged forcefully in the research: the power of prevailing imagery of family ties, and the degree to which the cultural importance of being dutiful and undemanding stifled women's articulation of stress or of complaint at their situations.

Permeating the accounts of the women who participated in the research were strong cultural images of proper family ties and women's place within them. As we have seen, women generally took it for granted that the family was the proper locus of care and that it was women's lot to be responsive to others and undemanding for themselves. As noted at the beginning of the chapter, this imagery underpins current social policy. If the Canadian situation continues to follow developments in the U.K. and the U.S., where economic recession and a conservative family ideology are more advanced, we can expect these cultural images to become increasingly entrenched.

Exploration of the ways these cultural images unfold in women's lives has suggested, however, that they do not correspond with their actual experiences but instead provide ill-fitting forms into which their realities are pressed. The imagery of the family communicated in political rhetoric, policy, and program planning implies a readily available pool of female care – in terms of both love and labour – and a population of elderly women ready to receive passively the support of younger female kin. We have seen, rather, women's recognition of the marginal claims of elderly women. Mrs. C, for instance, recognized that marginality over three generations of women: she remembers her own limits when her mother needed support, recognizes her daughters' limits now, and, in response, asks little and conceals her needs. Among the women I interviewed, there was consistent recognition of the primacy of the nuclear family – of husbands and dependent children – and of the relatively weak and tenuous entitlement of elderly mothers. These realities do not accord with the comfortable imagery of the extended family and intergenerational relations that is assumed in the vocabulary of social policies.

Women's awareness of the lack of correspondence between this official vocabulary and their everyday realities and family lives was experienced privately. The women who participated in my research did not speak easily of the tensions they felt: for older women, the tension between wanting to feel secure and the imperative to be undemanding; for younger women, the tension between wanting to be self-determining and wanting to be dutiful and caring of others. Unspoken, these dilemmas were experienced as personal struggles or failings. Speaking about them would occasion feelings of guilt and shame. Thus, as Mrs. S and Mrs. C illustrate, women concealed their concerns from their respective mothers and daughters and seldom shared them with their peers. In not sharing them, they did not, therefore, recognize their concerns as commonly experienced dilemmas and did not identify with other women in similar situations. This was especially true among older respondents like Mrs. S, who, rather than identifying with other old women, tended to distance themselves from them.

We can understand the silence surrounding women's experiences of the costs and tensions of receiving care as the result of entrenched cultural beliefs about independence and individualism, proper family ties, and feminine behaviour. Like all effective ideologies, these images make the possibility of other patterns of care and need-meeting seem unthinkable or impossible and render the present pattern "obvious" and "natural." The first step in making change and other possibilities thinkable is that they be speakable. Theorizing on the early stages of social movements suggests that, for individual experiences of stress to be transformed into publicly expressed claims for change, it is necessary that people talk about and share their difficulties and come to develop a sense of collective consciousness and identity (Henley, 1986; Leonard, 1984). Privately experienced strains are, thus, defined into the public realm and given public voice and visibility. They become "expressed" rather than "felt needs" and, as such, have a place in the political process (Bradshaw, 1972: 641).

For change to occur in the prevailing pattern of care of old people, breaking the silence that women experience as caregivers and care receivers will be a crucial step. In the small but growing literature on women and aging, we see some articulation of complaint and protest at the disadvantages that characterize women's life course and culminate in old age (MacDonald, 1984; Marshall, 1987). However, the experiences of the women in my research suggest the strength of ideological forces that repress complaint or challenge. As relatively privileged women in fair economic circumstances and with paid employment histories, they might have been expected to chafe against the constraints of caregiving and receiving more than women accustomed to less autonomy in their lives. That they were silenced and their difficulties individualized sounds a very pessimistic note for the future.

In the future, it will be crucial to foster the conditions in which women can speak about their experiences and make claims on their own behalf. We can learn from the, as yet, fairly isolated instances of women writing about their experiences and from women joining together formally and informally to structure the circumstances of their aging or their caregiving (e.g., the Association of Carers in the U.K. and the Older Women's Network here in Canada). In service structures, in the policy-making process, and in research conceptualizations of care, it will be important to seize opportunities to challenge prevailing images of dutiful daughters and undemanding mothers. Questioning taken-for-granted service patterns and advocating for women who do not conform to expectations can make small but incremental contributions to resisting care arrangements that systematically constrain women.

Remembering her mother's precariousness in old age, Mrs. C had once thought that, because of the autonomy she developed in the paid work world and her sense of competence in the face of complex family demands: "It'd be different for me." In fact, as we have seen, it was not. Mrs. C felt apprehensive and diminished, and concealed her struggles from others. Unless the material and, more importantly, the ideological underpinnings of the prevailing pattern of care of old people are recognized and resisted, there is no reason to expect this path into old age to be any different for future generations of women.

REFERENCES

The work reported in this paper was supported in part by: the National Health Research and Development Program of Health and Welfare Canada through a National Health Fellowship; the Program in Gerontology at the University of Toronto through a seed grant; and the Social Sciences and Humanities Research Council of Canada through a post-doctoral fellowship. For their comments on an earlier draft of this paper, I am grateful to: Roy Cain, Lynn Kearney, Dorothy Pawluch, Vera Tarman, and Eli Teram.

Allatt, P., and T. Keil. 1987. "Introduction," in P. Allatt, T. Kiel, A. Bryman, and B. Bytheway, eds., *Women and the Life Cycle: Transitions and Turning Points*. London: Macmillan.

Anderson, M. 1977. "The Impact on Family Relations of the Elderly of Changes Since Victorian Times in Governmental Income-Maintenance Provision," in E. Shanas and M.D. Sussman, eds., *Family, Bureaucracy and the Elderly*. Durham, N.C.: Duke University Press.

Arber, S., G.N. Gilbert, M. Evandrou. 1988. "Gender, Household Composition and Receipt of Domiciliary Services by Elderly Disabled People," *Journal of Social Policy*, 17, 2: 153–75.

Aronson, J. 1988. "Women's Experiences of Giving and Receiving Care: Pathways to Social Change," Ph.D. thesis, University of Toronto.

Binney, E.A., and C.L. Estes. 1988. "The Retreat of the State and its Transfer of Responsibility: The Intergenerational War," *International Journal of Health Services*, 18, 1: 83–96.

Bradshaw, J. 1972. "The Concept of Social Need," *New Society*, 30 (March): 640-43.

Briar, K.H., and R. Ryan. 1986. "The Anti-Institution Movement and Women Caregivers," *Affilia*, 1, 1: 20-31.

Briggs, A., and J. Oliver, eds. 1985. *Caring: Experiences of Looking After Disabled Relatives*. London: Routledge and Kegan Paul.

Brody, E.M. 1981. " 'Women in the Middle' and Family Help to Older People," *Gerontologist*, 21, 5: 471-80.

Brody, E.M. 1985. "Parent Care as a Normative Family Stress," *Gerontologist*, 25, 1: 19-29.

Canadian Medical Association. 1987. *Health Care for the Elderly*.

Chappell, N.L., L.A. Strain, and A.A. Blandford. 1986. *Aging and Health Care: A Social Perspective*. Toronto: Holt, Rinehart and Winston.

Cohen, L. 1984. *Small Expectations: Society's Betrayal of Older Women*. Toronto: McClelland and Stewart.

Crane, D. 1989. "Planning Now for the Burden of Elderly 'Boomers,' " *Toronto Star*, January 18: A27.

Dalley, G. 1988. *Ideologies of Caring: Rethinking Community and Collectivism*. London: Macmillan.

Doty, P. 1986. "Family Care of the Elderly: The Role of Public Policy," *Milbank Memorial Fund Quarterly*, 64: 34-75.

Eichler, M. 1988. *Families in Canada: Recent Changes and Their Policy Consequences*, Second Edition. Toronto: Gage.

Evers, H. 1981. "Care or Custody? The Experiences of Women Patients in Long-Stay Geriatric Wards," in B. Hutter and G. Williams, eds., *Controlling Women: The Normal and the Deviant*. London: Croom Helm.

Evers, H. 1985. "The Frail Elderly Woman: Emergent Questions in Aging and Woman's Health," in E. Lewin and V. Oleson, eds., *Women, Health and Illness*. London: Tavistock.

Finch, J. 1987. "Family Obligations and the Life Course," in A. Bryman, B. Bytheway, P. Allat, and T. Kiel, eds., *Rethinking the Life Cycle*. London: Macmillan.

Finch, J. 1989. *Family Obligations and Social Change*. Cambridge: Polity Press.

Finch, J., and D. Groves. 1980. "Community Care and the Family: A Case for Equal Opportunities?" *Journal of Social Policy*, 9, 4: 487-514.

Finch, J., and D. Groves, eds. 1983. *A Labour of Love: Women, Work and Caring*. London: Routledge and Kegan Paul.

Gilligan, C. 1982. *In A Different Voice: Psychological Theory and Women's Development*. Cambridge, Mass.: Harvard University Press.

Graham, H. 1983. "Caring: A Labour of Love," in Finch and Groves, eds., *A Labour of Love*.

Hagestad, G.O. 1986. "The Aging Society as a Context for Social Life," *Daedalus*, 115, 1: 119–39.

Hanmer, J., and D. Statham. 1989. *Women and Social Work: Towards a Woman-Centered Practice*. Chicago: Lyceum Books.

Hasselkus, B.R. 1988. "Meaning in Caregiving: Perspectives on Caregiver-Professional Relationships," *Gerontologist*, 28, 5: 686–91.

Health and Welfare Canada. 1986. *Aging: Shifting the Emphasis*. Working Paper. Ottawa.

Henley, N.M. 1986. "Women as a Social Problem: Conceptual and Practical Issues in Defining Social Problems," in E. Seidman and J. Rappoport, eds., *Redefining Social Problems*. New York: Plenum Press.

Hochshild, A.R. 1979. "Emotion Work, Feeling Rules and Social Structure," *American Journal of Sociology*, 85, 3: 551–75.

Leonard, P. 1984. *Personality and Ideology: Towards a Materialist Understanding of the Individual*. London: Macmillan.

Levin, E., I. Sinclair, and P. Gorbach. 1983. *Supporters of Confused Elderly Persons at Home*. London: National Institute of Social Work.

Lewis, J., and B. Meredith. 1988. *Daughters Who Care: Daughters Who Care For Mothers at Home*. London: Routledge and Kegan Paul.

MacDonald, B., with C. Rich. 1984. *Look Me In The Eye: Old Women, Aging and Ageism*. London: The Women's Press.

Marshall, D. 1987. *Silver Threads: Critical Reflections on Growing Old*. Toronto: Between the Lines.

Minkler, M. 1983. "Blaming the Aged Victim: The Politics of Scapegoating in Times of Fiscal Conservatism," *International Journal of Health Services*, 13, 1: 155–67.

Montgomery, R.J.V., and E.F. Borgatta. 1989. "The Effects of Alternative Support Strategies on Family Caregiving," *Gerontologist*, 29, 4: 457–64.

National Advisory Council on Aging. 1986. *Toward a Community Support Policy for Canadians*. Ottawa: NACA.

National Council of Welfare. 1989. *A Pension Primer*. Ottawa: Ministry of Supply and Services.

Ontario Ministry of Community and Social Services. 1988. *Planning Services for Persons with Dementia and Their Caregivers*. Issues Paper. Toronto.

Ontario Office for Senior Citizens' Affairs. 1986. *A New Agenda: Health and Social Service Strategies for Ontario's Seniors*. Toronto.

Patterson, J. 1987. "Winding Down Social Spending: Social Spending Restraint in Ontario in the 1970s," in A. Moscovitch and J. Albert, eds., *The "Benevolent" State: The Growth of Welfare in Canada*. Toronto: Garamond Press.

Peace, S. 1986. "The Forgotten Female: Social Policy and Older Women," in C. Phillipson and A. Walker, eds., *Ageing and Social Policy: A Critical Assessment*. Aldershott: Gower.

Qureshi, H., and A. Walker. 1989. *The Caring Relationship: Elderly People and Their Families*. London: Macmillan

Reinharz, S. 1986. "Friends or Foes? Gerontological and Feminist Theory," *Women's Studies International Forum*, 9, 5: 503-14.

Segal, L. 1987. *Is the Future Female? Troubled Thoughts on Contemporary Feminism*. London: Virago Press.

Shott, S. 1979. "Emotion and Social Life: A Symbolic Interaction Analysis," *American Journal of Sociology*, 84: 1317-34.

Smith, D.E. 1979. "A Sociology For Women," in J.A. Sherman and E. Torton Beck, eds., *The Prism of Sex: Essays in the Sociology of Knowledge*. Madison: University of Wisconsin Press.

Smith, D.E. 1986. "Institutional Ethnography: A Feminist Method," *Resources for Feminist Research*, 15, 1: 6-13.

Synge, J. 1980. "Work and Family Support Patterns of the Aged in the Early Twentieth Century," in V.W. Marshall, ed., *Aging in Canada: Social Perspectives*. Toronto: Fitzhenry & Whiteside.

Tarman, V.I. 1989. "Implications of Public and Private Sector Involvement in Long Term Care: Lessons From Ontario," paper presented at the 18th Annual Scientific-Educational Meeting of the Canadian Association on Gerontology, Ottawa.

Walker, A. 1985. "From Welfare State to Caring Society? The Promise of Informal Networks," in J.A. Yoder, J.M.L. Jonker, and R.A.B. Leaper, eds., *Support Networks in a Caring Community*. Dordrecht: Martinus Nijhoff Publishers.

Willocks, D., S. Peace, and L. Kellaher. 1987. *Private Lives in Public Places*. London: Tavistock.

CHAPTER VI

The Sexual Division of Poverty: The Consequences of Gendered Caring

Patricia M. Evans

> Women comprise half of the world's adult population but perform nearly two-thirds of all the work hours, receive only one-tenth of the world's income, and own less than one one-hundredth of the world's property. (UN figures, cited in Gunderson and Muszynski, 1990: 31)

INTRODUCTION

Women are more likely to be poor than men, and this vulnerability is captured in the phrase "the feminization of poverty." Women's poverty should not be interpreted as a recent phenomenon, however, because poor women have always outnumbered poor men. This chapter considers the impact of women's responsibilities for providing care to family members and argues that it contributes to the enduring nature of their poverty.

Women's poverty reflects their biographies as caregivers. Although it operates throughout the life cycle, its link to caregiving is most apparent in the two groups of women who are most likely to be poor: single mothers and elderly women. The undervaluing of women's work in the home and in the labour market results in poverty for a large proportion of single mothers, who are without the financial support of the traditional "breadwinner." The disadvantageous relationship between gender and employment accumulates to produce low pensions, and the inadequate income of older women frequently is the economic legacy of their caregiving. Not all caregivers are poor, and not all poor women are caregivers. However, as Hilary Graham (1987: 223) comments: "Poverty and caring are, for many women, two sides of the same coin. Caring is what they do; poverty describes the economic circumstances in which they do it."

In its exploration of the relationship between women's poverty and women's caring, this chapter examines the social policies that affect women as they respond to the competing demands of the "family ethic" and the "work ethic." The family ethic is a term introduced by Mimi Abramovitz (1988) to refer to the ideological norms that define women's roles in the family and in the workplace, and delegate to women the principal responsibility for caring for family members. The work ethic operates to reward self-sufficiency and to penalize economic dependency; it values work done in the "productive" market and contributes to the invisibility of women's work in the home. Both influence, often in contradictory ways, the policies and programs intended to alleviate women's poverty.

The first part of the chapter examines the growing visibility of women's poverty with the help of Statistics Canada tabulations. The consequences of assumptions regarding women's responsibility for child care and domestic tasks are considered in the second section. These consequences include work interruptions, low pay, economic dependency on a husband, and the undervaluing of women's work within the home. The third and fourth sections address in turn the situations of single mothers and elderly women, as the most visible of the female groups in poverty. The chapter concludes with a discussion of the general directions for, and the difficulties of, change.

THE INCREASING VISIBILITY
OF WOMEN'S POVERTY

For definitional purposes, poverty is usually measured through the use of a "poverty line," which separates the poor from the non-poor according to income. While such lines are useful yardsticks to monitor a nation's progress in combatting poverty, they are woefully inadequate reflections of an experience that, in addition to a lack of income, is so frequently accompanied by a sense of powerlessness, isolation, and stigma. More than thirty years ago, John Kenneth Galbraith (1958: 250) suggested the reasons for this:

> People are poverty-stricken when their income, even if adequate for survival, falls markedly below that of the community. Then they cannot have what the larger community regards as the minimum necessary for decency; and they cannot wholly escape, therefore, the judgement of the larger community that they are indecent.

Galbraith's comments also distinguish the "relative" conception of poverty, which incorporates prevailing standards of living into its definition, from an "absolute" or "subsistence" conception of poverty, which considers basic needs only. Statistics Canada's unofficial "poverty lines" are set in relation to the amounts that Canadians typically spend on food, clothing, and housing, and so to some extent reflect community standards in their approach. In keeping with general use elsewhere, Statistics Canada's poverty lines are adopted in this chapter, but it should be borne in mind that it produces the least generous of the Canadian poverty lines.[1]

The assumption that women's primary role is in the home, and that economic dependence flows as a natural consequence from these household responsibilities, has meant that until recently women's poverty has gone largely unrecognized. Even when Canada, along with the United Kingdom and the United States, "rediscovered" poverty in the late 1960s, it was male poverty that was rediscovered. The 1971 Report of the Special Senate Committee on Poverty devoted only two of its 200 pages to issues of maternal employment and child care, and selected a photograph of an elderly man for its cover. The alternative and radical report of the time also emphasized male poverty (Adams *et al.*, 1971). Only the 1970 Status of Women Report (Canada, 1970) documented the prevalence of poverty among women as one of its most unexpected and important findings.

Despite the gradual recognition of women's poverty, it continues to be underestimated in our focus on the household unit. It was not until 1980 that Statistics Canada published data on the overall numbers and distribution of poverty by sex in addition to the information it regularly generated on poverty by household type. Therefore, to examine the sexual division of poverty prior to 1980 it is necessary to obtain special tabulations of the Statistics Canada data.[2]

Data from these tabulations indicate that between 1971 and 1988 women were disproportionately represented in the ranks of the poor. Table 1 shows the female and male "shares" of poverty for selected years during this eighteen-year period and reveals that women represented 57–61 per cent of all the adults in poverty; the male share of poverty, therefore, ranged from a low of 39 per cent to a high of 43 per cent. This suggests that the phrase "the feminization of poverty" does not provide an accurate description of women's poverty over this period, because their poverty has been characterized more by stability than by change. Reference to the feminization of poverty may help to mask the reality that women have *always* been poor in greater numbers than men. It is the disproportionate nature of their poverty, and its relative intransigence, which is of such concern.

Although women's portion of the overall adult poverty in Canada did not dramatically alter between 1971 and 1988, there have been significant shifts in the way that poverty is distributed among different groups of women. The changing division of poverty among women is illustrated in Table 2, which shows a transfer of the burden of women's poverty from married women to women living on their own and single mothers. Married women, who in 1971 accounted for fully 55 per cent of all poor women, had reduced their share to 29 per cent in 1988. Between these years, however, single women under the age of sixty-five almost tripled their representation,

TABLE 1: Distribution of Poverty, by Sex
Selected Years, 1971-1988

Year	% Women	% Men
1971	56.9	43.1
1975	60.9	39.1
1979	59.4	40.6
1981	59.8	40.2
1984	58.1	41.9
1986	58.4	41.6
1988	60.4	39.6

SOURCE: Statistics Canada, Household Surveys Division, Survey of Consumer Finances, unpublished data.

increasing from 10 per cent to 27 per cent while the poverty share of elderly women on their own increased from 10 per cent to 21 per cent. Single mothers, only 7 per cent of poor women in 1971, more than doubled their share, which reached 18 per cent by 1988. The category of "other women" comprises never-married daughters living with parent/s, and they, like married women, were a smaller proportion of poor women in 1971 than they were in 1988.

The increase in the poverty profile of single mothers and women living on their own between 1971 and 1988 is an outcome of two factors. First, these women, always particularly vulnerable to poverty, grew in numbers between 1971 and 1988, reflecting changes in attitudes regarding divorce, separation, and single motherhood. Thus, single mothers increased their share of the total of women's poverty during this period. Second, the risk of poverty, which decreased for all groups of women between 1971 and 1988, declined very sharply for married women, in part due to their increased labour force participation.[3] Single mothers and women living on their own are not more vulnerable to poverty now than they were before, but their numbers are growing and their share of women's poverty expands as that of married women contracts.

TABLE 2: *Distribution of Adult Women in Poverty, 1971 and 1988*

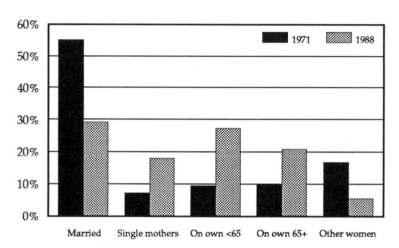

SOURCE: Statistics Canada, Household Surveys Division, Survey of Consumer Finances, unpublished data.

Women's poverty tends to be hidden in the household, and a woman is not counted as "head of household" except when she is without a male partner. Married women tend to get lost in those parts of the poverty statistics that count poverty according to the sex of the head of the household. The growing visibility of women's poverty, as we saw in Table 1, does not appear to be due to a significant increase in women's share of poverty. Rather than resulting from a change in the objective circumstances of women, its emergence is, in part, socially constructed. The increasing interest in women's issues and the emergence of a feminist perspective undoubtedly played an important role in focusing attention on the issue of women's poverty. Another possible factor in the growing recognition of women's poverty is suggested by Table 2. Their poverty is rendered more "visible" in the absence of a husband, particularly when it leads to the receipt of social assistance benefits.

Measuring poverty by reference to the household unit helps to mask women's poverty in other ways. It assumes that the financial resources in a household are equally available to all its members, an assumption that an accumulating body of research is challenging. Women may live in a non-poverty household but have access to only a poverty share of the resources. An emphasis on the household also obscures the particular burden poverty imposes on women as they attempt to absorb its impact and cushion the effects on their husbands and children (Millar and Glendinning, 1987a: 11). Paradoxically, poor single mothers may be "better off and worse off." Although their income drops significantly, their control over it increases, as a single mother from Nova Scotia who works part-time and receives social assistance explains: "we might be poorer now than before my husband left . . . but at least I know that there is money coming in regularly . . . and I don't have to worry about him spending it all after work" (cited in Gunderson and Muszynski, 1990: 12).

Women's poverty *is* coming out of the closet, but clearly the door is only slightly ajar. The growing visibility of women's poverty is presenting challenges to the traditional ways of understanding its causes, consequences, and solutions.

UNDERSTANDING WOMEN'S POVERTY: A FEMINIST PERSPECTIVE ON CARING

Low wages, limited labour force participation, and problems of welfare dependency have been the usual foci of investigations into women's poverty. Orthodox economic models identify the individual as the locus of disadvantage. The theory of "human capital," for example, suggests that women's low pay reflects a reluctance or inability to invest in training and other job-enhancing activities because of their expectation that their employment will be interrupted by domestic responsibilities. Women's employment decisions, therefore, result from a rational estimate of its costs and benefits (see, for example, Polachek, 1975). In attempting to explain why single mothers "choose" work or welfare, these models consider such factors as likely wages, costs of child care, the level of available welfare benefits, and the probabilities associated with each of these outcomes.

Other perspectives, however, look to the labour market, rather than to the individual, for an explanation of employment disadvantage. Dual labour market theory has sought to understand the processes at work in the labour market that both create barriers between "good" jobs and "bad" jobs and consign particular groups, notably women and visible minorities, to the lowest paid and least stable employment (for further discussion in relation to women, see Barron and Norris, 1976).

These frameworks for understanding women's poverty and their employment disadvantage provide, at best, only cursory attention to women's unpaid labour in the home. Orthodox economic models do not question the assumptions that give primacy to women's role in the household, and these models systematically undervalue their work both at home and in the paid work force. However, structural explanations that pay attention to the operation of the labour market have ignored the particular processes that identify women as targets for discrimination, as well as the ways in which the treatment of men and women workers may differ (Beechey, 1988: 46).

In contrast, a feminist framework understands women's poverty as the result of the intersecting processes of the family ethic and capitalism that assign men to work in the public world and women to work in the private domain of the household. This separation of the roles of men and women, the dichotomy between the public and private, "marginalises women's involvement in the labour market while at the same time [it] assigns little or no value to their caring and domestic work within the family" (Millar and Glendinning, 1987a: 3-4). This suggests that an analysis of women and poverty must be based on an understanding of the interrelationship between the labour women do in the home and their employment in the workplace.

The assumption that women are primarily caregivers and men are economic providers also affects women's earning capacities in important ways. Women's lower earnings reflect, in part, time spent out of the labour market engaged in caregiving responsibilities. However, over and above this direct impact, the gendered division in responsibilities and the lack of value attached to women's work in caring contribute in important ways to the segregation and general devaluation of the work women do in the labour market. These direct and indirect effects of caregiving on women's employment will be examined in turn.

Caregiving and Work Participation: A Direct Impact

Perhaps the most obvious, well-documented, and uncontroversial impact is that women are much more likely than men to work part-time and to interrupt employment to take care of family and to discharge household responsibilities. A 1984 survey of 7,194 women in Canada who had been employed at some time for at least six months found that more than half (58 per cent) had interrupted their employment for at least a year. Almost seven out of ten of these women cited family reasons for their work interruptions (Robinson, 1987: 10, 27).

While children are the most visible beneficiaries of women's care, we should not underestimate the responsibilities women often have for other dependent adults. A 1984 British survey revealed that one in five women over the age of forty was responsible for caring for dependent adults (cited in Lewis and Meredith, 1988: 2). Another British study found that 12 per cent of employed women, as well as 23 per cent of those not employed, reported that caring for elders limited the nature of their employment, the number of hours they were able to work, or whether they were able to undertake paid work at all (Hunt, 1988: 166).

Although some of the discrepancy between male and female earnings can be attributed to differences in employment histories, the major portion of the wage gap cannot be accounted for by variations in work experience and hours worked (Ornstein, 1983: 29). Women pay a greater "price" for their household responsibilities than can be justified on purely economic grounds. The next section examines other factors that contribute to women's low wages and increase their vulnerability to poverty.

Occupational Segregation: An Indirect Impact

The second impact of the sexual division of labour is reflected in the continuing segregation of women's work. This has persisted in spite of important occupational changes in the labour force and efforts to remove barriers to women's employment. Throughout time and across cultures, there has been a nearly universal tendency to place a lesser value on the work identified as "women's work," regardless of its contribution or complexity. Even when jobs in the workplace are comparably evaluated in terms of skill and responsibility, occupations in which females dominate command only 80 per cent of the wages earned in the male occupations (Gunderson, 1985: 9). Indeed, women's concentration in low-wage occupations has been found to be a more important factor than education or work experience in explaining the male-female wage gap (Ornstein, 1983: 30).

Much of the work that women do in the labour market mirrors their work in the household and incorporates a significant component of personal service. In 1988, the top ten occupations, which accounted for almost three-quarters of working women, included secretaries, sales clerks, bookkeepers, cashiers, nurses, waitresses, kindergarten and elementary school teachers, receptionists, and office cleaners (calculated from Statistics Canada, 1990b: 82; Parliament, 1989: 6). Employment that closely replicates the caring work women do in the home attracts little status and is poorly paid. In 1989, the Ontario government raised the basic hourly wage rate of homemakers to $7.25 in provincially funded services; this was at a time when the provincial average hourly wage was $12.90 (Statistics Canada, 1990a: 119). Despite the important increase in women's labour force participation rates, occupational segregation in the "female" clerical, sales, and service sectors continues to increase. Although women have made gains in some male-dominated occupations, men are also making inroads into elementary school teaching, traditionally one of women's higher-paying occupations (Connelly and Mac-Donald, 1990: 33).

The idea that women constitute a dispensable labour force working for "pin money" is used to justify women's segregation into insecure and low-paying employment. It is viewed as a mutually satisfactory arrangement that suits both the female worker, who is able to enter and exit the labour market with ease, and the employer, who benefits from her "dispensability" (England, 1982). This perspective persists, despite the increase in the number of single mothers and the growing evidence that the employment income of married women is an important factor in keeping families out of poverty (Ross and Shillington, 1989: 92).

Wage equity continues to be difficult to achieve. Initially conceived as "equal pay for equal work" and now as "equal pay for work of equal value," wage equity has been particularly elusive for women of colour. A report on the Federal Employment Equity Act (1989), which requires federally regulated employers and Crown corporations to implement programs to eliminate employment barriers, found that visible minority women work under a double disadvantage. The majority (53 per cent) of all women working full-time in 1988 earned less than $25,000 per annum; this was true for almost two-thirds (62 per cent) of women of colour. In contrast, only 13 per cent of men, taken as a whole, and 21 per cent of men from visible minorities earned less than $25,000 (Employment and Immigration Canada, 1989: 29, 62). It is sobering to note that the poverty rate of U.S. black single mothers who are employed full-time throughout the year is virtually identical to the rates reported for non-working white households (Pearce, 1985: 450).

The male-female wage gap is slowly closing. Between 1971 and 1987, the earnings of female employees who worked full-time and throughout the year increased from 60 to 66 per cent of that of male workers in full-time employment (Statistics Canada, 1990b: 97). Trends in the labour market, however, suggest that the prospects for many working women are deteriorating as jobs in the lower-paying service sector increase and employment opportunities in the better-paying manufacturing sector decline (Lindsay, 1989: 20). In addition, part-time work is on the increase, and not because this is what women want. Between 1976 and 1985, part-time employment among women in the clerical sector increased at five times the rate of full-time work. During the same period, the proportion of women who worked part-time because they could not find full-time employment more than doubled (Cohen, 1989: 5-6).

The view of men as breadwinners and significant players in the "public marketplace" has important consequences for women. As we have seen, women's work in the labour market has consistently been underpaid and women's work in the household remains hidden in the private domain, despite estimates that its economic value totals more than one-third of the GNP (*Canadian Social Trends*, 1986: 42). Thus, the gendered division of labour helps to structure women's economic vulnerability, both at home and in employment. Efforts to improve the economic position of women through strategies that begin at the workplace door can only have a limited impact.

WOMEN IN POVERTY

The observation that a woman is frequently "only a man away from poverty" highlights women's proximity to poverty and the economic vulnerability of women who are on their own. The remainder of the chapter focuses on two groups of women for whom the gendered assumptions of caring have resulted in an extremely high risk of poverty – single mothers and elderly women. The impact of the family ethic and the work ethic on their poverty is explored, and the social policies that reflect expectations about work and family responsibilities, which are so very important to poor women, are examined.

A Profile of Single Mothers
There have been significant changes in Canadian single-mother families over the last twenty-five years. First of all,

they are an increasingly common type of family. Between 1966 and 1986, the number of single-parent families grew by 130 per cent, more than three times the increase in husband-wife families. Over the same period, they increased their share from 8 per cent to 13 per cent of all families (Moore, 1987: 31). This does not, however, represent an all-time high. Fifty years ago, almost one in seven of Canadian families was headed by a single parent, but for different reasons (Boyd, 1988). The changing pathways to single mothering reflect differences in marital attitudes and practices. In 1951, two-thirds of all single mothers were widowed; in 1981, the majority were separated and divorced. During the same thirty-year period, the number of single mothers who had never been married increased, reflecting in part a growth in the number of women aged 20–34 who chose to bear children outside of marriage. Nonetheless, the fact that single mothers are more likely to be separated and divorced, rather than widowed, means that single mothers, and the children they care for, are younger now than ever before (Statistics Canada, 1984).

Single mothers, as a group, face a number of specific problems. There is little doubt that they are more likely to experience stress and social isolation than women who parent with a partner (Kamerman and Kahn, 1988: 190–91). It is, however, the economic vulnerability of the single mother, rather than the lack of a male partner *per se*, that is likely to be a major source of stress. In her examination of the consequences of divorce on U.S. women, Lenore Weitzman (1985: 339) labels marriage breakdown a "financial catastrophe." She found that women at the end of the first year following divorce experienced on average a 73 per cent decline in their standard of living, while men's improved by 42 per cent. In his time study of employed women in Toronto, William Michelson (1985: 91) suggests that "low income should be kept in mind as perhaps the most prominent feature of the situation of the single mother." Contrary to other studies (cited by Kamerman and Kahn, 1988), Michelson finds that time spent on "obligatory activities" such as employment, housework, and child care is greater for married women than for single mothers. The single mother, however, is almost twice as likely to worry about money, more likely to be concerned about not spending enough time with her children, but less likely to worry about housework than her married counterpart.

Single mothers are more likely to be poor than any other group. In 1988, almost half (48 per cent) of single mothers with children under the age of eighteen had incomes below the poverty line. The poverty rate for two-parent families, in contrast, was 8 per cent, and only one out of ten single fathers lived in poverty (Statistics Canada, Household Surveys Division, Survey of Consumer Finances, unpublished data).[4] Not surprisingly, government transfer payments (social assistance, unemployment insurance, Family Allowance) are particularly important to single mothers, although they do not appear to be very effective in raising their income above the poverty line. In 1987, transfer payments made up 27 per cent of their income, although these accounted for only 6 per cent of the income of husband-wife families and 8 per cent for single fathers (Statistics Canada, 1990b: 106).

Although the *risk* of poverty among single mothers was somewhat lower in 1988 than in the previous years, their relative economic position had deteriorated. Between 1980 and 1988, their average income declined by 4 per cent, while the income of two-parent families increased by 5 per cent. While employment reduces the risk of poverty for the single mother, it is clearly not a panacea. Without earnings, almost all single-mother households are poor (94 per cent), but even with earnings, more than four in every ten (44 per cent) single mothers are poor (Statistics Canada, 1989: 23).

The single mother's exceptional vulnerability to poverty can be attributed to three factors: obstacles to adequate earnings, lack of child support, and low rates of social assistance. The barriers to adequate earnings – low pay and occupational segregation that confront all women in the labour market – make it extremely difficult for single mothers to earn an income that brings the household above the poverty line. In addition, as Evelyn Ferguson discusses in Chapter III, the availability of adequate and affordable child care is extremely limited, imposing a particular burden on low-income single mothers. Second, income from child support payments is frequently inadequate and often non-existent. The judicial criteria used in calculating the amount of awards are uncertain, the amounts awarded tend to be low, and there is a high rate of default on the payments ordered (Canadian Advisory Council on the Status of Women, 1987). Finally, many single mothers must rely on provincial social assistance programs for financial support, and all provinces provide an income to the single mother and her dependant(s) that falls significantly beneath the poverty line (National Council of Welfare, 1987).

These facts, however, do not reveal very much about either the impact of the continuing financial pressures that so many single mothers experience or the worry and guilt that result from incomes too low to permit these mothers to provide as they want to for their children or to meet society's expectations. The National Council of Welfare (1979: 10–11) describes the feelings expressed by a woman more than a decade ago; unfortunately, they continue to be relevant for today's single mothers. Lorraine, a single mother with three children, lost her husband and her house:

> Now more than two years later, she despairs of ever getting out of the welfare trap. She has had people call her stupid, crafty, dishonest, lazy and irresponsible. Her constant worry is adequate food and clothes for her children. She knows that their perennial diet of bread, macaroni, rice and hamburger, which is all she can afford, is not good for their health. "I don't mind refusing them potato chips or cookies," Lorraine says, "but it's really upsetting to have to say 'no', you can't have a banana."

It is hardly surprising that a recent study found that 65 per cent of the families using a Toronto food bank are headed by single parents, even though they represent only 15 per cent of Metro families (Daily Bread Food Bank, 1989). Single mothers are also overrepresented in their involvement with the child welfare system. This should not surprise us, given its focus on "mothering" and the very close connections between child welfare and problems of poverty, which Karen Swift explores in Chapter VIII.

Work and Welfare: The Family Ethic and the Work Ethic

Over time, social assistance and employment weave complex patterns in the lives of many single mothers as they negotiate the competing demands of the labour market and their work at home. Longitudinal studies demonstrate that most single mothers who receive social assistance do so for fairly limited periods. A recent Ontario study, for example, found that more than half (54 per cent) of the 10,000 single mothers who came onto the Family Benefits caseload in 1981 left within three years (Evans, 1987).[5] For many single mothers, then, social assistance provides necessary economic support during a period of transition and adjustment to the break-up of a marriage, the loss of employment, or the need to stay home to care for children. Unfortunately, many of the women who leave social assistance find they must return to it again. More than one in four (27 per cent) of the single mothers who came onto Ontario Family Benefits in 1975 had left *and* returned by 1987 (Evans, 1987).

The assumption that single mothers are *either* in employment *or* relying on social assistance oversimplifies the situation of many low-income single mothers as they struggle to meet the responsibilities of household and children and the demands of employment. This complex reality is illustrated by the "mix" of work and welfare that, over time, so frequently characterizes their lives. A study of 200 low-income single mothers from Winnipeg found that nearly one in three (30 per cent) reported income from both employment and social assistance over a three-year period, 1972–74. In contrast, 44 per cent were employed and did not receive social assistance, while the remaining 26 per cent relied on social assistance without wages (Evans, 1984). Only one in four, then, was not employed at any time during this three-year period. However, the obstacles encountered in remaining employed are highlighted by a single mother in Nova Scotia whose temporary contract as a community worker is about to expire. She worries about the future:

> I am panicked right now . . . what am I going to do to get me through this winter? . . . I have to do something . . . I have to find work . . . but then I look around and there are only jobs

like the department stores hiring part-time . . . or waitress-
ing . . . I cannot afford to work for those wages or to work
shifts. (Quoted in Gunderson and Muszynski, 1990: 78)

A recurring theme throughout this book is the contradictory demands made on women and the ambiguous messages
given to them. The development, form, and content of social
assistance policies have been shaped by the family ethic and
the work ethic, and single mothers have been subject to their
conflicting requirements. Over time, the dictates of social
assistance programs have ebbed and flowed between supporting single mothers to care for their children at home and
encouraging them, or pressuring them, to enter the labour
force. The history of income support to single mothers reflects
society's views about families, beliefs about the appropriate
division of roles and responsibilities between the sexes, and
notions of "worthiness."

Mothers' Allowance legislation, enacted in a number of
provinces between 1916 and 1920, established, for the first
time, an entitlement to a regular if meagre allowance to single
mothers in economic need as long as they were deemed
eligible (Strong-Boag, 1979). Assumptions about which mothers were "deserving" of the benefit excluded many categories
of single mothers. Ontario's statute of 1920, for example, did
not include women who were either unmarried mothers or
the wives of prisoners. In addition, mothers were not eligible
if they had only one child, because it was assumed that they
could, or should, support themselves (Kierstead, 1925: 21).
Finally, before the allowance was granted, the mother had to
be viewed as a "fit and suitable person" to care for her
children. The influence of the family ethic is particularly
apparent in the concern to exclude women and children
whose husbands should be providing for them, even if they
were not.

Divorced women became eligible for financial aid in Ontario in 1955, unmarried mothers in 1957. However, the family
ethic continues to dictate a breadwinner-dependent homemaker model of the family for social assistance purposes. For
example, a single mother is still generally not able to claim
social assistance if she is living with a man. In all provinces,

with the exception of Ontario and Quebec, it is assumed that a woman is the economic dependant of a man even when he has no legal obligations to support her. As Margaret Leighton (1987) points out, this limits the freedom and privacy of women to form relationships and, if they reject these restrictions, places them at economic risk by denying them benefits. In 1987, Ontario abolished the "man in the house" rule and extended eligibility to women who are living with men, as long as the man owes no financial obligation under the Family Law Reform Act, which in effect means until a child is born or they have lived together for a three-year period.[6]

The family ethic has not operated in isolation; the work ethic has also had an important influence on programs to provide financial assistance to the single mother. When first instituted, Mothers' Allowance was designed to ensure adequate care and supervision of children by providing an alternative to full-time maternal employment (Splane, 1965: 269). However, part-time work was positively encouraged in the early days to diminish the "pauperizing" potential of the allowance. Following World War Two, when the needs of the returning male work force dictated the return of the women to their homes, even part-time employment for single mothers was discouraged (Ontario Ministry of Community and Social Services, 1984).

The increasing numbers of single mothers on the social assistance caseload, the dramatic rise in the labour force participation of women with children, and a desire to contain social spending have converged to redefine the employment expectations for single mothers on social assistance. Programs are in operation to encourage work through a variety of measures, which range from the "carrot" to the "stick" and include opportunities for education and training, subsidized child care, incentives to increase the financial gains from work, as well as lowering or cutting off benefits (Evans and McIntyre, 1987). However, these efforts have no discernible impact on the ability of single mothers to support themselves, and have not effectively addressed such important obstacles as affordable and available child care and the lack of jobs that pay women sufficient incomes (Evans, 1988). One single mother with two children put it this way:

After five months on Family Benefits [Ontario's long-term social assistance program], I decided that we couldn't continue to live this way. Fortunately, I found full-time employment as an office manager. Working did little to improve our life-style. My net monthly income was $1,100. But with the added expenses of working – like work, clothing, transportation, and day care (which was partially subsidized) – we still struggled. In addition, I lost my drug card when I started working. I came home from work too exhausted to offer my children anything emotionally. I felt like a robot. They needed two parents and didn't even have one. After working for nine months, I had to give up my job and return to Family Benefits. (Ontario Ministry of Community and Social Services, 1988: 183)

The income support system reflects the contradictions and ambiguities between women and the welfare state. First, social assistance, through reinforcing the family ethic, has played a part in regulating women's lives and women's dependency. This is particularly apparent in the "man in the house" regulations and the failure to create programs to help single mothers overcome employment obstacles. At the same time, social assistance provides an important source of economic support for women, which allows them to provide full-time caring to their children, albeit at a significant economic disadvantage and in some places for a limited period of time (Evans and McIntyre, 1987). Gillian Pascall (1986: 27) comments: "Social policies, then, often serve to enhance reproductive work to which women are often committed. If, at the same time, they undermine women's position – especially in the reproductive sphere – we should not be surprised."

A recent review of policies toward single mothers in several Western European countries suggests that Sweden's focus on full employment and development of policies to facilitate working and parenting have played an important role in improving the economic position of Swedish single mothers. These policies include a generous family allowance and subsidized child care, as well as an extensive and imaginative system of parental leave designed to alleviate the tension between working and parenting, particularly important for the single mother.[7] Single mothers are also guaranteed child support through a government administered scheme that collects from fathers, distributes to mothers, and substitutes or supplements these payments as needed. In addition, about 70 per cent of single mothers also receive an income-related housing allowance. As a result, a relatively small percentage (16 per cent) of single mothers use social assistance (Kamerman and Kahn, 1989).

Although Swedish single mothers are also economically disadvantaged in contrast to two-parent families, this disadvantage is comparatively small. A cross-national study comparing the ratio of incomes of single-parent families to two-parent families in six countries ranked Canada fifth out of six countries, while Sweden came first (Hauser and Fischer, 1986). Sweden's example suggests that our policies must emphasize the continuity rather than the compartmentalization of women's experience.

Policies that help to combine employment and parenting roles are extremely important to all mothers and are becoming more important to fathers. As long as we divide the problem of single-mother poverty from the problems of mothers and women as a whole, we will not find solutions. This does not mean that increases in the rates and benefits of social assistance are not important; in the short term, they are. However, any significant improvement in the economic vulnerability of the single mother will require policies recognizing that her poverty stems from the difficulties of achieving an adequate family income from a labour market that consistently undervalues her work and from a social welfare system that defines her as a worker or a homemaker, but does not make it easy to do both.

The Poverty of Older Women
Canada's elderly are one group for whom there has been real progress in reducing poverty. Between 1969 and 1986 the poverty rate for families headed by an adult sixty-five years old or older was cut by three-quarters, from 41 per cent to 10 per cent (National Council of Welfare, 1988: 1). However, the poverty rate for individuals living on their own has not fallen as dramatically, and the burden of poverty among the elderly

continues to fall disproportionately on women. In 1988, more than one-third (36 per cent) of all women over the age of sixty-five and living on their own were poor, compared to one in five elderly men. As Alan Walker (1987: 178) suggests, "gender is one of the clearest lines along which the economic and social experience of old age is divided."

The poverty of older women is not primarily a problem of aging. Rather, it results from assumptions that men will provide for women and the contradictory message women receive that "encourages us to be passive and dependent and then punishes us for these same qualities when we are old and alone" (Cohen, 1984: 126). It is essentially the consequence of women's caregiving responsibilities and the related labour market inequalities we examined earlier in this chapter. Sheila Neysmith (1984: 17) comments:

> Poor old women are not exotic plants that live in the special conditions of retirement – rather, poor old women are perennials, their roots are laid down in youth, their poverty merely comes into full flower in later life.

Unfortunately, once in flower, their poverty is unlikely to fade or wilt. Autonomy, dignity, and health are all the more difficult to retain in the face of poverty, as Mary, a sixty-seven-year-old woman, relates:

> Emergencies come up, grandchildren have birthdays, clothes wear out, cleaning products run out, bus rates go up. How do we manage? We pay our rent and utilities and eat less. We live in fear. Fear of the future, of more illness, less money, less pride. (National Council of Welfare, 1979: 12)

The poverty of older women, like the poverty of single mothers, also reflects the tension between the family ethic and the work ethic. As discussed earlier, the family ethic encourages women to provide care for their children and husbands as their primary task, which in turn helps to devalue their work in the labour market. The impact of the family ethic is particularly powerful for the current cohort of older women, who have generally spent less time in the work force than younger women are likely to. The next section examines how the work ethic and the family ethic, operating through the retirement income system, play a significant role in the poverty of older women.

The Pension System: Multipliers of Inequalities

Why poverty so often accompanies women's old age in Canada can be understood by examining three major layers of the retirement income system to assess the extent to which they reinforce women's disadvantaged position. These layers comprise government benefits, public pensions, and private pensions. The first layer provides elderly Canadians with a basic guaranteed income and includes three separate, government-provided benefits that are not based on previous contributions or labour force participation. The central provision is the universal, flat-rate Old Age Security. In addition, those with incomes below a designated level are also entitled to at least some portion of the Guaranteed Income Supplement (GIS). In 1989, almost half of Canada's elderly received this benefit (National Council of Welfare, 1989: 8). Finally, a Spouse's Allowance is available to low-income spouses or widows (or widowers) aged 60–64, but not to low-income individuals who have never married.

These three elements in the first layer of the retirement income system are considerably more important for women than for men. In 1986, the combined income from OAS and GIS comprised almost half of the income of older women; by contrast, one-quarter of the income of older men was derived from these sources (Lindsay and Donald, 1988: 23). This is the only part of the income system for the elderly that does not reinforce women's disadvantage. Nonetheless, the combined benefits from all levels of governments, including additional supplements provided by some provinces, fail to keep from poverty the single elderly person, the majority of whom are women (National Council of Welfare, 1989: 17).

The second tier of the income system for the elderly comprises the government-provided and work-related Canada/ Quebec Pension Plan (C/QPP). Instituted in 1966, this plan provides retirement, disability, and survivors' benefits, which vary according to earnings and the time spent in employment. The survivors' benefit is particularly important to women and is quite low: the average benefit paid in June, 1989, was $2,350 per annum (National Council of Welfare, 1989: 30). The C/QPP illustrates clearly the contribution of the family ethic and the work ethic to women's poverty in old age. The work ethic helps to identify contributory, earnings-related pensions as an increasingly important plank in the retirement income system, while the family ethic ensures that most women cannot take full advantage of it.

The accumulated effects of low-wage, part-time, and discontinuous employment, discussed earlier in this chapter, result in lower pension entitlements for women. The overwhelming majority of men are eligible for at least 80 per cent of the maximum pension available under the CPP, and yet half of the women who benefit receive less than 40 per cent (National Council of Welfare, 1989: 29). The increasing rates of women's labour force participation, however, suggest that in the future, benefits for women eligible under the C/QPP will improve. In 1983, the "drop-out" provision was instituted to allow mothers (or fathers) to exclude the years they spent out of the labour force rearing young children. This has the effect of protecting the level of their lifetime earnings, which is used in calculating pension entitlement. In view of the persistence of the wage gap and the increasing amounts of female part-time employment, this provision is an important one: it is estimated that it may raise pensions by 22 per cent for those able to take advantage of it (National Council of Welfare, 1989: 31).

Private pension schemes comprise the third and final layer of the retirement income system; they magnify the problems of the public pension scheme and are even more disadvantageous to women. Women, so frequently employed in poorly paid and low-status jobs, are much less likely than men to be covered by private pensions. They are also unlikely to be indirect beneficiaries, because most private plans do not include survivors' benefits, although plans regulated by federal and some provincial laws now require this option to be offered (National Council of Welfare, 1990: 58). In 1985, only 21 per cent of Canadian older women reported income from private pension plans in comparison to 46 per cent of elderly men (Oja, 1988: 18, 48).

Thus, both the public and private employment-related layers of the retirement income system serve to perpetuate into old age the inequalities women experience throughout their lives. Men who are out of the labour market or employed in low-paid and unstable jobs will also benefit less from employment-related programs, a disadvantage that reflects the inequities of class. However, the interaction between class and gender places a particularly disproportionate burden on women. While women's entitlement to c/QPP is formally equal to men's, the consequences of the family ethic on women's employment produce an inequitable distribution of benefits. Although OAS/GIS remains the most significant source of income for the elderly, its importance is declining while pension income is increasing (Oja, 1988: 25). In the absence of full equity in the labour force, women must necessarily lose out in a system that places increasing reliance on work-related pensions.[8]

DEFEMINIZING POVERTY

This chapter has examined the connections between women's poverty and women's responsibilities for caring. Of course, not all women who have caregiving responsibilities for others are poor. However, the family ethic and the work ethic structure women's economic vulnerability. The family ethic directly affects woman's earnings through limiting her availability for paid work. Less obviously, but at least as important, is the way that the work ethic, with its emphasis on market-based "productivity" buttressed by the family ethic, operates to discount the significance of women's work in the labour market and to devalue its importance in the home. The relationship between the family ethic and the work ethic, as reflected in social welfare policies, has been explored, as have the ways in which these policies, at best, fail to redress effectively women's economic vulnerability and, at worst, reinforce the poverty of single mothers and elderly women. This final section considers the dilemmas and potential for change.

Recognizing the Economic Value of Caregiving: Problems and Prospects

Each chapter of this book explores, from different reference points, an important theme: the impact of the continuing and systematic undervaluing of women's caring in the private sphere. One of the most important contributions of feminist analysis has been its attention to the significance of women's domestic labour and its relationship to their disadvantaged position in both private and public domains. As a result of this growing awareness, homemakers' "pensions" and the related concept of homemakers' "wages" are proposed as a constructive way to recognize the significance and value of women's household labour. The objective of homemakers' pensions is to extend pension coverage to women while they are at home caring for dependants, entitling them to pensions and improving their economic position when they are older.

The goal of homemakers' wages, in contrast, is to provide some type of cash payment to adults (almost always women) who are currently at home with dependants (usually children) to recognize the value of this work. Only a minimal value was placed on women's caring in the recent addition to the Child Tax Credit, which provides on an income-tested basis a token payment of $200 to mothers caring for children under the age of six on a full-time basis.

Proposals for homemakers' pensions have received recent support from the National Action Committee on the Status of Women, as well as from the 1983 Parliamentary Task Force on Pension Reform.[9] Although appealing to some, they raise important dilemmas. Providing homemakers' pensions, it is argued, is an effective way to recognize the economic value of women's work and to improve the economic position of women. Critics, however, identify a range of concerns, which also apply to proposals for homemakers' wages. These include the creation of inequities between women in employment who also have caregiving responsibilities and those who work full-time in the home, and the favouring of one-earner families over two-earner families at the same level of income. Further, others argue that the universal benefit of Old Age Security is a much more effective channel to improve the economic position of older women (Cohen, 1984; Wolfson, 1987). The National Council of Welfare (1984: 22) suggested that homemaker pensions are an idea that has "come too late," in view of the diminishing number of women who work as full-time homemakers. But perhaps the most telling argument is captured by Jane Lewis (1986: 97):

> It is in many ways easier for government to give a measure of recognition to women's traditional work than it is to promote significant change in the sexual division of labour in order to improve women's position in the workforce and persuade men to do more of the caring work at home.

Restructuring the Gendered Division of Labour

Women's high rates of poverty must not be considered out of context and viewed as the result of particular individual traits or characteristics. While lower levels of education *do* distinguish poor single mothers from those who are not poor (Ross and Shillington, 1989: 48), differences in educational achievement do not explain why female single parents are almost three times as likely to be poor as male single parents (Statistics Canada, 1989: 171). Improvements in social assistance benefits and expanded opportunities for education and training will make important differences for some women, but these changes will be at the margin for poor women as a whole, including most women on social assistance, unless the structure of women's disadvantage is altered.

The economic position of women will not be altered fundamentally through strategies that simply recognize the value of a woman's labour in the home but pay little attention to her position in the labour market. Similarly, her economic independence will not be secured by attending to labour market inequities while ignoring the reality of the caregiving that must be accorded to children and dependent adults. However, equity in the allocation of caring responsibilities is not easily achieved and will require, as Sheila Neysmith outlines in Chapter IX, changes in ideology about the family ethic, a shift toward more collective values, and a more vigorous role for the state. These are long-term changes for which there is no simple or single remedy; such changes are more likely to be accomplished in an evolutionary and incremental fashion, rather than by a few radical and dramatic steps. The remainder of this chapter points to some of the directions to pursue and the pitfalls to avoid if we are to reduce the economic vulnerability of women, visible in its most extreme form in the poverty rates of single mothers and elderly women.

First, in the absence of a sharing of caregiving responsibilities and equal access to resources, formal models of equality will be of limited value to women and are likely to be harmful. Their limitations were apparent in our examination of the Canada Pension Plan, which, while not overtly discriminating between men and women, reproduces in its benefits the inequities women confront in the labour market. Similarly, the ways in which women's financial and legal protections may be eroded through family law reforms intended to promote "equal treatment" after the ending of a marriage have been well documented (Weitzman, 1985; Mossman and MacLean, 1986).[10] It is essential that any changes truly operate to women's advantage. Resources are better directed to improving child care rather than to instituting a homemakers' pension or wage whose value may be more symbolic than real and may tend to support, rather than to mitigate, women's economic disadvantage. The exclusive assignment of caring responsibilities to women is the issue, not simply the level of the payment accorded to this caring.

Second, we must work to develop policies that explicitly acknowledge women's "complex allegiances and claims, and offer them more choice" (Lewis, 1986: 97). In turn, this means a very careful and sensitive evaluation of social policies for their impact on individuals in families and on different family forms. As Margrit Eichler (1988) points out, social policies may favour the breadwinner family or the two-earner family, and social benefits may use either the family or the individual as the basic unit for claiming purposes. Traditionally, our social welfare system has supported the breadwinner model of the family, which assumes that the father provides economically for his family and that the mother is available to provide care to family members. We can see this in operation in social assistance through the "man in the house" rule, which dictates that a single mother is the breadwinner until she lives with a man. Social policies based on the bread-winner model will reinforce women's economic dependency. Without accompanying changes, however, entitlements to social welfare based on individual rather than family claims will offer little relief to women's poverty, as the discussion of the Canada Pension Plan revealed. In addition, translating family-based benefits to individual entitlements conflicts with the goal of income redistribution as it favours the two-earner family and may result in an increase in means-tested rather than more universal benefits (Lewis, 1986; Millar and Glendinning, 1987b).

In part, this dilemma adds further weight to the necessity of considerably more state support for services such as day care and policies that attach benefits to children. In other words, casting the problem in terms of a more equitable sharing of responsibilities within families is not good enough. It too neatly returns the problem back to the family for resolution as "private troubles," which will advantage two-parent families and families with resources to purchase caring services. Avoiding public responsibility for the caring work done by women in families continues to give families these responsibilities without providing the necessary resources to carry them out.

Third, efforts to achieve equity in the workplace must be accompanied by efforts to make women's work in the labour market and at home more compatible. This means that men must increase their work at home, that employers must see employees as mothers and fathers, and that the state must also accept an active role in the sharing of care. As Evelyn Ferguson's chapter illustrates, Canadian social policies have recognized little responsibility for child care. In comparison to most European countries, Canada's provisions for mater-nity leave benefits are limited in coverage, benefits, and duration. As a result, it was estimated that in 1985 only 55 per cent of employed pregnant women claimed maternity bene-fits under unemployment insurance (Status of Women Can-ada, 1986: 25). The additional ten weeks of parental leave benefit recently implemented under UI is unlikely to prove more popular – the benefit is still set at 60 per cent of insurable earnings.

In 1962, the Swedish government recognized that women's equality in the workplace depended on making parenting and employment more compatible. The resulting policies include a generous and extremely flexible parental leave policy and a universal and heavily subsidized child-care system. But it is still overwhelmingly mothers who take advantage of the parental leave, although the number of fathers who do is increasing. In addition, there are not sufficient spaces available in Sweden's excellent, but expensive, formal child-care sector. Nonetheless, Sweden has firmly rejected the principle that the care of young children is largely a private and family responsibility and instead has acknowledged a collective responsibility for both children and dependent adults. However, it seems to have been less successful in changing normative assumptions of the "good" employee or the profile of what constitutes a career path. Although interruptions in employment histories for caring duties are allowed, even legally protected, the ideal of the traditional full-time-plus commitment to work remains intact and those using these hard-fought-for policies suffer in comparison to those who do not have to use them.

The family ethic and the work ethic have operated to women's disadvantage and helped to structure their poverty. While there are no easy solutions to women's economic vulnerability, the costs of failing to address it are extremely high. And these costs are increasing, as more and more women are parenting on their own and our population ages. At the same time, the changes taking place among Canadian women, and in Canadian families, highlight the inadequacy of our traditional assumptions and strengthen both the demand and the necessity for a more equitable distribution of the costs and the benefits of caring. Specifically, an image of citizenship must recognize the value of the contribution people make to the welfare of society as persons who care for others, as well as that recognized for direct contributions to the economy.

NOTES

1. In 1989, for example, the "poverty lines" set for a family of four included $27,597 by the Canadian Council on Social Development and $30,204 from the Budget Guides produced by the Social Planning Council of Metropolitan Toronto. Statistics Canada's "poverty line" ranged from $18,121 to $26,619, depending on size of population (Ross and Shillington, 1989: 6–11). Ross and Shillington (1989) also point out that Statistics Canada's commitment to a relative approach to defining poverty is limited – estimates are based on expenditure surveys from 1969 and 1978, and only in the appendix are they reported with reference to the 1986 survey.

2. These tabulations are based on the "census" rather than "economic" definition of family. The census definition is more restricted – "family" only includes husband, wife, and any single and unattached children. The economic family includes all individuals living together who are related by blood, marriage, or adoption, and will generally produce a higher poverty rate.

3. Between 1971 and 1988 the incidence of poverty decreased from 29 per cent to 7 per cent for married women; from 59 per cent to 36 per cent for women over the age of sixty-five and living on their own; from 40 per cent to 32 per cent for non-elderly unattached women; and from 62 per cent to 48 per cent for single mothers with children under the age of eighteen. Source: Statistics Canada, Household Surveys Division, Survey of Consumer Finances, unpublished data.

4. These are lower percentages than are often cited, due to differences in definitions. See note 2.

5. This underestimates the total time on social assistance as single mothers will initially go on General Welfare Assistance, Ontario's short-term program, where they typically stay for three-six months before moving to Family Benefits.

6. Quebec uses a similar basis to that of Ontario but deems a man responsible after living with a woman for one year. The possibility of challenges under Canada's Charter of Rights and Freedoms has also encouraged other provinces to make changes, which have, in theory at least, shifted the onus of proof of "man in the house" from the woman to the provincial authorities, and generally have removed the worst forms of intrusiveness from these investigations (information from Ministry of Community and Social Services, by telephone interview).

7. Despite Sweden's focus on "parental" leave, it is important to note that, although increasing numbers of fathers are making use of leave,

it is still overwhelmingly mothers who use it more frequently, and for longer periods of time (Moen, 1989).

8. Changes announced in the 1989 budget further erode the importance of the OAS. Beginning in 1990, the highest-income elderly will have their OAS fully recovered through the tax system. Apart from the concerns this raises regarding the principle of universality, the income levels are not fully indexed, so that over time, increasing numbers of the elderly will lose at least some of their benefits (National Council of Welfare, 1989b).

9. It is interesting to note that the Task Force proposals would have provided pension benefits for women with no children but who were at home looking after their husbands (National Council of Welfare, 1984).

10. For an excellent discussion of the dilemmas in the two contrasting models of gender equality, equality based on the assumption of "sameness" vs. "difference," see Cossman, 1990.

REFERENCES

Abramovitz, Mimi. 1988. *Regulating the Lives of Women: Social Welfare Policy from Colonial Times to the Present*. Boston: South End Press.

Adams, Ian, William Cameron, Brian Hill, and Peter Penz. 1971. *The Real Poverty Report*. Edmonton: Hurtig.

Barron, R.D., and G.M. Norris. 1976. "Sexual Divisions and the Dual Labour Market," in Diana Leonard Barker and Sheila Allen, eds., *Dependence and Exploitation in Work and Marriage*. London: Longman.

Beechey, Veronica. 1988. "Rethinking the Definition of Work: Gender and Work," in Jane Jenson, Elisabeth Hagen, and Ceallaigh Reddy, eds., *Feminization of the Labour Force: Paradoxes and Promises*. Oxford: Polity Press.

Boyd, Monica. 1988. "Changing Canadian Family Forms: Issues for Women," in Nancy Mandell and Ann Duffy, eds., *Reconstructing the Canadian Family: Feminist Perspectives*. Toronto: Butterworths.

Canada. 1970. *Royal Commission on the Status of Women in Canada*. Ottawa: Information Canada.

Canadian Advisory Council on the Status of Women. 1987. *Integration and Participation: Women's Work in the Home and in the Labour Force*. Ottawa: CACSW.

Canadian Social Trends. 1986. "The Value of Household Work in Canada," adapted from an article by J.L. Swinaner. Ottawa: Statistics Canada, Autumn.

Cohen, Leah. 1984. *Small Expectations: Society's Betrayal of Older Women*. Toronto: McClelland and Stewart.

Cohen, Marcy. 1989. "The Changing Structure of Women's Employment Opportunities: The Policy Implications for the 1990s," paper presented at the Fourth National Conference on Social Welfare, Toronto, October 24-27.

Connelly, M. Patricia, and Martha MacDonald. 1990. *Women and the Labour Force*. Ottawa: Minister of Supply and Services Canada, Cat. 98-125, February.

Cossman, Brenda. 1990. "A Matter of Difference: Domestic Contracts and Gender Equality," *Osgoode Hall Law Journal*, 28, 2 (Summer): 303-80.

Daily Bread Food Bank. 1989. "The Kids are Hungry," Toronto: Daily Bread Food Bank.

Eichler, Margrit. 1988. *Families in Canada Today: Recent Changes and Their Policy Consequences*, Second Edition. Toronto: Gage.

Employment and Immigration Canada. 1989. *Employment Equity Act: Annual Report 1989*. Ottawa: Minister of Supply and Services.

England, Paula. 1982. "The Failure of Human Capital Theory to Explain Occupational Sex Segregation," *Journal of Human Resources*, xviii, 3 (Summer): 358-70.

Evans, Patricia M. 1984. "Work and Welfare: A Profile of Low-Income Single Mothers," *Canadian Social Work Review*: 81-96.

Evans, Patricia M. 1987. "A Decade of Change: The FBA Caseload, 1975-1986," report prepared for the Ontario Social Assistance Review Committee, June.

Evans, Patricia M. 1988. "Work Incentives and the Single Mother: Dilemmas of Reform," *Canadian Public Policy*, xiv, 2 (June): 125-36.

Evans, Patricia M., and Eilene McIntyre. 1987. "Welfare, Work Incentives and the Single Mother: An Interprovincial Comparison," in *The Canadian Welfare State: Evolution and Transition*. Edmonton: University of Alberta Press.

Galbraith, John Kenneth. 1958. *Affluent Society*. Boston: Houghton Mifflin.

Graham, Hilary. 1987. "Women's Poverty and Caring," in Caroline Glendinning and Jane Millar, eds., *Women and Poverty in Britain*. Brighton, Sussex: Wheatsheaf Books.

Gunderson, Morley. 1985. "Discrimination, Equal Pay, and Equal Opportunities in the Labour Market," in W. Craig Riddell, ed., *Work and Pay: The Canadian Labour Market*. Toronto: University of Toronto Press.

Gunderson, Morley, and Leon Muszynski, with Jennifer Keck. 1990. *Women and Labour Market Poverty*. Ottawa: Canadian Advisory

Council on the Status of Women, June.

Hauser, Richard, and Ingo Fischer. 1986. "The Relative Economic Status of One-Parent Families in Six Major Industrialized Countries," LIS-CEPS Working Paper #6, Luxembourg: Centre d'Études de Populations, de Pauvreté et de Politiques Socio-économiques, January.

Hunt, Audrey. 1988. "The Effects of Caring for the Elderly and Infirm on Women's Employment," in Hunt, ed., *Women and Paid Work: Issues of Equality*. London: Macmillan.

Kamerman, Sheila B., and Alfred J. Kahn. 1988. *Mothers Alone: Strategies for a Time of Change*. Dover, Mass.: Auburn.

Kamerman, Sheila B., and Alfred J. Kahn. 1989. "Single-parent, female-headed families in Western Europe: Social change and response," *International Social Security Review*, 1: 3–34.

Kierstead, W.C. 1925. "Mother's Allowances in Canada," *Canadian Congress Journal*, IV, 7 (July): 27–29, continued in IV, 8 (August): 21–23.

Leighton, Margaret. 1987. "Handmaids' Tales: Family Benefits Assistance and the Single-Mother-Led Family," *University of Toronto Faculty of Law Review*, 45, 2: 324–54.

Lewis, Jane. 1986. "Feminism and Welfare," in Juliet Mitchell and Ann Oakley, eds., *What is Feminism? A Re-examination*. New York: Pantheon.

Lewis, Jane, and Barbara Meredith. 1988. *Daughters Who Care*. London: Routledge and Kegan Paul.

Lindsay, Colin. 1989. "The Service Sector in the 1980s,"*Canadian Social Trends*, No. 12 (Spring).

Lindsay, Colin, and Shelley Donald. 1988. "Income of Canada's Seniors," *Canadian Social Trends* (Autumn).

Michelson, William. 1985. *From Sun to Sun: Daily Obligations and Community Structures in the Lives of Employed Women and Their Families*. Totawa, N.J.: Rowman and Allanhead.

Millar, Jane, and Caroline Glendinning. 1987a. "Invisible Women, Invisible Poverty," in Glendinning and Millar, eds., *Women and Poverty in Britain*. Brighton, Sussex: Wheatsheaf Books.

Millar, Jane, and Caroline Glendinning. 1987b. "Towards the Defeminisation of Poverty," in Glendinning and Millar, eds., *Women and Poverty in Britain*.

Moen, Phyllis. 1989. *Working Parents: transformation in gender roles and public policies in Sweden*. Madison: University of Wisconsin Press.

Moore, Maureen. 1987. "Women Parenting Alone," *Canadian Social Trends* (Winter).

Mossman, Mary Jane, and Morag MacLean. 1986. "Family Law and

Social Welfare: Toward a New Equality," *Canadian Journal of Family Law*, 5, 1 (Summer): 79-110.

National Council of Welfare. 1979. *Women and Poverty*. Ottawa, October.

National Council of Welfare. 1984. *Better Pensions for Homemakers*. Ottawa, May.

National Council of Welfare. 1987. *Welfare in Canada: The Tangled Safety Net*. Ottawa, November.

National Council of Welfare. 1988. *Poverty Profile 1988*. Ottawa, September.

National Council of Welfare. 1989a. *A Pension Primer*. Ottawa, September.

National Council of Welfare. 1989b. *The 1989 Budget and Social Policy*. Ottawa, September.

National Council of Welfare. 1990. *Pension Reform*. Ottawa, February.

Neysmith, Sheila M. 1984. "Poverty in Old Age: Can Pension Reform Meet the Needs of Women?" *Canadian Women Studies*, 5, 3 (Spring): 17-21.

Oja, G., in collaboration with R. Love. 1988. *Pensions and Incomes of the Elderly in Canada, 1971-1985*. Statistics Canada Cat. No. 13-548. Ottawa: Minister of Supply and Services, June.

Ontario Ministry of Community and Social Services. 1984. "One-Stop Service," Report of the Joint Steering Committee on Integration, Monitoring and Evaluating, December.

Ontario Ministry of Community and Social Services. 1988. *Transitions*. Report of the Social Assistance Review Committee. Toronto: Publications Ontario.

Ornstein, Michael. 1983. "Accounting for Gender Differentials in Job Income in Canada: Results from a 1981 Survey," Ottawa: Labour Canada.

Parliament, Jo-Anne B. 1989. "Women Employed Outside the Home," *Canadian Social Trends* (Summer): 2-6.

Pascall, Gillian. 1986. *Social Policy: A Feminist Analysis*. London: Tavistock.

Pearce, Diana M. 1985. "Toil and Trouble: Women Workers and Unemployment Compensation," *Signs*, 10, 3 (Spring): 439-59.

Polachek, Solomon. 1975. "Discontinuous Labour Force Participation and its Effect on Women's Market Earnings," in Cynthia B. Lloyd, ed., *Sex Discrimination and the Division of Labour*. New York: Columbia University Press.

Robinson, Patricia. 1987. *Women and Work Interruptions: Results from the 1984 Family History Survey*. Ottawa: Statistics Canada, Cat. 99-962.

Ross, David P., and Richard Shillington. 1989. *Canadian Fact Book on*

Poverty: 1989. Ottawa: Canadian Council on Social Development.

Special Senate Committee. 1971. *Poverty in Canada*. Ottawa: Information Canada.

Splane, Richard. 1965. *Social Welfare in Ontario 1791-1893: A Study of Public Welfare Administration*. Toronto: University of Toronto Press.

Statistics Canada. 1984. *Canada's Lone-Parent Families*, Cat. 99-993. Ottawa: Minister of Supply and Services, May.

Statistics Canada. 1988. *Survey of Consumer Finances*. Household Surveys Division, unpublished data. Ottawa.

Statistics Canada. 1989. *Income Distributions by Size in Canada, 1988*, Cat. 13-207. Ottawa: Minister of Supply and Services Canada, November.

Statistics Canada. 1990a. *Employment, Earnings, and Hours*, Cat. 72-002. Ottawa: Minister of Supply and Services Canada, January.

Statistics Canada. 1990b. *Women in Canada*, Cat. 89-503E. Ottawa: Minister of Supply and Services Canada, February.

Status of Women Canada. 1986. *Report of the Task Force on Child Care*. Ottawa: Minister of Supply and Services.

Strong-Boag, Veronica. 1979. " 'Wages for Housework': The Beginnings of Social Security in Canada," *Journal of Canadian Studies*, 14, 1 (Spring): 24-34.

Walker, Alan. 1987. "The Poor Relation: Poverty Among Older Women," in Glendinning and Millar, eds., *Women and Poverty in Britain*.

Weitzman, Lenore J. 1985. *The Divorce Revolution: The Unexpected Social and Economic Consequences for Women and Children in America*. New York: Free Press.

Wolfson, Michael. 1987. *Homemaker Pensions and Lifetime Redistribution*. Ottawa: Statistics Canada, Social and Economic Studies Division.

CHAPTER VII

For Better or For Worse: Caring and the Abused Wife

Imogen Taylor

INTRODUCTION

Most of the literature on caring has centred on the care given to persons who, by reason of age or disability, cannot care for themselves. Kari Waerness (1984), however, has also identified another dimension of women's caring – the care of healthy men. Women, in many and perhaps most marriages, are not only expected to care for dependent individuals in the family, they are expected to care for and provide nurture to their husbands – care that may be characterized as "personal service."

This chapter explores the relationship between society's expectations of women's caring and the occurrence of wife abuse. Although the research findings of the London, Ontario, Battered Women's Advocacy Clinic suggest that a number of factors contribute to the victimization of women (Greaves, Heapy, and Wylie, 1988), the impact of caring on wife abuse is a factor that has received little attention in either the caring literature or the literature on abused women.

What assumptions are made about the care provided by a wife to a husband who physically, sexually, or psychologically abuses her? Where possible this discussion is based on data about women in Canada, and it begins by highlighting the salient facts about the incidence, prevalence, and demographics of wife abuse and the experiences of the well-publicized case of one Canadian woman, Jane Stafford (Vallee, 1986). Although abuse in gay and lesbian relationships is increasingly being reported and may contribute to our understanding about the relationship of caring, gender expectations, and abuse, there is very little research available and this area is not discussed here.

ABUSED WIVES

Definitional Issues

Language used to describe violence against wives takes many forms. Terms such as "family violence," "domestic violence," and "spouse abuse" are neutral and obscure the dimensions of gender and power fundamental to understanding that it is men who use violence against women as a powerful means of controlling them (Bograd, 1988; Breines and Gordon, 1983; Schecter, 1982; Sinclair, 1985).

In spite of some concerns about the terms "wife" and "husband," these are preferred to the term "partner" as they are gender specific and will be used to encompass an intimate relationship whether or not sanctioned by marriage. The terms "abuse" and "assault" are used interchangeably. The term "batterer" is largely avoided as it implies serious injuries requiring hospitalization and that other kinds of abuse are less significant (Sinclair, 1985).

An adequate definition of wife abuse is elusive. There is no unified feminist perspective on wife abuse, although there is general agreement that the constructs of gender and power are extremely important and that the social institutions of marriage and the family, as they have traditionally been conceived, promote and maintain men's use of physical force against women (Bograd, 1988).

Linda MacLeod, who has undertaken two studies of wife abuse in Canada (1980, 1987), defines wife abuse as:

a loss of dignity, control, and safety as well as the feeling of powerlessness and entrapment experienced by women who are direct victims of ongoing or repeated physical, psychological, economic, sexual, and/or verbal violence or who are subjected to persistent threats or the witnessing of such violence against their children, other relatives, friends, pets, and/or cherished possessions by their boyfriends, live-in lovers, ex-husbands or ex-lovers, whether male or female. (MacLeod, 1987: 16)

This definition captures the multifaceted nature of abuse as well as the often neglected fact that a significant amount of abuse occurs after separation or divorce (Giles-Sims, 1983).

Incidence and Demographics

Wife abuse has been viewed as a private matter and has for centuries remained hidden. As a result, incidence figures are usually based on estimates and projections. Furthermore, the only national studies of the problem have focused on women in shelters (MacLeod, 1980, 1987). A frequently quoted statistic in Canada is that one in ten wives is abused by her husband, although experts working in the field consider this to be an underestimate and suggest that a conservative guesstimate would be that almost one million women in Canada are abused by their husbands each year (MacLeod, 1987).

Wife abuse cuts across demographic lines and repudiates the lower socio-economic and educational status stereotype of abused women (Greaves, Heapy, and Wylie, 1988; Kincaid, 1982). A review of fifty-two American studies found that income, educational level, and race do not discriminate victims from non-victims (Hotaling and Sugarman, 1986).

Another common stereotype is that abuse stops once the wife leaves. However, 44 per cent of American women who

The Abused Wife

never returned to their husbands after they left a shelter reported at least one violent incident involving their husbands (Giles-Sims, 1983). Twenty-three per cent of Canadian wives slain by their husbands between 1974 and 1983 were separated from their killers (Wilson and Daly, 1987). Homicide statistics draw attention to the fears that many abused women constantly live with. During the period 1974–83, 1,060 Canadians were killed by their spouses: 812 wives and 248 husbands. The 812 wives who were victims represent 41 per cent of all adult (fifteen years of age or older) female victims of homicide (Wilson and Daly, 1987).

What happens to make marriage a nightmare – even ending in violent death – for so many women? Assuming that when a man and woman choose to become husband and wife there is an element of mutual caring present, what happens to this?

CARING AND WIFE ABUSE

As discussed in Chapter I, the literature on caring has been divided and fragmented according to disciplinary boundaries, restricting our understanding of the experience for the individual woman. Nevertheless, it is essential to disentangle the concepts to understand the place of caring in wife abuse.

The work of Waerness explicitly addresses caring for a healthy man and has implications for our understanding of wife abuse. She discusses the caring that occurs between two people where "one of them (the carer) shows worry, consideration, affection, devotion towards the other (the cared for)" (Waerness, 1984: 70). In principle this kind of caring among healthy adults is based on norms of reciprocity, but as caring is usually assumed by women there is often an absence of mutual exchange. Waerness introduces the concept of "personal service," which refers particularly to those services provided over and above a reciprocal exchange of caring, where a partner, usually the woman, is in a subordinate position with respect to status and power. "When women provide these services for husbands or other adult healthy members of the family, it can be experienced as something they are 'forced' to do, not as a consequence of their concern for others well being but as a consequence of their subordinate position in the family" (1984: 70). Waerness does not extend this further to include force by the threat of, or use of, abuse.

Although the concept of "love and labour" was developed in relation to children, adults who are disabled or chronically ill, and the frail elderly, women's work within the family and the marital relationship is also filled with emotional expectations as well as the performance of many household responsibilities. Early in a marriage there may be a reciprocity of love, if not labour. However, "love can very quickly become labour quite devoid of any of the feelings of affection which are meant to be its cornerstone" (Finch and Groves, 1983: 10). This is certainly true for many abused women.

The distinction between "caring about" and "caring for" (Dalley, 1988) parallels the concept of love and labour. "Caring for" comprises the tasks of tending for another person; and, "caring about," the feelings about the other person. As will be discussed later, the distinction between the two kinds of caring is blurred in the situation of wife abuse. The enforced requirement for a wife to "care for" her husband, or to offer him "personal service," may come to symbolize her "caring about" him.

Relationships can be viewed on a continuum, from a relationship based on mutuality and shared power to a relationship characterized by physical, psychological, or sexual expression of male dominance (Kelly, 1988). Caring can be characterized on the same continuum, from mutual and reciprocal labour and love, to the relationship where love is eroded and may be extinguished, while the expectations of labour are sustained by force. In between is what continues to be the norm, the relationship dominated by the man, in which the wife is expected to offer personal service.

The concept of a continuum, although it risks oversimplifying the highly complex institution of marriage, is a useful one because it reflects the reality that "Wife abuse is not viewed as a rare and deviant phenomenon that results from the breakdown of family functioning, but as a predictable and common dimension of family life as it is currently structured in our society" (Bograd, 1988: 14). A continuum also highlights the shifting forms a marriage can take. This is demonstrated in the ground-breaking study by Rebecca and Russell Dobash (1979) of 109 abused women in Scotland. Apart from a few exceptions where violence occurred prior to the marriage, most marriages initially were located at the centre of the continuum; however, after three years of marriage, 84 per cent had shifted into the realm of wife abuse.

What happens to a woman whose position in a marriage shifts from one in which there is some reciprocity of caring and where personal service is "willingly" provided, to a position characterized by abuse as she is compelled to provide service? To better analyse the abused wife's experience, the socialization of women will be explored, including the patriarchal imperative that women care as well as the psychological influences. Together, these influences all too often set the scene for abuse and entrap a wife in an abusive marriage. By examining both patriarchal and psychological factors, we can begin to integrate the public and private worlds of women, which takes wife abuse beyond an explanation centred on individual pathology.

Patriarchy

What bearing does patriarchy have on wife abuse and caring? There are two important dimensions to the patriarchal message: (1) woman's place is in the private world of the home; and (2) her position in the public world of work is secondary to that of men. The expectation that men demand care or personal service makes many wives vulnerable to abuse and makes it extremely difficult for them to leave a marriage once abuse has occurred. Hierarchical legal, political, religious, and economic institutions have reinforced the power of patriarchy, ensuring the continuing domination of men and relegating women to positions of subservience. Acceptance of this structure is reinforced by ideology. As the Dobash (1979: 31) study points out, "Women's place in history often has been at the receiving end of a blow." Home is often not the haven hoped for.

The cultural legacy of patriarchy dictates not only that a woman should become a wife and mother, it also prescribes how domestic work is to be carried out and the womanly feelings that should accompany it. This means assuming "the major responsibility for domestic work and child care and providing emotional comfort, psychological support, and personal service to all family members in a spirit of extreme commitment and selflessness" (Dobash and Dobash, 1979: 76). The prescription for what is seen as natural and right for women prevails across different class and ethnic groups and during different historical periods.

Patriarchy gives men power over women, and this may include the use or threat of force. According to Schecter (1982: 226), "Her work, maintaining a home and caring for children, becomes the terrain for his inspection and potential discipline." Reinforced by the legal system, wife abuse in Canada as recently as the 1960s was beyond the law. The "rule of thumb" principle, derived from English Common Law, gave a husband the right to chastise his wife with a weapon no wider than his thumb. Although wife abuse is now a criminal offence, enforcement of the law remains an ongoing struggle. Patriarchal influences are also evident in the continued economic discrimination faced by women. A wife in the traditional nuclear family, often wageless or a low-wage earner and dependent on her husband but at the same time responsible for the care of the home, is extremely vulnerable to violence (Schecter, 1982).

Psychological Influences

Two psychologists, Jean Baker Miller and Carol Gilligan, have made significant contributions to feminist analysis of the psychology of women. They help us understand the power of the requirement that a wife care for a husband. Central to their work is the recognition that a woman's identity is formed in relation to others, in contrast to a man's identity, which is developed in relation to the external world: "Women not only define themselves in a context of human relationships but also judge themselves in terms of their ability to care. Woman's place in man's life cycle has been that of nurturer, caretaker, and helpmate, the weaver of those networks of relationships on which she in turn relies" (Gilligan, 1982: 17).

What happens to the wife who is the nurturer, caretaker,

and helpmate when she is abused by her husband? It might be expected that caring would be withdrawn; indeed, in some marriages this is exactly what happens. Frequently, however, the first episode is not treated as though it is the beginning of a violent relationship; it is only understood this way in retrospect. The first episode is "at the same time dramatic and insignificant" (Dobash and Dobash, 1979: 94). The physical effects are often insignificant compared to what happens later; it is dramatic in that both husband and wife usually respond with shock, shame, and guilt.

Jane Stafford's experience demonstrates this. After almost two years of living with Billy and six months after their son was born, Jane was beaten for the first time when Billy assumed (incorrectly) that Jane had been "making eyes" with Richard, a friend of Billy's:

> Billy slapped her face and began punching and kicking her. "That was my first real beating, and I didn't know why." Billy was sheepish the next morning at breakfast. "I'm sorry," he said. "I'll never do it again. I promise." (Vallee, 1986: 62)

Billy's promise was frequently and appallingly broken.

Yet Jane Stafford struggled to find ways to cope with Billy's violence. Baker Miller (1977) argues that when women suspect they have caused men to feel angry, they tend to assume guilt. As a result, personal service may increase as the wife "attempts to comprehend the violence in terms of her own behaviour, to see her own 'guilt,' and both to forgive her husband (for perhaps merely overreacting) and to seek a solution by changing her behaviour so as to give him no further reason for hitting her" (Dobash and Dobash, 1979: 96). Jane Stafford experienced this: "I wondered, 'Did I look at Richard like he said I did?' Just maybe I did. To me no one got that angry or violent without a reason. So I must have been the reason" (Vallee, 1986: 62). This assumption is often reinforced by others who also believe the abused wife is responsible for her plight. Even if an abused woman begins to acknowledge the significance of the violence, women whose identity and status are very largely defined by their role as wives and mothers risk a great deal in admitting that they have failed to make their marriage work (Greaves, Heapy, and Wylie, 1988; Kincaid, 1982; Pahl, 1985).

An abused wife may believe it is wrong to leave a husband who is in distress. Angela Browne (1987) found in her study of women who ultimately murdered their abusive husbands that they empathized with the husband's feelings so his pleading for them not to leave was often effective. Leonore Walker found that wives "see themselves as the bridge to their man's emotional well being" (1979: 68). In this study, 10 per cent of the abusing husbands killed themselves after their wives left. When Jane Stafford told Billy she was considering leaving him, he selected an equally if not more potent controlling device: he told her he would kill her family, and she had every reason to believe him.

For the abused woman, particularly in the early stages of an abusive relationship, the prospect of leaving the marriage and experiencing the lack of caring and the isolation of the external world may feel more dangerous than the violence itself. In addition, life as a single woman in a patriarchal society organized around heterosexist options may be unthinkable, particularly at a time when her psychological resources are diminished by the abuse (Greaves, Heapy, and Wylie, 1988).

Women's vulnerabilities at home correspond with the uncertainties they experience in the public sphere. Baker Miller (1977) suggests that women often do not perceive themselves as having the right to act or make decisions that would be for their own direct benefit. The wife in a subordinate position attends to her own needs subject to her husband's approval. Stafford found herself in this situation when her employers at the Home for the Elderly suggested she take a cooking course, all expenses paid:

> I told them I would give them an answer by the end of the week. That gave me four days to catch Bill in a good mood and get his approval. Deep inside I knew it was no good to get my hopes up, but I wanted to go so badly. (Vallee, 1986: 89)

The patriarchal and psychological influences on a woman to care are frequently woven into a dangerous net as the wife is initially abused and then becomes entrapped in an abusive marriage. In the next section, specific areas of marriage in which violence is most likely to occur are analysed, and the way that the requirement to care sets the scene for abuse and limits the options for change is explored.

WHERE CARING, MARRIAGE, AND VIOLENCE INTERSECT

Dobash and Dobash (1979) have identified the three most common situations preceding violence: the husband's jealousy of the wife, differing expectations about domestic responsibilities, and the allocation of money. An additional aspect of marriage in which violence frequently occurs is pregnancy. A discussion of this, expanded to include motherhood, completes the next section of this chapter.

Jealousy
Studies of abusive marriages have found sexual jealousy to be a key factor in disputes leading to violence (Browne, 1987; Dobash and Dobash, 1979; Kincaid, 1982; Walker, 1979). Possessiveness toward and isolation of women may begin even prior to marriage as women begin to give up their circle of friends. This was highlighted in the Dobash study: "When they did go out they were more likely to engage in activities like movie going in order to ensure there would be no doubt in their boyfriend's mind about whether or not they were seeing other males" (1979: 83). At the time, possessiveness may well be romantically interpreted by women as evidence that men really care, which prevents them from understanding how commitment and control become inextricably linked.

Once a couple is married, a pattern may develop in which they spend less time going out together – the wife stays at home while the husband increases his evenings out. The Dobash study points out that "her [the wife's] commitment to marriage demands an exclusivity not demanded of the husband and this exclusive commitment to the relationship must be constantly demonstrated" (Dobash and Dobash,

1979: 89). Such commitment is frequently manifested by acts of personal service.

Browne (1987: 43) describes a similar pattern in which the husband always needed to know the wife's whereabouts and did not want her to interact with people other than himself. They "cut their partners off from family and friends, refused to let them work outside the home, and treated activities the women wanted to pursue without them as a personal affront." This was also the experience of Jane Stafford:

> When I went anywhere, I avoided talking to anyone. I was terrified if anyone spoke to me. When that happened I told Bill as soon as I got home. I was that paranoid. Bill was a very jealous man although he had no reason to be. (Vallee, 1986: 90)

Billy's jealousy extended beyond other men to friends and family, even to the church: "I wasn't even allowed to attend church or speak of the Lord. I wasn't allowed to have a Bible, and I wasn't even allowed to have any pictures of any members of my family in the house" (Vallee, 1986: 90).

Can an abused wife ever convince her husband that she is faithful and cares about him? Once again there is a juxtaposition of commitment and control as caring about or commitment is enforced by the control of threat or use of violence. For a wife this often means increased isolation and entrapment. She is cut off from possible sources of emotional and material support at a time when she needs it most, thus limiting the option of leaving her marriage. As we will see, this is compounded for women who are isolated by language, culture, or geography.

Domestic Labour

Domestic labour refers to the unpaid daily housekeeping activities that support the "survival and refreshment of members of the household" (Task Force Report to the General Synod of the Anglican Church, 1986: 17). Despite gains made by the women's movement, housework and child care continue to be seen as primarily the responsibility of the wife even for highly educated, professional couples (Eichler, 1988).

This is as true for the woman at home full-time as for the woman employed outside the home who is doing "double work."

The Dobash study found that in traditional marriages in the middle of the relationship continuum, as discussed above, wives have primary responsibility for domestic labour but lack decision-making authority. Even in areas where husbands believe wives should have authority, if there is disagreement his wishes prevail. In the process of the inevitable negotiation that ensues, violence frequently begins.

Jane Stafford's ordeal was somewhat different. She did not attempt to negotiate with Billy, but tried to avoid abuse by complying with his expectations that she take responsibility for all the domestic work. Jane describes the tremendous burden she carried, which for her was exacerbated by living in a rural area and not having the amenities of city life. In addition, she was employed outside the home.

> I worked harder than any man. We had no well, and until 1980 I brought water from where I worked or carried it from a spring half a mile from our house. I carried all the water for cleaning, cooking, and laundry. There was no stove in the house until I got a second hand electric one at the end of 1979. (Vallee, 1986: 74)

To make matters worse, Billy frequently and deliberately created a mess for Jane to clean up, often turning this into a demeaning and humiliating experience by psychologically abusing her. Billy's expectations of Jane were extreme but not unusual among husbands who abuse:

> The cleanliness of the house, the preparation of the meals, and the care of clothing often serve as symbols that a wife is committed to her husband, that she takes care of him and respects his authority and serves him, and that she has been well prepared for these tasks. (Dobash and Dobash, 1979: 91)

In this way, the tasks of caring *for* another person are regarded as confirmation of a woman's affection – the caring *about* her husband. However, caring in this way is often provided not from concern but from fear, and caring about may indeed be eradicated.

Allocation of Money

The third common source of disputes leading to violence is derived from the wife's request for housekeeping money and the husband's expenditure on individual pursuits (Dobash and Dobash, 1979). Even if wives are employed outside the home, their income is generally earmarked for domestic requirements and women have little control over financial decisions. As Jane Stafford recalls: "Right from the start, my wages bought groceries and paid bills. If I managed to have a few dollars left, he would steal it right out of my purse" (Vallee, 1986: 60).

Without money the abused woman is dependent and forced to save and hide a few cents at a time in order to be able to acquire the resources to leave. This is a risky process because some husbands force their wives to account for every penny.

Caring, Abuse, and Motherhood

Pregnancy and motherhood are a double-edged sword for the abused woman. During pregnancy, abuse may begin or increase. Motherhood may entrap a woman in a marriage "for the sake of the children" and, if children are abused, it may provide the needed momentum to leave. Caring for and about her children and her family presents a contradiction – it can be a source of both strength and weakness.

Although the literature indicates that violence often begins at the time of pregnancy, there has been surprisingly little research done on this issue (Hotaling and Sugarman, 1986). Gelles (1977) suggests that pregnancy increases a woman's dependency, which may be a factor in the occurrence of violence. This concurs with the argument made in the Dobash study (1979) that the dependent status of the wife gives the husband the right and obligation to control her and justifies abuse. It is also likely that jealousy, discussed earlier as a key precipitant in violent incidents, would include jealousy of children, including a child still in utero.

Jealousy in relation to children appears to have been a factor in Billy's abuse of Jane. Psychological abuse increased during pregnancy. After the birth of their first child Jane was advised not to do any heavy work for six to eight weeks because she had a difficult delivery and required surgery, but when she came home from hospital with their newborn baby, Billy insisted on the usual attention: " 'Well, what the hell are you waiting for?' Billy said with a sneer. 'Can't you see all the work that needs doing around here? Put that little bastard in the crib and get busy' " (Vallee, 1986: 58). Soon after this the beatings began.

The most common reason for a wife to stay in an abusive relationship is her belief that a broken home is worse for the children than a violent one (Dobash and Dobash, 1979). For many women this is combined with the enormous practical obstacles to leaving. As the number of children living with an abused woman increases, the probability of her leaving decreases (Greaves, Heapy, and Wylie, 1989). Yet, an increasing body of Canadian research documents that children who witness wife abuse are high-risk candidates for long-term emotional adjustment problems (Jaffe, Wilson, and Wolfe, 1988; Pressman, 1984). Jan Pahl (1985) notes that many women decided to leave when it became evident that the eldest child was aware of the situation. This suggests it is useful to raise the awareness of abused women of the effect witnessing violence may have on their children.

There is evidence that if children become direct targets of abuse, then the need to care for them takes precedence, causing the mother to leave (Dobash and Dobash, 1979). Typically, however, children are not the targets of direct attack unless they come to the defence of the mother or fail to meet the father's unrealistic expectations. An important area of future study should examine the link between the abuse of children and women. Linda Gordon's (1988) historical study of family violence concluded that many women sought help from child protective agencies as a means of gaining help for themselves.

In everyday life, the areas of tension and conflict identified in cases of wife abuse are also areas of tension for many couples, irrespective of their place on the continuum of marriage relationships. However, the daily realities of life for abused women are compounded by their inability to escape from economic and psychological dependence. This is reinforced by social and legal institutions that identify personal service as an important aspect of women's caring. Two groups of women who are particularly vulnerable and deserve special consideration are Canadian aboriginal women and recent immigrants.

ABUSED ABORIGINAL AND
IMMIGRANT WOMEN

Aboriginal women who are abused face the added obstacle of confronting social and legal institutions not responsive to them and that frequently revictimize them. There has been a long history of racism in Canada, and both aboriginal and immigrant women may view the dominant culture as the primary aggressor and choose loyalty to their cultural group rather than expose the violence they are experiencing. Linda MacLeod (1987) suggests that the vulnerability of abused aboriginal women is also increased by the high value they attach to family life, privacy, and the authority of men. Such values put a particular onus on women to care for and about others.

Abused aboriginal women also suffer from a particular lack of responsiveness on the part of the social welfare system. If they live on a reserve with its own police and services, they are faced with the dilemma of seeking help from a system internally controlled by regional councils that may have an interest in maintaining the status quo. Off the reserve they frequently experience discrimination and a lack of resources culturally attuned to their particular needs. They are distrustful of the criminal justice system. They may also have experienced discrimination in shelters, both from staff and from other residents (MacLeod, 1987).

There are some encouraging signs of change. One example is portrayed in the 1986 National Film Board series *The Next Step*, three films that demonstrate the need for services to abused women. The second film in the series, *A Safe Distance*, looks at services and programs designed to meet the needs of abused women in rural, northern, and native communities. It features the women of the West Bay Reserve in Ontario and the mutual caring that exists as together they build a shelter, an important sign that they will no longer tolerate violence.

Similar to aboriginal women, abused immigrant women are confronted with additional complications and have fewer options than women born in Canada (Ruitort and Small, 1985). The term "immigrant women" refers particularly to women born outside Canada whose mother tongue is neither English nor French and who therefore are culturally and socially separated from mainstream society even though they may have been in Canada many years (Ruitort, 1986). While there are many differences among immigrant women based on their particular ethnic origin, there are also areas of similarity. An important common factor is that, like aboriginal women, immigrant women may find other forms of oppression more urgent than violence from husbands. Racism makes family and community ties primary and women may choose to remain side by side with men for survival (Schecter, 1982).

Once again, there is limited research about the situation of abused immigrant women, particularly those who do not seek the help of shelters. In 1982, 53 per cent of the residents of Interval House, a Toronto shelter, were born outside Canada and 24 per cent of these were sponsored immigrants (Ruitort, 1986). These figures are high and may in part reflect Toronto's high concentration of immigrants relative to many other parts of Canada. In Canada, in 1985, 6 per cent of women in shelters were reported as legal immigrants and an additional 2 per cent were illegal immigrants or temporary visitors (MacLeod, 1987). It is generally agreed by service providers who work with immigrant women that many will not go to shelters and that these figures underrepresent the problem of wife abuse.

The pressure for immigrant women to care for husbands and children is particularly strong because traditional sources of support (mothers, sisters, cousins, mothers-in-law, etc.) are no longer available. Language barriers frequently compound the isolation. For many immigrant women, not to fulfil the roles of wife and mother also represents personal failure (Szado, 1987; Zambrano, 1985). Zambrano outlines such expectations for Latina women in the United States and highlights the centrality of their role in the family and the expectation that the needs of husband and children are of primary importance. In addition, "many immigrant women are under strong pressures to protect their husbands from public shame. An assaulted immigrant woman often faces social ostracism if she exposes her husband's violence to public scrutiny" (Ruitort and Small, 1985: 2). Fear of ostracism can be particularly controlling because an immigrant woman may be set apart from other possible social supports by language and cultural differences.

Whether wife abuse is more likely to occur in particular immigrant groups is controversial. However, there may well be a relationship between traditional expectations and the woman's ability to leave an abusive relationship. A recent study of ethnic differences among Anglo, black, and Hispanic women in a Texas shelter found that not only were Hispanic women burdened by language differences but also by larger families, less personal income, and more binding marital norms (Gondolf, Fisher, and McFerron, 1988).

The plight of the abused immigrant woman has been largely ignored by the social welfare system. Susan Schecter (1982) has documented the racism within both the battered women's movement and the broader system in the U.S. It would be dangerously complacent to assume the situation is different in Canada. The failure of the system in Canada to respond to the needs of the abused immigrant woman has been complicated by the problems associated with their admission to Canada. Many immigrant women enter Canada sponsored by their husbands and are therefore not eligible for a training allowance or subsidized day care to enable them to attend English-language classes, which reinforces their isolation. MacLeod's study (1987) also suggests that the fear of deportation and possible negative experiences with police in their home country are other factors serving to isolate the abused immigrant woman. Should a sponsored immigrant wish to leave her husband, the welfare office must be convinced that the sponsorship relationship has been dissolved before they will offer financial assistance. To obtain long-term financial assistance involves satisfying Employment and Immigration Canada that sponsorship has been severed. The complex procedures involved are mystifying and intimidating, particularly to women who do not speak English and are fearful of being deported.

However, some policy and program changes that attempt to redress the disadvantages experienced by immigrant women have been instituted. One example is the Cultural Interpreter Service Project recently funded in several communities by the Ontario Ministry of Citizenship and Culture. A cultural interpreter is someone who speaks English and another language, is ethnic-sensitive, and has knowledge of the issues of wife abuse. The Project provides cultural interpretation to abused women, shelter workers, and, where funding allows, to other service providers. Such projects symbolize an increasing recognition of some of the difficulties faced by abused immigrant women and the need for government support to address them. In addition, shelters are being specifically designed to meet the needs of different groups of immigrants.

THE SUPPORT OF FAMILY, FRIENDS, AND NEIGHBOURS

When women are confronted with abuse, they most often turn to informal sources of help (Pahl, 1985). Natural support networks are based on mutual caring and have played an important role in providing women with the first indication that there are options available to them. Some women have found it difficult to seek and receive help from friends and family. Other women are isolated and have limited friends to whom they can turn. The hurdles are particularly difficult for two groups: those who keep the abuse to themselves and those who reach out but do not find the help they are looking for. The boundary between these two groups is fluid. A woman's perceptions about the availability of help may influence the likelihood of her seeking it. As well, the pattern of seeking help may change throughout the marriage (Dobash and Dobash, 1979).

The factors that deter a woman from reaching out to her family, friends, or neighbours include her belief that the violence will stop without outside intervention, her feelings of shame and guilt that she is failing in her marriage, and her internalization of the value of privacy and the sanctity of the home (Dobash and Dobash, 1979). These values and attitudes are socially and culturally determined, and they encourage women to believe "they would do better to continue to cope with the known, hidden problem than to take on the unknown, public risks associated with identifying themselves as a victim of battering" (Greaves, Heapy, and Wylie, 1988: 46).

Whether the informal network is told or simply knows, however, "A conspiracy of silence often develops" (Walker, 1979: 145). Friends and family are as much imbued with the values and attitudes identified above as are the abused woman and her husband, and they are often not supportive, or only are so in very restricted ways. Rebecca and Russell Dobash found that when an abused woman approached her parents she was generally looking for help in the form of a sympathetic ear and temporary shelter. Both may be offered, although not in all instances, but the message to the daughter is that she should not stay for long and that the parents do not have the right to intervene. As the Dobash study (1979: 174) noted: "Much of the emotional and material assistance offered battered women reflects various beliefs about the privacy of the home, the inviolability of marriage and the family and the hierarchical relationship between husbands and wives." The duty to care for her husband and children may override the need for an abused woman's own care and safety.

Like family members, neighbours may be ambivalent about providing support to an abused woman, and indeed may not have the resources to do so. Concerned about maintaining a respectable and untroubled community, neighbours are usually reluctant to become involved in what they consider private domestic disputes. High-profile cases such as that of Joel Steinberg and Hedda Nussbaum in New York, which involved extreme child and wife abuse, highlight the failure of neighbours to intervene, despite their knowledge of abuse (*Newsweek*, 1988).

In Jane Stafford's case, her parents, her in-laws, her friends and neighbours, and her co-workers knew at some level that Jane was being abused. Her father comments:

Jane never mentioned it to me. I guess if it would have got out, well, he'd probably have killed her for sure. Jane used to wear dark glasses, but I didn't know this was going on. If she had a bruise or something, I'd say, "How'd you do that Jane?" She'd tell me she bumped into something. (Vallee, 1986: 83)

Jane's father had, on one occasion at least, been the target of Billy's violence himself.

Despite the limitations of friends, families, and neighbours – traditional networks of support – in meeting the needs of abused women, they have been instrumental in bringing the issue of wife abuse to the attention of the public. Natural helping networks, while offering necessary emotional support to abused women, cannot be expected to provide on-going material support such as housing and financial help. These needs have been more commonly identified by the feminist movement, which has played an important role in developing programs and resources for battered women.

SERVICES FOR ABUSED WOMEN

The provision of services for abused women increased dramatically in the 1980s. Much of this has been undertaken by the transition house movement in Canada, which has extended its services to include support and counselling as well as emergency shelter.[1] As well, there has been an effort to expand resources for a more diverse group of women, such as aboriginals, immigrants, and the disabled. Abused women themselves have worked to achieve changes in the service delivery systems.

The pressures abused women face in caring for and about their families are gradually being recognized by shelter workers, who are demonstrating a greater understanding of the experience of abused women. Co-operating and sharing ideas and knowledge among women from shelters operating under different auspices have further facilitated knowledge about wife abuse and the ways in which women have coped with violence. MacLeod's study highlights how staff have gained an increased awareness of the difficulties facing the abused woman:

> When we first started this house I guess in retrospect some of us just assumed that if a woman came to us, she must want to leave her husband. We also thought that if she didn't want to leave, she should because no woman should live with brutality. We didn't want to make decisions for her, to force her to do anything she didn't want to do. We just wanted to do what was best for her. . . . We now know that most of the women we see aren't ready to leave their husbands and may never want to leave. We've tried to see the men through slightly more sympathetic eyes, in the way their wives see them. (MacLeod, 1987: 55)

By comprehending the contradictions that women's caring poses for women, transition house staff are less likely to condemn or reject the women who return to abusive marriages.

While these changes can be applauded, there has also been a drive to "professionalize" shelter staff, which may increase the distance between abused women and shelter workers. An emphasis on credentials, the hiring of male staff, the adoption of hierarchical administrative structures, and the development of "professional" boards of directors are abrupt departures from the feminist ideology underlying the transition house movement. Some shelter workers have expressed their concern that transition houses are becoming mainstream and may end up revictimizing women (MacLeod, 1987).

Although shelters are gradually becoming part of the formal social welfare delivery system and have become more responsive to the needs of abused women, other more traditional social service organizations have not made the same gains in expanding their resources or support for abused women. The relative poverty most women experience if they leave their husbands is a critical factor in their decision to separate (Greaves, Wylie, and Heapy, 1988). In Chapter VI, Patricia Evans clearly outlines the poverty experienced by so many single mothers. The drop in income is significant not only in economic terms but also because it brings with it a loss of stability of environment and social contact (Eichler, 1988).

Lack of affordable housing remains a central problem. For some abused women who leave, the first stop is a shelter. As noted above, the number of shelters in Canada has more than quadrupled since 1979, but there remains an acute shortage of space. Women in rural areas have few resources available to them and are particularly disadvantaged. Inadequate funding for existing shelters causes serious problems for ongoing operations and future planning. Although strides have been made in developing public awareness about the problem of wife abuse, it has coincided with government cutbacks on social service spending that have severely retarded the development of outreach, preventive, or follow-up programs for abused women (MacLeod, 1989). Of equal concern are the limited second-stage housing options available for women who choose not to return to their husbands but require a longer stay than most shelters will allow.

For the abused woman whose psychological, social, and economic resources are already severely depleted, the path of separation and divorce is a daunting one. Although social workers and others involved in counselling might be expected to show a greater understanding of wife abuse, this is often not the case (Maynard, 1985). One major problem is that professionals often see their function as keeping the family together (Dobash and Dobash, 1979). Wife abuse is understood all too often as a symptom of family pathology, with the resulting effect that the victim is held responsible for the violence (Bograd, 1984). Again, there are some encouraging signs of change with the gradual inclusion in social work curricula of the issue of wife abuse and the use of manuals, such as those by Deborah Sinclair (1985) and David Currie (1988), for in-service training.

Abused women often report experiences of revictimization by other social institutions. Attempts to draw attention to the failure of the "system" to act on behalf of abused women have been illustrated in a number of Canadian films. A poignant example of this is portrayed in *Loved, Honoured and Bruised*, the National Film Board (1980) story of Jeannie, a woman from a farm in Manitoba who after sixteen years of abuse leaves her husband and takes her children to Winnipeg. The film shows how the judicial and welfare systems revictimize her, although with support from other women she is ultimately strong enough to survive. Wife abuse is now a criminal offence, yet institutions continue to a greater or lesser extent to reflect the patriarchal attitudes that justify it (Dobash and Dobash, 1979; Pagelow, 1981; Pahl, 1985).

The criminal justice system has taken some positive steps to respond to abused women. In 1982, the Solicitor General issued a policy directive that the police must lay charges in all cases of wife abuse where reasonable and probable grounds exist. There is evidence of the success of this policy in London, Ontario, where the implementation of police guidelines resulted in a dramatic increase in the number of charges laid, an increased feeling of support from the police by victims, and a decrease in recidivism (Jaffe, Wolfe, Telford, and Austin, 1986). These findings, however, cannot be generalized to other communities where there are no clear procedures and where the police often choose not to lay charges, suggesting rather that the woman lay them herself (Freedman, 1985; MacLeod, 1989). When women fail to do this, the response is often "victim blaming" (Burris and Jaffe, 1984). The lack of sanctions for abusive men can only give wives the message that it remains their individual problem, and husbands the message that they can use force with impunity (Carmody and Williams, 1987).

Medical personnel are often the first ones an abused woman will turn to for help. Although she may not offer information about the source of her injuries, studies reveal that she is often not asked. An American study found that only one in thirty-five abused women who went to an emergency room for treatment was identified (Stark, Flitcraft, and Frazier, 1979). When abused women are recognized they are often viewed negatively (Dobash and Dobash, 1979). Interviews with physicians showed that over a half do not view the detection and management of wife abuse as "real medicine" (Borkowski, Murch, and Walker, 1983). Some shelter workers in Canada continue to express concern that family physicians are "still telling women to try to be a better wife and their husband will behave" (MacLeod, 1987: 103). The quality of medical care will often determine whether a woman will follow through with a referral to social services, legal, and other health care agencies (Mehta and Dandrea, 1988). A Canadian physician, Barbara Lent (1986), also suggests that a physician's response to wife abuse has important implications for preventive health care.

Nonetheless, there are signs of change. Gradually, medical training is incorporating knowledge about wife abuse. The Ontario Medical Association set up a Committee on Wife Assault in 1986, which is doing some important educative and advocacy work. In over half the provinces, protocols have been developed to help hospital staff respond more effectively to the problem.

The clergy have also encountered difficulties in responding to the needs of battered women. Ministers are often viewed by these women as lacking knowledge and sensitivity (Fortune, 1983). In her Foreword to the Task Force Report to the General Synod of the Anglican Church of Canada (1986: 3) on violence against women, Marie Fortune argues that the church needs to acknowledge "its collusion in the patriarchal prerogative . . . its role in prescribing abuse as fitting behaviour for husbands . . . its role in promulgating a theory which excuses wife battering . . . its savage ignorance which has rendered it helpless to minister to women's suffering."

While these are only some of the criticisms levelled against social institutions, abused women can provide more powerful examples not only of how they did not receive the care they were seeking but of how the interventions that were made were destructive, revictimizing them and their children. Jane Stafford's experience illustrates how her perception that help would not be available or effective dictated her actions, compounded by the difficulty of access to services experienced by rural women.

> Billy Stafford's parents, my parents, and the entire community (including the RCMP) knew him and what he was capable of. Yet everyone was helpless. . . . I knew nothing about women's crisis centres. Even if I had known, I had no telephone or transportation. (Vallee, 1986: xi)

Jane Stafford survived her marriage by killing her husband. During her trial she was asked by the crown attorney, Blaire Allaby:

> You never enquired about any way the situation could be relieved other than killing Billy?
> Jane: If I'd have left there would have been a lot more people killed than Bill.
> Allaby: That was your feeling?
> Jane: That I knew. (Vallee, 1986: 162)

Jane now lives in Nova Scotia and, after qualifying as a nursing assistant, works in a caring capacity and continues to be involved in advocating for abused women. Other women, such as Francine Hughes, whose story is told in *The Burning Bed* (McNulty, 1981), and the women interviewed by Angela Browne (1987), are also pushed to the desperate extreme of homicide in order to achieve freedom. In the next section we will briefly examine one particular program designed to prevent women from having to endure the kind of nightmare that drives them to homicide as the only way out.

CHANGE: AN EXAMPLE

Many of the effective programs designed to resolve the problem of wife abuse have been developed by women – those who have been abused and women committed to feminism. The telling of Jane Stafford's story is an example of one kind of public education:

> I want this book to be written, not for myself but for all of those others out there who are living the same hell as I did. If even one person picks up the book and is helped by it, that will be reward enough. I hope it also helps professionals understand the dynamics of abusive relationships. (Vallee, 1986: xii)

Any proposed solution to wife abuse must go beyond attempts to offer service to the women who have been abused and to the men who have abused them (MacLeod, 1989). Providing adequate funding to programs directed at second-stage housing and to treatment programs for the children who have witnessed violence and are seen as high-risk candidates for long-term emotional adjustment problems are immediate goals (Jaffe, Wilson, and Wolfe, 1988).

One innovative example of an attempt to change the values and attitudes that institutionalize the power of men over women was started in 1986 by the Lincoln Public School Board of Education in Ontario, which introduced a kindergarten to grade 12 curriculum, *Personal Safety: We Care*. The goal is to provide students with age-appropriate knowledge, skills, and attitudes to enable them to respond to problems posed by child abuse, sexual assault, and wife abuse. The project includes a curriculum guide for all grades, a program of in-service training for school staff, orientation sessions for parents, and a series of pamphlets for students and their parents to be used at home. The initial evaluation from teachers, students, and parents has been positive, as has feedback from teachers and students that the goals of the program are generally being achieved (Lincoln County, 1986). On the basis of this evaluation, the program is continuing.

Changes in values and attitudes are slow and must be evaluated over time. It is hoped that other school boards will build on the work of Lincoln County and demonstrate the same kind of commitment to children. Programs such as *Personal Safety: We Care* must be recognized as essential and given adequate financial support if the values and institutions that condone and perpetuate wife abuse are to be changed.

However, whether individually focused or directed at crisis intervention or prevention, programs need to be developed along with policies that take into consideration the work of women in both the private and public spheres of life. More far-reaching strategies are essential to achieve long-term change in the structures and values that institutionalize the power of men over women. In marriage this includes the institutionalization of the norms of equality, mutuality, and reciprocity, as opposed to those of personal service and enforced compliance. As long as caring for and about others remains solely women's work, the wife in most marriages will continue to be relegated to a subordinate position and vulnerable to abuse.

CONCLUSION

This chapter has explored how the concept of caring adds to our understanding of wife abuse. It has been argued that the imperative to care is a causative factor in wife abuse and the entrapment of a wife in an abusive marriage. As such, it interacts with other social, economic, psychological, and physical factors.

The focus has been on women entrapped in abusive marriages. Some women do manage to overcome the many obstacles and leave. "It is the pragmatic weighing of the risks and benefits (or potential for improvement) on all dimensions . . . that determines the decision to stay or to leave" (Greaves, Heapy, and Wylie, 1988). The latter study suggests that women may be most ready to leave when their hopes for improvement in the marriage, generated by change in one or several factors, are dashed by new violence. The "final straw" is inflicted and the wife is no longer prepared to stay.

It is important that the strengths of caring that women have offered within marriage, and which have often forced them to remain in highly turbulent relationships over long periods of time, be recognized as strengths that can be generalized "to leaving, to beginning a new life, to survival, and to the establishment and maintenance of more constructive relationships in the future" (Browne, 1987: 87). In analysing the dynamics of caring there is a danger that caring will be construed as a weakness and that the ideal will be perceived as opting for the safety of a model of autonomy, thus avoiding the risks inherent in providing care. For women it is a question of being in a relationship where the strengths of caring are nurtured through respect and reciprocity.

NOTE

1. In 1987, there were 230 shelters for abused women in Canada, an

increase from the seventy-one that existed in 1971 (MacLeod, 1987: 50).

REFERENCES

Baker Miller, J. 1977. *Toward a New Psychology of Women*. Boston: Beacon Press.

Bograd, M. 1984. "Family systems approach to wife battering: A feminist critique," *American Journal of Orthopsychiatry*, 54: 558–68.

Bograd, M. 1988. "Feminist perspectives on wife abuse: An introduction," in K. Yllo and M. Bograd, eds., *Feminist Perspectives on Wife Abuse*. Beverly Hills: Sage Publications.

Borkowski, M., M. Murch, and V. Walker. 1983. *Marital Violence: The Community Response*. London: Tavistock.

Breines, W., and L. Gordon. 1983. "The new scholarship on family violence," *Signs: Journal of Women in Culture and Society*, 8: 490–531.

Browne, A. 1987. *When Battered Women Kill*. New York: Free Press.

Burris, C.A., and P. Jaffe. 1984. "Wife battering: A well-kept secret," *Canadian Journal of Criminology*, 26, 2: 171–77.

Carmody, D., and K. Williams. 1987. "Wife assault and perception of sanctions," *Violence and Victims*, 2, 1.

Currie, D. 1988. *The Abusive Husband: An Approach to Intervention*. Ottawa: Health and Welfare Canada.

Dalley, G. 1988. *Ideologies of Caring: Rethinking Community and Collectivism*. London: Macmillan.

Dobash, R.E., and R. Dobash. 1979. *Violence Against Wives: A Case Against the Patriarchy*. New York: Free Press.

Eichler, M. 1988. *Families in Canada Today: Recent Changes and Their Policy Consequences*. Toronto: Gage.

Finch, J., and D. Groves. 1983. *A Labour of Love*. London: Routledge and Kegan Paul.

Fortune, M. 1983. *Sexual Violence: The Unmentionable Sin*. New York: Pilgrim Press.

Freedman, L. 1985. "Wife assault," in C. Guberman and M. Wolfe, eds., *No Safe Place: Violence Against Women and Children*. Toronto: Women's Press.

Gelles, R.J. 1977. "Violence and pregnancy: A note on the extent of the problem and needed services," *Family Co-ordinator*, 26: 81–86.

Giles-Sims, J. 1983. *Wife Battering: A Systems Theory Approach*. New York: Guildford Press.

Gilligan, C. 1982. *In a Different Voice*. Cambridge, Mass.: Harvard University Press.

Gondolf, E.W., E. Fisher, and J.R. McFerron. 1988. "Racial differences among shelter residents: A comparison of Anglo, Black, and Hispanic battered," *Journal of Family Violence*, 3, 1: 39-51.

Gordon, Linda. 1988. *Heroes of Their Own Lives*. New York: Viking Press.

Greaves, L., N. Heapy, and A. Wylie. 1988. "Advocacy services: Reassessing the profile and needs of battered women," *Canadian Journal of Community Mental Health*, 7, 2: 39-51.

Hotaling, G.T., and D.B. Sugarman. 1986. "An analysis of risk markers in husband to wife violence: The current state of knowledge," *Violence and Victims*, 1, 2: 101-24.

Jaffe, P., W. Wilson, and D. Wolfe. 1988. "Specific assessment and intervention strategies for children exposed to wife battering: Preliminary empirical investigations," *Canadian Journal of Community Mental Health*, 7, 2: 157-63.

Jaffe, P., D. Wolfe, A. Telford, and G. Austin. 1986. "The impact of police charges in incidents of wife abuse," *Journal of Family Violence*, 1, 1: 37-49.

Kelly, L. 1988. *Surviving Sexual Violence*. Minneapolis: University of Minnesota Press.

Kincaid, P.J. 1982. *The Omitted Reality: Husband-Wife Violence in Ontario and Policy Implications for Education*. Concord, Ont.: Belsten Publishing.

Lent, B. 1986. "Diagnosing wife assault," *Canadian Family Physician*, 32: 547-49.

Lincoln County Board of Education. 1986. *Personal Safety: We Care*.

MacLeod, L. 1980. *Wife Battering in Canada: The Vicious Circle*. Ottawa: Canadian Advisory Council on the Status of Women.

MacLeod, L. 1987. *Battered but Not Beaten . . . Preventing Wife Beating in Canada*. Ottawa: Canadian Advisory Council on the Status of Women.

MacLeod, L. 1989. "Wife Battering and the Web of Hope: Progress, Dilemmas and Visions of Prevention," discussion paper for Working Together: National Forum on Family Violence. Ottawa: Health and Welfare Canada.

Maynard, M. 1985. "The response of social workers to domestic violence," in J. Pahl, ed., *Private Violence and Public Policy*. London: Routledge and Kegan Paul.

McNulty, F. 1981. *The Burning Bed*. New York: Bantam Books.

Mehta, P., and L.A. Dandrea. 1988. "The battered woman," *American Family Physician*, 37, 1: 193-99.

Newsweek. 1988. "A Tale of Abuse," December 12: 56-61.

Pagelow, M.D. 1981. *Woman-Battering: Victims and Their Experiences*. Beverly Hills: Sage Publications.

Pahl, J., ed. 1985. *Private Violence and Public Policy*. London: Routledge and Kegan Paul.

Pressman, B.M. 1984. *Family Violence: Origins and Treatment*. Guelph, Ont.: Children's Aid Society of the City of Guelph and the County of Wellington.

Ruitort, M. 1986. "Violence and The Immigrant Woman," paper presented at the Faculty of Social Work, University of Toronto.

Ruitort, M., and S.E. Small. 1985. *Working with Assaulted Immigrant Women: A Handbook for Lay Counsellors*. Toronto: Education Wife Assault.

Schecter, S. 1982. *Women and Male Violence: The Visions and Struggles of the Battered Women's Movement*. Boston: South End Press.

Sinclair, D. 1985. *Understanding Wife Assault*. Toronto: Ontario Ministry of Community and Social Services.

Stark, E., A. Flitcraft, and W. Frazier. 1979. "Medicine and patriarchal violence: The social construction of a 'private' event," *International Journal of Health Services*, 9, 3: 461-93.

Szado, D. 1987. "Social roots of wife battering: An examination of the phenomenon in Mediterranean immigrant communities," *Canadian Women Studies*, 8, 2: 41-42.

Task Force Report to the General Synod of the Anglican Church of Canada. 1986. *Violence Against Women: Abuse in Society and Church and Proposals for Change*. Toronto: Anglican Book Centre.

Vallee, B. 1986. *Life with Billy*. Toronto: Seal Books.

Waerness, K. 1984. "Caring as women's work in the welfare state," in H. Holter, ed., *Patriarchy in a Welfare Society*. Oslo: Universitetsforlaget.

Walker, L. 1979. *The Battered Woman*. New York: Harper and Row.

Wilson, M., and M. Daly. 1987. "Spousal Homicide in Canada," paper presented at the Third National Family Violence Research Conference, University of New Hampshire.

Zambrano, M. 1985. *Mejor Sola Que Mal Accompanado: For the Latina in an Abusive Relationship*. Washington: Seal Press.

CHAPTER VIII

Contradictions in Child Welfare: Neglect and Responsibility

Karen Swift

INTRODUCTION

This chapter deals with the issue of caring for children. It examines both the concept of child neglect and the caring work performed by women, which has remained a hidden reality of the issue of child neglect. I will explore ways in which caring has come to be discounted and ignored in the public and professional discourse about child neglect and examine the problems faced by mothers on child welfare caseloads in caring for their children. The analysis focuses on two themes. First, the traditional relationship between the state and the private family is shown to be crucial to the way we think about caring for children. The social work response to neglect, characterized by contradictory mandates both to help the family and to exercise authority over negligent mothers, is a reflection of this relationship. The second, and closely related theme, is the gendered division of labour in our society through which mothers become the primary and often the only providers of care for children. Through an elaboration of these themes, I will propose how we might learn to understand and to address the issues of neglect and caring very differently.

The analysis presented here is based partly on a research project carried out in a Canadian child welfare agency. The study is an example of "institutional ethnography," a research design that facilitates an understanding of the actual operation of an organizational setting (Smith, 1987). The project focused on verified cases of child neglect and involved a detailed study of the case files of selected families, followed by interviews with workers about these families. I wanted to find out how child welfare workers come to identify and understand neglectful behaviour in the context of an organizational setting.

The analysis was accomplished through an alternate view of understanding and developing knowledge about child neglect than that which has ordinarily been employed in child welfare research. This approach is grounded in the writing of Marx and Engels (1947), has been expanded through the work of ethnomethodologists (Garfinkel, 1967; Cicourel, 1976), and more recently has been used in feminist research (Smith, 1987). In this approach, reality is not viewed as obvious. Instead, it contains surface realities, which appear to us as self-evident, as well as hidden realities, which enter into and organize that which appears on the surface. With respect to child neglect, the case material upon which so much knowledge about neglect has been based can be viewed as the surface reality. An exploration of the underlying processes through which case material is produced can suggest new understandings of the surface realities and the social purposes they serve. In this chapter, the underlying realities are represented by two central themes – state-family relationships and the gendered division of labour.

The value of this approach is that it allows us to perceive and examine features of experience that otherwise remain submerged under the rubric of "fact," and it directs us to use this knowledge for change. We read many "facts" about child neglect, and we are encouraged to understand social policies and programs as the logical responses to these facts. My purpose is to probe the realities underneath the apparent facts in order to understand the effects of our policies and to identify new directions. I will briefly sketch the "facts of neglect" as they are usually presented in child welfare literature and review the main components of the social policy response to it. I will pose this view against an analysis based on the model described. Finally, I will propose some ideas for change in our current social response to the care of children.

CHILD NEGLECT: A BRIEF HISTORY

The concept of child neglect reflects an historical relationship between the state and the family. The fundamental concept shaping this relationship is known as *parens patriae*, literally meaning "parent of the nation." *Parens patriae* is deeply rooted in English history, with its origins in the medieval reign of Edward I (Custer, 1978). The doctrine was codified in English law in 1765 and later became part of both the American and Canadian legal structures. It is a doctrine that can be used with the humanitarian intent of protecting children from the excesses of their parents, but it also provides a power and rationale for considerable state intervention into private family life. This doctrine and the power of the state provide the framework for child welfare as we know it, and the concept underlies the legislation and social policy that have developed to deal with neglect and other child welfare issues (Farina, 1982).

Linda Gordon (1988) notes that child neglect as we currently think of it was "discovered" in North America around the turn of the century. The issue of neglect in Canada, however, has its roots in the poverty and abandonment of large numbers of children in the earliest years of industrialization. Although many children were an asset to their parents in the early years of settlement, by 1799 sufficient numbers of children had been orphaned or abandoned in Upper Canada that legislation for their protection was thought to be necessary. The first legislation was the Act for the Education and Support of Orphans or Children Deserted by their Parents, and it provided for the binding out of children as apprentices. Through this Act, public responsibility for protecting children outside the family was established in Canada.

Toward the end of the nineteenth century, several sets of conditions conspired to produce organizational and legislative action for more explicit measures to protect children. During these years, thousands of homeless children were sent to Canada from the United Kingdom and placed as apprentices. Some placements did not work out and many of these children eventually made their way to urban centres, especially Toronto, where their poverty became a visible problem (Sutherland, 1976). In addition, the intensity of the processes of industrialization during the 1880s and 1890s produced conditions of homelessness and exploitation for many Canadian children of the working class. These same processes also produced a new middle class whose standard of living rapidly increased. The social context for this group, especially for women with increased leisure, allowed time and energy for social change. The efforts of these women to effect change are explored by Carol Baines in Chapter II.

Out of these conditions grew a social reform movement directed toward improving the living conditions of deprived children, known at the time as "child saving" (Jones and Rutman, 1981). This movement helped to establish the first Children's Aid Society in Canada in 1891 and was instrumental in promoting legislation in Ontario that applied to children living with their own families as well as to those who were abandoned or orphaned. Ontario legislation in 1888 articulated the principle of the state's right to evaluate the suitability of a child's environment and to remove a child from that environment if it is deemed to be in the child's interests. This Act laid the groundwork for more specific child welfare legislation passed in 1893, addressing the Prevention of Cruelty To and Better Protection of Children. A neglected child was defined by this legislation in the following ways:

- a child who is found begging or receiving alms;
- a child who is found wandering about without any home or proper guardianship;
- a child who is found associating or dwelling with a thief, drunkard, or vagrant and growing up without salutary parental control;
- a child who is found in any house of ill-fame or the company of a reputed prostitute;
- a child who is found destitute, being an orphan or having a surviving parent undergoing punishment for crime.

Assumed in these definitions is that children require safe and stable living conditions and that these conditions should be provided by parents or suitable guardians. The role of the state is to ensure that this occurs. In this we see an important feature in the relation of state and family codified in law: that the first responsibility of the state is not that of supplying care for children but of enforcing needed care through the medium of the family. This perception of the role of the state grew out of ideas firmly embedded in English Common Law identifying parental responsibilities for the maintenance, protection, and education of their children. As Farina (1982) notes, these ideas, published by Blackstone, who codified English Common Law in the latter half of the eighteenth century, produced the framework for subsequent family law in Canada.

The 1893 legislation also established several of the cornerstones of child welfare practice designed to protect children when parents failed to provide adequately. The newly formed Children's Aid Societies, the administrative arm of the law, were charged with enforcement of standards of care and parental behaviour. Thus, the focus for the societies was from the beginning organized around the case-by-case supervision of particular families. Also, the reformers believed, along with their American counterparts, that the family was the proper source of nurture for children (Falconer and Swift, 1983). They opposed group and institutional care and fought successfully for the incorporation into the legislation of a foster care model of substitute care for children who could not or did not live in families of their own. Finally, although poverty and exploitation became relevant issues in the fight for Mothers' Allowances early in the twentieth century, the early reformers did not include these "social" issues in their reform agenda. Consequently, built into the legislation and organizational policy from the beginning was the idea that the family was primarily responsible for its own destiny and the state was responsible for the enforcement of this ideal.

The traditions of the "friendly visitors" inherited by the first child welfare workers perpetuated and elaborated this approach (Lubove, 1965). The duties of visitors were spelled out early on. They were to "visit each applicant, to examine particularly into her moral character, her situation, her habits and modes of life, her wants and the best means of affording relief" (Treudley, 1980: 136). Child welfare workers retained the investigative functions of the early visitors along with some discretion to establish the eligibility of clients for whatever resources might be available. In the early years of child welfare, extra resources were rarely available, and often consisted of personal contributions from the workers themselves.[1] Nevertheless, in principle, the responses established through the original legislation and by the first child welfare workers represent the same three elements of service that Kadushin (1967: 23) outlined as the basis of child welfare: (1) protection, to help parents "enact their roles in a more socially acceptable manner" and the "apprehension" or removal of children from homes found to be unsuitable; (2) supplementary services, the "second line of defense"; and (3) substitute services, both temporary and permanent. Thus, even at this early stage, the contradictory roles of enforcement and help were enshrined in child welfare practice.

CURRENT ISSUES

The stage set by the first legislation and reformers remains a framework for understanding child neglect in contemporary times. The emphases on the moral attributes of individual parents, especially mothers, and on enforcing and improving care of children within the family continue to be primary issues for the attention of child welfare authorities. The power of the state to intervene in family life continues as the dominant force in child welfare.

Neglect was the issue around which child welfare legislative and administrative activity revolved until the 1960s. In the last three decades, physical and sexual abuse have become more prominent issues than neglect, although a great deal of the day-to-day work in child welfare agencies continues to fall into the category of neglect. Diminished attention to neglect is reflected by the fact that this term has become less prominent in some provincial legislation,[2] as well as by the relatively small proportion of recent child welfare literature dealing with this topic. When neglect has served as the focal point, the debate centres on how intrusive the power of *parens patriae* should be.

The discretionary use of this power by social workers has been strenuously criticized. The basic dispute, in an era characterized by rights movements of all kinds, has been whether state intrusion into private family life has occurred too frequently and too extensively. Critics such as Wald (1976) and Mnookin (1973) suggest that social workers are imposing middle-class values of child care on poor and culturally different populations. They suggest a criterion of actual and demonstrable harm to a child as the minimum grounds necessary to justify child welfare intrusion into the family. The definition of harm as "physical injury" and "emotional disability" contained in recent provincial legislation indicates that legislators have moved to the position of stronger protection of family autonomy. Manitoba's legislation states, for example, that families and children have a right to the "least interference" with their affairs compatible with "the best interests of children," a phrasing that emphasizes the role of enforcement rather than one of support and assistance.

In Canada, the "rights" issue has been sharpened and expanded by critics from the native community. Although native families complained for many years about the treatment they received from child welfare agencies and workers, only in the 1970s and 1980s did these complaints become political issues. Published work, by Patrick Johnston (1983) for example, documented the "sixties scoop," a term that refers to the vast numbers of native children permanently removed from their families during the 1960s, often on charges of neglect. Native leaders criticized authorities for failing to understand the cultural differences in family life and child care between natives and the dominant culture, and also for failing to realize the difficulties of caring for children under the conditions of poverty and dislocation experienced by so many natives. The politicization of these issues has also resulted in specific legislative changes aimed at protecting the rights of native families and children, and in some cases has also led to the development of child welfare organizations run by and for natives.[3]

DEFINING NEGLECT

Closely related to the rights question is the issue of defining neglect. A precise definition, it is suggested, would provide child welfare workers with clear guidelines as to when intrusion into the family is necessary. Consequently, a good portion of scholarly discussion of neglect is taken up with definitional problems. Typically, neglect is referred to in the social work literature as a "problem of omission," whereas abuse is viewed as a "crime of commission." Neglect is usually characterized descriptively: "the child is found to be living in filth, malnourished, without proper clothing, unattended and unsupervised" (Kadushin, 1967: 210). Such descriptions generally distinguish among the different "types" of neglect identified in child welfare literature: physical, emotional, moral, and educational.

Research concerned with neglect has often involved intensive efforts to define neglect in more precise terms. Polansky (1972, 1981), for instance, developed a complex scale based on the concept of "adequacy of caring." The scale was used to rate mothers along a continuum from poor to excellent, with ratings at the lower end of the scale suggesting neglect. Giovannoni and Becerra (1979) asked both professional and lay people to respond to a series of vignettes in an attempt to determine what various sectors of the population define as neglect and abuse. James Garbarino (1981) based his work on an "ecological" model emphasizing interaction between the family and its surroundings. He defines maltreatment of children as a violation of community or scientific standards of the expected development of children, an approach that explicitly relies on social norms as a feature of the problem definition.

This concept that social norms are intrinsic to the definition is sometimes expressed in child welfare literature as the "relative" nature of neglect, meaning that what is seen as neglect in one context may not be seen as neglect in another context. This phenomenon has been well documented in recent research. Isabel Wolock (1982), for instance, found that workers rate specific cases of neglect in relation to the prevailing norms in their area. Workers in districts with more severe cases of maltreatment used a lower standard of care to define a case as neglect. Jill Korbin (1980) discusses neglect from a cultural perspective and shows that child-care practices considered normal by North American parents would be considered neglectful by parents of other cultures. Others (e.g., Austin, 1981) have shown that the way a case is categorized relates to resource availability; thus, if funding and programs are not available to assist in problems characterized as neglect, then a case is less likely to be assessed as neglect.

In summary, a great deal of energy has been devoted to determining what constitutes neglect, in order to clarify for social workers appropriate grounds for intervention into the private family. Both the definitional and the rights debates are closely related to and, in fact, grow out of the framework established by the original child welfare legislation, which relies on the investigation of individual families to ensure that specific parental duties are carried out.

THE CAUSES AND CURES OF NEGLECT

Although not often explicitly expressed, discussions of neglect always imply that mothers are responsible. Fathers are rarely mentioned in this literature. When fathers are mentioned, it is usually to exonerate them (McCord, 1983) or to connect them to the mother's inadequacy in choosing them (Polansky *et al.*, 1972). Mothers are seen as so central to the issue of neglect that some definitions of the problem specifically name them. David Gil (1970: 31), for instance, defines neglect as a "breakdown in the ability to mother."

The dominant perspective on causation in the child welfare literature is that neglect is caused by the immaturity of particular mothers. Neglecting mothers are described as "children themselves" (Young, 1964); "child-like, pleasure-seeking, irresponsible and impulsive" (Katz, 1971); and "infantile" (Polansky, 1972, 1981). Since mothers are so heavily implicated in the cause of neglect, the literature on treatment is generally aimed at changing the behaviour of mothers and improving their performance in the mothering role (Swift, 1988). Suggestions over the past two decades have focused on meeting the mother's emotional needs and, more recently, have concentrated on upgrading the mother's "parenting skills."[4]

A prominent sub-theme of causation, and one upon which virtually all students of neglect agree, is that neglecting mothers are poor. Why this should be so has been the subject of considerable attention in the literature. The problem usually attended to by researchers is the question of why some poor mothers neglect while others do not (Jones and McNeely, 1980). Traditionally, this issue has been explained by psychological inadequacies in the mothers (Young, 1964; Polansky, 1972). Leroy Pelton (1981) takes a different view, arguing that the material circumstances of poverty increase "the hazards of a mother's neglect."

A more comprehensive approach has been to examine the interaction of several factors to explain neglect. Jeanne Giovannoni and Andrew Billingsley (1970) identify poverty, single-parent status, marital disruption, and number of children as important interacting factors related to neglect. Isabel Wolock and Bernard Horowitz (1979) suggest that deprivation of the parents themselves, social isolation, and higher than average numbers of children are significant factors. In a later study, these researchers returned to a more clearly social explanation, finding neglecting parents to be "the poorest of the poor" (Horowitz and Wolock, 1981). Even though poverty has been found by some to be the root cause of neglect and by others as a critical factor in producing neglect, this theme remains mysteriously in the background of literature on the issue. The bulk of literature continues to be treatment-oriented and to focus on the deficiencies of particular mothers (for Canadian exceptions, see Callahan, 1985; Martin, 1985).

THE STATE'S RESPONSE TO CHILD NEGLECT

Social work has become more professional and bureaucratic during the past century. However, agencies continue to be directed by the three basic functions of protection, supplementary care, and substitute care. The primary feature of the state's response to child neglect continues to be one of "protecting" children through enforcement of parental duty, with support and substitute care available in some measure when the family's care is deemed to be inadequate. Social workers continue to investigate, supervise, counsel, and provide advice and resources.

The supplementary role of child welfare has broadened considerably, especially over the past two decades. A wide array of support services can be made available to clients of child welfare agencies. Examples of these include income support, medical services, recreational groups, child care, educational resources, housing, homemakers, and institutional settings for disturbed children. One of the main tasks of workers in present-day settings is to ration these services and account for their distribution to particular clients. Thus, over time, resource provision has become more prominent, based on what we believe is needed to assist parents in their own homes.

Substitute care, when it is offered, continues to be based on the foster care model. The legal processes through which children may be removed temporarily or permanently from their homes have become complex over the past several decades. Court procedures and the worker's role in bringing a case to court require considerable time and effort. The "least intrusive" principle has been incorporated into some recent child welfare law and signifies the importance of "family autonomy" in our society and the political intent of present governments to preserve it. As Gillian Dalley (1988) points out, the growing conservatism of Western governments promotes the idea of family life as a buttress against the intrusions of the state. In child welfare, this principle means that workers are obligated to provide the least intrusive assistance compatible with protection of the child in the home, with removal only as a last resort. Thus, the time of workers is increasingly consumed by the legal process, and often there is little left over to devote to "helping" clients.

THE CURRENT PERCEPTION OF CHILD NEGLECT: SUMMARY

Neglect is usually viewed as the failure of individual mothers to carry out their responsibilities. Because the issue is embedded in a legislative context providing permanent removal of children from their natural families when mothers fail, a great deal of attention has been paid to definitional issues and to whether the family's right to autonomy should prevail over the right of children to be protected. The traditional and contemporary response of the state has been to provide an investigative service, mounted through provincially run child welfare departments or Children's Aid Societies, and legal channels through the courts to protect the rights of both parents and children. In this sense, neglect, along with other child welfare problems, has been "legalized"; that is, it generally becomes a visible issue through legal processes established to identify and act on it.

The professional social work response has been to provide various kinds of "treatment programs" aimed at the rehabilitation of inadequate mothers. Social work research on the issue has sought to understand neglect as a disease requiring treatment procedures. In this sense neglect has been "medicalized"; the help offered is ordinarily some kind of "treatment" designed to restore mothers and produce a higher or healthier level of mothering for their children.

RECONCEPTUALIZING CHILD NEGLECT

The account of neglect outlined above covers the main themes, issues, and problems described in the literature. The usual presentation of neglect, including its current interpretations, debates appearing in academic literature, and the state apparatus designed to address the issue, is ideological in form. By "ideological," I mean that the account masks and distorts the reality of everyday lived experience; society and social relations are instead represented "from the standpoint of their ruling and from the standpoint of men who do that ruling" (Smith, 1987: 2). This traditional account depends on the acceptance of the concepts and "facts" of neglect forming the "official view," and on the acceptance of state and professional responses as more or less appropriate, since they follow from this perspective.

Beneath these official views and responses, however, lies a world remaining to be explored. This is the often contradictory world of women, of mothers, of their work and caring activities, and of the context within which this occurs. This is a world organized by social, economic, and political forces of which we are usually aware, which are sometimes invoked by the relevant literature, but which are not ordinarily brought into the debates and discussions of child neglect. In this section the images and "instructions" for understanding that underlie this meaning of child neglect are examined. These socially structured images distort or direct our attention away from social forces that shape reality, and they are sustained through the discourse about neglect, that is, the "ongoing interchanges among 'experts' doing research and developing theories" (Griffith and Smith, 1987: 96). Discourse is not confined to academia or to the formal literature, but also provides ideas for newspapers, magazines, and television. In addition, it supplies links to educational material, so that ideas receive wide public dissemination, not only among adults but also among school-age children. Discourse on child neglect intersects and interacts with related discourses, for instance on the family and on mothering. I will examine two methods through which the usual presentation of neglect glosses over significant portions of reality. The first is through use of language, the second, certainly closely related, is through the presence of an implicit underlying schema for understanding both the issue itself and the state's response to it.

The Language of Neglect

In discourse, neglect is characterized by contradictory presentations of reality. For the most part, the usual language of research is employed. Such language assumes a fact-finding tone that suggests a disciplined search for truth. Polansky *et al.* (1972), in studying neglected children, asked the question why some children "come to live so poorly." In order to "advance theory" on this issue and to bring about change, the researchers considered a range of possible causes of neglect, which were eventually narrowed to two – poverty and the "pervasive inadequacy in the maternal personality." Mothers were then identified as the "crucial variable" in neglect.

Posed against this neutral language is the human face of suffering revealed in the descriptive language of the case example, as we see in this social worker's description of neglected children:

> they had sore crusts on their arms and legs. They were indescribably dirty, hair matted, body and hands stained and covered with spilled food particles. Sitting on a urine soaked and soiled mattress in a baby carriage behind them was a younger child. (Kadushin, 1967: 212)

Such a presentation invokes in the reader an immediately sympathetic response, and sometimes outrage. Most of us are touched by such suffering, and our sense of outrage is quite naturally directed at the responsible parties. We may notice that while the official research language directs our attention to mothers, the descriptive language evoking sympathy is usually about children. This contrast provides implicit instructions to readers as to how to regard mothers. We do not feel sympathetic toward them as we do toward the children; instead, we hold them responsible for the children's suffering. Often explicit reasons for doing so are provided, as in this example from my research, taken from the notes of a night-duty worker:

> Mom is drinking again. There was a passed-out male in the house, and a fire almost started as he was cooking when he collapsed. Kids say mom is drinking and they are "afraid of the guy." Place was a mess, empty beer bottles were scattered all over. Kids appeared neglected, baby was soaked, not changed for some time, and reeked of stale urine. No diapers in the house. Kids anxious to go with worker and were apprehended.

The mandates and organizational structures of child welfare agencies, which produce case material, also provide basic instructions for the way child neglect can be spoken about. Along with other child welfare issues, neglect is perceived and examined on a case-by-case basis. Investigations take place in the private domain, with particular families as their focus. It is important to recognize that these processes necessarily produce a particular view of the issue. The case-by-case approach instructs us to see the problem as individualized; our attention is directed to the unique circumstances and behaviours occurring in this particular family and to the specific effects on particular children. The legislative mandate tells us that neglect is an issue demanding intervention into these individual families by some system of justice. This way of organizing child welfare moves the social and economic issues affecting these families to the background. The tasks of workers are structured around determining the culpability of individual families and acting on those determinations. An issue such as poverty is not made actionable in such a system; data about its existence and effects are not gathered, and workers have no organizational or legal mandate to act on poverty as a problem. What becomes visible through this system must inevitably be questionable behaviours of individuals, and the language of case files reflects this.

As we have also seen, neglect of children always implicates parents, usually mothers. As Gerald DeMontigny (1980) points out, the mandate of child welfare does not entitle workers to protect children from environmentally caused dangers or from violence in the streets. This fact alone substantially narrows the mandate for protecting children. It suggests no social responsibility for the well-being of children, but rather, as we have seen, social responsibility only for enforcing minimal care by parents.

Further, while the category of neglect may appear on the surface to be gender-free, implicating "parents" as responsible for care, we can easily see that almost all people accused of neglecting their children, both historically and at present, are mothers (Gordon, 1988; Polansky and Polansky, 1975; Gil, 1970). It is interesting that although this fact is "common knowledge" among researchers, virtually no one writing about neglect has examined the issue from the perspective of women's lives.[5] Instead, we almost always speak of the neglect of children by their "parents." Use of the gender-free term "parent" performs at least two functions in directing our thoughts. The word "parent" suggests a non-sexist and fair approach, and its frequent use implies that our concern is equally with fathers and mothers. When coupled with research findings that mothers are the "crucial variable," the implication is that fathers and mothers have been submitted to identical scrutiny, and it is the mothers who are clearly "causal variables."

The language of neglect also emphasizes certain aspects of the parent-child relationship at the expense of others. The term "to parent" is relatively new. It refers us to complex, modern images of tasks involved in child care: providing consistency, teaching the child to behave appropriately, coordinating the child's relationship with schools and day care, supervising diet and television viewing, careful discipline, and so on. In this construction, the affective component of the relationship is valued and expressed largely through carrying out these tasks. Thus, a worker is able to say of a loving but inconsistent mother, "she can't parent her children." Carried into the processes of legal adjudication, this thought process has important implications, for it means that the evidence collected by workers focuses on the completion of those parenting tasks that can be observed and measured. The resulting evaluation can then be seen as a reflection of the quality of affection a mother feels for her children.[6]

Finally, the category "neglect" carries explicit instructions, formalized by definitions in the discourse of child welfare, to see the problem as one of passivity, as "omission" of some kind of necessary care (Kadushin, 1967). Polansky (1972: 81) solidifies this idea with his extensive work on the "apathetic-futile mother," a term conjuring images of ragged children in the care of a depressed and hopeless mother. The reality beneath the surface for many of these mothers, however, is the life of violence and abuse by fathers, husbands, and lovers that Imogen Taylor explores in Chapter VII. Random examples of ongoing violence can easily be found in the case files of neglect, although they are not usually presented as explanatory factors or as features of life associated with the kind of care the children are receiving. Instead, episodes of violence appear as background information, as the reason for opening a case, or as an occasion for intervention by the worker. Children in neglect cases are also often subjected to substantial violence. Some are sexually abused by relatives, boy-friends, or others who have access to their homes; some are physically attacked or threatened. Children are present at drunken brawls and drug parties that sometimes lead to serious illness or death of participants. Many of these children live in neighbourhoods where violence is a regular occurrence.

The concept of neglect, however, does not take account of violence as a factor in the lives of children or in the quality of care provided by the mother. Protection of the children is seen as the responsibility of the mother, and the instructions of neglect tell us to perceive violence to the children as a sign of her apathy or incompetence. Violence that the mother herself is subjected to may be viewed, as one worker commented, as "just another crisis on a list of many for her," and the problem for the mother of producing consistent, quality care of children in violent, abusive situations is ignored. A judge in one neglect case shows clearly how these instructions are incorporated into the legal mandate:

> Always remember this: the Court is not concerned so much with your problems . . . the Court's paramount concern is with respect to the welfare of the child . . . the whole objective of the law [is] to ensure that the child receives a decent upbringing and is looked after carefully. . . . So if you people don't, somebody else will.

WOMEN CARING:
THE UNDERLYING SCHEMA

Upon what foundation are such directives built? These "instructions of neglect" may be more easily understood if the concept is placed in its historic and social context. The concept of "the family" is a necessary basis for understanding the surface reality of neglect.

As we have seen, responsibility for the care of children on a day-to-day basis has been relegated almost exclusively to "the family," which has come to mean the nuclear family in modern times. We are familiar with the idea that this outcome has occurred through processes of urbanization and industrialization, which have fragmented the extended family and produced a separation between this private domain of caring and the public domain of paid work. The notion of parents as the usually exclusive caregivers for their children is closely wedded to the individualistic philosophy so basic to our social and economic life. The consequences of this for women and our models of child care are spelled out by Evelyn Ferguson in Chapter III. Individualism provides the logic and moral force supporting the delegation of caring responsibilities to individual parents and families, regardless of the resources needed to carry them out. Self-reliance is the "dominating virtue" that "justifies the shutting of doors firmly in the faces of those unable to be self-reliant" (Dalley, 1988: 118).

The separation of private and public life, as Phillipe Aries (1962) points out, corresponds to a definition of the family as organized around the education and protection of children (Andrew, 1984), tasks that are time-consuming and expensive in modern society. In the social and economic division of labour, the work of caring for children has traditionally been allocated to women. In modern times, this division has been justified on the grounds that women are naturally suited to nurture, and this leads logically to suitability for the work involved. Because of the complexities now involved in caring for children, these responsibilities are onerous and becoming more so, as the literature of "parenting" discovers more and more possibilities for nurturing children so that they may develop to their full potential.

Embedded in assumptions about mothers' suitability to care is also the obverse: that fathers (and men) are not suited for "caring" and therefore need not be responsible for the tasks involved in the care of children. Their role, it is assumed, should be the more removed and distant one of breadwinning. When we speak of the nuclear family, then, we refer not only to the configuration of two parents living in a private dwelling with their children; a gender-based division of labour is also implied.

This nuclear family as an ideal of adult life and child-rearing, as Michele Barrett and Mary McIntosh (1982) forcefully show, has become all-encompassing. The family is romanticized by the media and structured into all forms of social organization. As all the chapters in this book reveal, the very structure of the welfare state in fact assumes a functioning nuclear family as both goal and reality. Recent child welfare legislation, for example, continues to promote this concept of the family in statements of principle. Manitoba legislation from 1985, for example, states:

> The family is the basic unit of society and its well-being should be supported and preserved. The family is the basic source of care, nurture and acculturation of children and parents have the primary responsibility to ensure the well-being of their children.

This statement may remind us of parental responsibilities articulated by Blackstone two centuries ago. References to the family we take to mean the nuclear family, in which financial provision is made primarily by the father, perhaps supplemented by the mother, and the care of children is carried out by the mother, perhaps supplemented by the father. This ideal performs the ideological function of concealing important features of modern reality. For instance, the image of the nuclear family does not take account of class, race, or ethnicity, nor does it consider the realities of life for single mothers (Gordon, 1988; Dalley, 1988). Nevertheless, as Gordon persuasively argues, this image provides the underlying schema for understanding neglect, because the image of the nuclear family provides us with the standards against which care can and should be measured. It dictates the division of labour in the family and tells us precisely what mothers ought to be doing with and for their children.

What Does It Mean To Care?

While the tasks of modern motherhood are very specifically covered in the discourse of parenting, the everyday realities of caring for children remain hidden, only now coming to light in feminist discourse. That this is so is especially ironic, given the enormous attention paid to mothers in the literature of child neglect. This almost exclusive focus on mothers makes it appropriate and in fact essential to take up the issue of neglect from the perspective of women, the lives they lead, and their actual capacity to do the work of caring.

Efforts to examine the concept of caring usually begin with the idea that caring involves both feelings and activities (Waerness, 1984) or "caring about" and "caring for" (Dalley, 1988). According to Dalley, these two aspects of caring merge in modern motherhood. They are thought of as inseparable, probably because of our strongly held belief that it is "natural" for mothers to both love and labour for their children. Mothers who attempt to separate these aspects of caring – and this is often the case in neglect – are seen as deviant. Thus, as Dalley (1988: 8) notes, "cleaning the lavatory and washing the kitchen floor are invested with as much significance as is reading a bedtime story." Examples of neglect complaints show that we ordinarily do take this to be the case. Two contrasting images from case files from my research make the point: "Apartment reeked of stale urine; dirty diaper lying around"; "Mom lives with kids in a tiny apartment which she keeps clean." Although neither observation relates directly to care of children, we are easily able to infer the quality of a mother's care of the children from comments about cleanliness. Not only do the writer and the reader understand this to be so, but the mother herself knows that a clean apartment reflects well on her capacity to mother.

Fathers, it must be noted, will not be assessed by virtue of clean kitchens. In accordance with the ideological model posited by the nuclear family, they may be judged by their efforts at provision. However, they will not be judged at all unless they are present. If they are not living with the mother and children, only the standards of financial responsibility remain as an issue for evaluation. From here, it is a simple step to expand our expectation of the mother to both provide and care, and we do not often explore in any detail how she goes about achieving a reasonable standard of living for her children or how the work of caring is affected by the disappearance of the father. "The prevailing ethos of family-based care suggests that normal tasks are being performed, that the roles enacted are straightforward, expected and unproblematic" (Dalley, 1988: 10).

Arlene Kaplan Daniels (1987) suggests that the activities of "caring for" children are invisible because in our society only *paid* activities are classified as "work." Work in the labour market has "moral force and dignity," while unpaid work does not and thus remains unnoticed. Feminists are now exploring the work of caring and identifying its complexities. Caring involves both the obvious physical activities such as feeding and diapering babies, but also the minutiae of caring such as finding lost mittens, fetching drinks of water, and bandaging wounds. Caring also involves the considerable "emotional work" of attempting to meet the needs of others. Daniels (1987) suggests some of the components of emotional work include tailoring tasks to meet special circumstances, meeting others' deadlines, and lobbying on behalf of family members. These tasks are carried out in a particular context that, depending on the circumstances, may promote or hinder their successful completion.

In examining cases of neglect, circumstances often must be inferred because written records usually omit all descriptions of the work of caring, as well as the context of its occurrence. In one case record, for instance, medical personnel are repeatedly critical of a mother of six for her failure to visit one of the children who is in hospital. The lack of visits form part of an argument that is being built in the written record to show the mother as unconcerned for the welfare of the child. Although it is noted at one point that the mother did visit when supplied with transportation money, no further notice is taken of poverty as a possible explanation for her failure to visit, nor is it anywhere discussed how her other children could be cared for should she attempt to make the visits. This is a fairly typical example of the way in which practical problems of caring are treated in the written files of child welfare. The actual tasks remain unexamined and may instead be construed as having psychological significance.

Since the child welfare mandate involves a search for problematic care, it is not surprising to find that successful efforts to care are usually missing from case files. If no problems are perceived, this is likely to be noted in such phrases as "no immediate concerns"; "family does not require assistance of this agency"; or "other support systems are in place." How the mother does the work of caring not only remains unrecorded, but it may be assumed that it is accomplished through institutionalized services rather than by the mother herself. This does not mean that workers fail to see resourceful efforts of the mother – often they do. However, it is not the worker's job to account for good mothering but to attend to those features of a mother's behaviour that are relevant to establishing the existence of neglect. The child welfare mandate directs the attention of the worker to the issue of neglect through a variety of organizational routes, including the layout of reporting forms and instructions, the principles of the legislation the caseworker is authorized to enforce, exposure to child welfare literature and training opportunities, and so on. As a result of these processes, neither the case records nor the academic literature about neglect include discussion of how successful caring is managed by these mothers.

BREADWINNING AND THE SINGLE MOTHER

From the outset, as Gordon's (1988) work clearly shows, single mothers have been greatly overrepresented in the population of neglecting mothers, and this remains the case today. At times, these women have been charged with neglect because they could not, simultaneously, work for pay outside the home and be at home with their children, but neither could they afford to pay others to care for their children (Spearly and Lauderdale, 1983). Prior to the existence of accessible welfare for single mothers in Western industrialized countries, the death or abdication of the father inevitably put women in this precarious position unless they had extended family or inherited wealth to rely on.

With the advent of Mothers' Allowances in Canada, this contradictory experience for mothers has been reduced, as they are usually able to apply for some form of welfare. This step has provided some small independence for single mothers, although the help they receive is inadequate, as clearly outlined by Pat Evans in Chapter VI. One of the effects of this financial aid may be that a mother is dependent on her children for her income, and often for her housing as well. If the children of a single mother are apprehended by child welfare authorities, she loses the benefits she receives on their behalf, her "baby bonus," and frequently her housing as well, since she needs those benefits to pay the rent. Sometimes she loses her belongings, too: "When the workers come to pick the kids up out of the home, they just pick up the kids. And if the mum is sort of transient and sort of down and out, the belongings get sent to some Salvation Army by the landlord." If she is not pursuing the return of her children, the mother may also lose contact with her Children's Aid worker and whatever resources that contact has represented, since the mandate of the agency is not to offer support to women but to offer help in keeping families together.

If children remain in agency care for any length of time, then, a mother may find herself in the position of starting over, looking for housing, re-establishing her benefits, and creating a new set of relationships with various workers. In line with the individualist ethic underlying the ideal of the nuclear family, the onus is on her. Child welfare workers encourage her to recognize that she has to achieve independence if she is to have the children back. "She's going to have to learn to be very strong for herself, because she is going to have to ask for service, she won't be able to handle all her children herself, so it's a skill that she's going to have to acquire." Workers do this because they recognize the social reality that awaits the mother, a reality based on the belief that individuals in our society can and must "make it on their own." The proof of self-reliance in the context of child welfare is a mother caring for her children with minimal or no assistance; failure to achieve this goal will have drastic consequences for all concerned.

When Caring Is Impossible

The care of children by single mothers poses potentially serious problems, since there is no automatic or immediate backup should the mother become incapacitated. Specific issues, not uncommon in neglect caseloads, are alcohol and drug addictions. Professional literature on alcoholism usually alludes to this condition as a disease. For child welfare workers, however, an alcoholic mother means poor care for kids. Even if the father is present, the mother is still expected to be the primary caregiver, and the onus for recovery will be on her. She will be expected to choose a recovery program, to follow through, and to maintain sobriety. The worker may have difficulty understanding how a mother could fail in this attempt, given that her children's lives are at stake, and ask, as did one worker from my study: "How many times do your children have to be in care before you decide to stop drinking?"

Child welfare workers are quite naturally upset and frustrated by such a situation, for they see the anguish of the children as they are shuttled back and forth to foster placements, and they are aware of the risk and harm children sustain as dependants of an addict. As onlookers, we yearn for such a mother to right herself and get the family back together. Behind this yearning is again the image of "the family" – happy children at home with their mother. When the problem is constructed in this way, the work of caring merges into affect and becomes invisible. We assume that the mother can be cured if she chooses, and that the joys of children, the rewards for a mother of having them with her, should constitute sufficient motivation to overcome addiction.

If we look at the mother's problem from the perspective of her caring work, however, we see a different picture. We see the children increasingly upset and perhaps difficult to manage as they move back and forth from home to foster care, each move accompanied by attendant strains of loss of friends, schools, belongings, and so on. To maintain the support services the mother receives through her status as a child welfare client, she has to submit to ongoing scrutiny and criticism when the children are in her care. In fact, the support staff who help her will also act as scrutineers and may testify in court against her. The mother may often be required to make "contracts" with the worker imposing conditions on her lifestyle and relationships. If she has relatives with similar addictions, she may be asked to sever ties with them, which means cutting herself off from the very family we are taught to revere, and she will then be even more reliant on the agency to supply needed supports for her child-caring responsibilities.

The reality for such a mother if she keeps her children with her is a difficult and poverty-stricken life, involving attempts to manage several children on resources below the poverty line, often living in barren cold quarters, possibly in an unsafe neighbourhood. The children will share this poverty-ridden existence with her, based on the rationale that she has a right to the "least intrusive" alternative. Such a case will be seen as having a "successful" outcome on the grounds that the family is together. Since the child welfare mandate does not include protecting children from poverty or helping the mother enrich her own life, the case will likely be closed – until the next crisis. The rewards of sobriety, in short, may come to seem doubtful.

When addiction produces repeated placements of the children, court proceedings to determine the mother's fitness may eventually be invoked. In this instance, the workers involved must choose between the mother's right to her children and the rights of the children to be protected from her problematic behaviour. A decision will be made based on the "best interests" of the children.[7] When the mother has been seen to fail repeatedly, foster care or adoption may seem the desirable options. Although the failures of the foster care system have been well documented (Johnston, 1983; Hepworth, 1980), we will likely perceive this outcome as a successful "rescue" operation because we witness a solution to the immediate problem. The children then disappear into another system, their "case" as victims of neglect is closed, and their fate as foster or adopted children is not pursued.

THE LITERATURE REVISITED

Having explored some of the hidden realities beneath the surface of neglect, I now return to issues posed by the literature to suggest how we might view them differently. Literature on neglect represents the problem primarily as a failure in mothering, although this failure has not been defined in clear and unequivocal terms. The resulting ambiguity, it is argued, has permitted social workers and the child welfare system to impose white, middle-class standards on the poor and culturally different.

While this argument has some merit, it is oversimplified and ideologically based. Social workers do recognize the problems of poverty faced by clients. As the critique developed by and about native children has begun to expose, the work of caring has been concealed and consequently not examined for the kinds of standards we assume can and ought to be carried out. In addition, these standards include a growing number of components, as the social sciences develop and test methods of measuring "appropriate" child development. Further, the native critique of child welfare does not include an examination of gender. The assumptions of class and the dominant culture embedded in our ideas of caring for children and assumptions about the division of labour, both within the family and in the society in general, need to be revealed if a less ideological understanding of neglect is to be achieved.

With these divisions in mind, prominent research problems, such as predicting who is most likely to neglect their children and what factors are most likely to be associated with neglect, are rendered unimportant. If the underlying schema of neglect rests on the ideal of a two-parent, middle-class, dominant-culture family, it is quite logical that parents not matching this ideal are the most likely to become clients of the child welfare system – the poor, single mothers and those who are culturally different. And – no surprise – this has traditionally been the caseload (Johnston, 1983; Horowitz and Wolock, 1981; Gordon, 1988).

Also important to note is the liberal form of arguments concerning the definition of neglect. The heavy focus on "rights," with the contradictory and seemingly unsolvable tensions between the rights of children and the rights of parents (read mothers), has reduced the issue of child neglect to the question of determining specific harms to a child. Such a framing of the question does not address, and therefore conceals, the issues of care: who performs caring work, what resources are required, what problems are faced by caregivers. At the same time, the intersection of two discourses, one on neglect and one on parenting, produces two vastly different pictures of child care, with the effect of pushing the ideal "standards" of care ever higher. The picture of the maltreatment of children suggests dirty, ragged, underfed, unhealthy children, in the care of an apathetic mother. In contrast, the large and growing discourse on parenting provides detailed images of excellent care, including attention to every facet of a child's development by both parents. Preparing nutritious meals, attending home-and-school meetings, reading at bedtime, giving birthday parties, and soothing a sick child are examples of the images of good parenting we receive on a daily basis through women's magazines, advertising, and television programs. Thus the job of child welfare workers appears more contradictory as time goes by. On the one hand they are dealing with a legal mandate reduced to proving harmful effects on children. On the other, they are exhorted to move "neglecting" parents toward standards of parenting that even those families conforming to the outlines of the nuclear family find difficult to approach. Of course, simple failure to match the ideal does not bring the child welfare worker to the door. However, once a mother is under suspicion, her failures can and will be used as evidence in court.

When children are removed from the care of their mothers, the proposed remedy is the "rescue" of the child(ren) from the mother, usually leading to the substitution of another mother for the original deficient mother. That the work and responsibility is passed on to another woman is seldom questioned. As White (1986, cited in Dalley, 1988) notes, any number of failures in foster care will be tolerated so that the image of family care can be produced and reproduced. The child welfare system as it stands today has set the parameters for caring, in effect pitting women against each other, competing to provide "the best" individual care of children. While the nuclear family model suggests the presence of an active and caring father, this is not often the case even in two-parent families, and rarely in families on child welfare caseloads. The current professional focus on treatment of deficient mothers has successfully directed attention away not only from the foster care system but also from fathers, both individually and collectively. It has also concealed the effort required and the resources needed to perform caring work in the home, as well as ignored many structural obstacles, such as the high cost of housing, that women confront in their efforts to provide care.

Nor are the needs of the women themselves legitimated in current approaches. While the standard of the nuclear family requires the woman be dependent, this does not mean she will be cared for:

> . . . for women, the experience of dependency is contradictory. Their dependent status – as housewives, mothers, dutiful daughters – is not absolute, but is conditional upon their being simultaneously depended upon by others. Thus for many women, being a dependant is synonymous not with receiving care but with giving it. (Graham, 1983: 24–25)

RECONCEPTUALIZATION

What is required for genuine change? Arguments for the structural change necessary to provide adequate incomes, reasonable housing, and employment opportunities for mothers have been made elsewhere, and I will not repeat them here (see, e.g., Garbarino, 1981; Wolock and Horowitz; 1984; Pelton, 1981). My analysis suggests, however, that these critiques have remained in the background of child neglect. Changes within child welfare itself must be sought if this is to change. The child welfare mandate needs to be broadened to include the protection of children not only within their families, but from social forces that affect families. Further, child welfare workers and administrators are well placed to collect and publicize data about the material deprivation experienced by their clients and about the social structures that oppress them. These workers are aware of, and sympathetic to, the problems faced by their clients, but they must create the organizational means to make this knowledge visible and actionable. This is a difficult but exciting task. As the recent history of native political action shows, it is possible to create important legal and administrative changes in child welfare.

A second question is whether we can produce a serious and thorough critique of child welfare that takes account of the hidden realities of caring work. This is both possible and necessary; further, beginning to develop needed changes depends on questioning the very foundations of child care in our society. As Kari Waerness (1984) points out, caring for children within the confines of individual families is relatively new. Yet for us, who have never experienced child-rearing differently, it seems the only possible way. It is risky to propose something else, for of all our social directives the call to motherhood is surely the most powerful and dangerous to challenge. Further, it is not clear that women themselves wish to challenge it.

A small but interesting literature dealing with this issue is beginning to emerge. Caroline New and Miriam David (1985), for instance, challenge the mystique of mothering, citing a wide variety of collective forms of child care in the present as well as in the past. Along with Gillian Dalley (1988), they argue that collective forms of care not only free mothers from the exclusively held responsibilities that now exist, but can help to shield children from unnecessary threat and produce high-quality care for the many children who are not living in the ideal nuclear family.

It is essential to recognize that children do need good and consistent care. The "rights" debate of the 1970s and 1980s, while claiming concern, actually ignored the issue of the care that children received. The defence of families against state intrusion inevitably operates to deny children access to badly needed services. Debates based exclusively on protection of class and cultural rights may also operate to deny children needed care, although this has not necessarily been the intent.

Until the components of care are made visible and until caring work is legitimized as a social value, the issue of child neglect will continue to be viewed from traditional and individualistic perspectives. Many social workers have recognized that the visible signs of child neglect represent a serious social problem. However, the attention to punishment and treatment encouraged by our legal and medical approach to child welfare has served to obscure rather than to reveal the fundamental nature of the problem. It has become increasingly clear that in failing to address the material circumstances of life for the caregiver, neither legal nor medical approaches can work.

Our current response system does provide the appearance of social responsibility. Dalley's (1988) distinction between social responsibility and social forms of care is useful in this regard. Social responsibility to provide, she suggests, is a principle of the welfare state. It is closely related to the values of individualism that encourage both public and private "charity" to those in need of care, rationed according to principles of deservedness. This model leads logically to individualized solutions to problems of caregiving, delivered in the private sphere. Of course, a commitment to social responsibility is important, but we need to be aware that this approach has not led to satisfactory forms of caring for children.

Social or "collective" forms of care, on the other hand, presuppose that those who provide care and those who receive care are part of a reciprocal network. Such a model stands in opposition to the charity approach we currently employ, in which the carer (i.e., the welfare agency) is invested with moral virtue while the virtue of the one cared for (i.e., the mother) automatically comes up for review. Collective caring suggests a greater emphasis on group living and group interactions, as opposed to the isolation and fragmentation of current care models. Group interaction allows carers and cared-for to come to know each other personally and to develop concern for each other. This model of caring also allows for those being cared for to move eventually into roles of assisting in caregiving, rather than being consigned forever to a position of moral inferiority. Smith and Smith (1990), for example, studied a child welfare project based on a collegial rather than hierarchical model of fostering. Their study shows that when the agency encouraged this approach, foster mothers adopted a "familial" and sympathetic attitude toward natural mothers.

These ideas, of course, run counter to our beliefs in privacy and individualism, yet they hold possibilities for much more effective kinds of care for children currently at risk, without inevitably causing damage to both mother and children. To illustrate, I return to the case of an addicted mother to examine how we might treat this differently. At present, treatment programs house the mother for set periods of time to help her through withdrawal and to provide some counselling and support. During this time, the children must be placed in substitute care, and the household is likely to be dismantled. Upon release, the mother begins again. She is probably homeless and penniless as she attempts to reclaim her children. Can we imagine collective forms of living that provide children with ongoing care when their mothers are in trouble, in which mothers and fathers can help each other through crises and receive ongoing support and treatment in their living situations following release from treatment? Collective forms of living can mean that children have ties to other caretakers, which obviates the need to leave their homes, schools, belongings, and friends should their mother require further treatment. Finally, collectives can allow the mother a socially useful role in helping others through problems she has experienced.

A collective approach allows us to face the fact that in some situations the work of caring cannot or will not be done by the natural mother. It requires courage and honesty to begin to challenge the centrality of the mother in the lives of her children. As women, we fear a loss of our own importance within the family circle, and we fear that giving permission for a few mothers to "resign" may lead to desertion of responsibility on a massive scale. However, history shows that, for whatever reasons, mothers almost invariably pursue relationships with their children regardless of the obstacles they encounter. Threat of removal of a child from its mother nearly always evokes a fearful resistance (Gordon, 1988). Perhaps we believe that only ideology keeps mothers firmly fixed in their responsibilities. If this is so, our fears should lead us to a deeper examination of the actual experience of caregiving in the mothering role, and to the collective responsibility for improving that experience.

The concept of caring can be used to re-evaluate how we view a mother in distress and what the state response might be. At present, repeated failures to "care for" mean a potential decision to remove the children, often with permanent cutting of ties, regardless of whatever feelings of "caring about" exist between mother and child. By separating caring for from caring about, we can begin to give value to affection, recognizing that caring about has value for children even when caring for is sporadic or impossible. Both children and their mothers are paying a high price for our failure to make this distinction.

And what of fathers? Missing almost completely from the picture of "parenting" to date is a clear analysis of the abdication of so many fathers.[8] We must begin to address this issue in child welfare planning, not only in the interests of the immediate care of children, but to help to prevent reproducing traditional gender roles into their future. In utterly ignoring the disappearance of fathers, the message we give to these children, most assuredly, is that fathers count for nothing, a message that fathers themselves may also have received. For girls, this is a prediction of the responsibilities they may expect when they become mothers; for boys, this picture provides a script for avoiding responsibility in the future. As many child welfare workers know, taking an active interest in an absent father sometimes produces an unexpected resource for children and may produce a new and important life interest for the father, as was the situation in one of the cases used in my research. Certainly if we wish to socialize and share the work of caregiving, we must begin to consider how fathers can play a part in this different configuration of responsibility.

The kinds of resources we typically deploy in child welfare must also be questioned. The value of our "professional" help has rightly been questioned by critics of the current system. We may need research to demonstrate what we already know: the resources we put in are largely ineffective, and are primarily used for evidence-gathering purposes. In addition, our charity-based notion of care invests care providers with moral virtue but casts the cared-for as individuals of doubtful moral worth. Our present allocation of resources carries a very strong moral message that stigmatizes mothers for requiring help. Even well-intentioned individuals providing care cannot overcome the moral divisiveness implicit in present models of care. As some feminists are now arguing, the ethics of care require that acts of caring confirm rather than deny the other's sense of self-worth (Noddings, 1984).

In explicating the actual work involved in doing a good job of caring for children we provide ourselves with some direction, but we must go further, to ask how this caring is to be supplied, thus raising the issue of care for the caregivers. Studies of neglect typically show that these mothers lead impoverished lives, emotionally as well as physically. They often have no one to care for them, and may have never had the experience of being cared for. Instead of supplying support as a way to improve their child-caring capacities, the needs of mothers for care and self-care need to be legitimized as having value in their own right. Mothers can be helped toward both self-care and mutual care, as demonstrated by guided self-help projects (Lovell, Reid, and Richey, 1988).

Revealing some of the hidden realities of child neglect helps to outline a way of changing and expanding old debates.

While the critique of child welfare practices has been necessary and useful, it has proven insufficient. As Timpson (1990) argues, these debates have tended to reduce the problem to "cultural ignorance and frivolous workers" while overlooking the arduous and underfunded nature of child welfare work and the serious inattention to issues such as health, education, and employment that affect child welfare clients and make the work of caring so difficult. A different strategy is needed for deploying resources to those families who are already having difficulties in providing adequate care. We will have achieved some success in child welfare, I would argue, when a reasonable standard of care can be provided children without the necessity of impoverishing, stigmatizing, and coercing mothers to do the caring work.

NOTES

1. Jones and Rutman (1981) describe in detail the budget shortages that plagued Ontario Children's Aid Societies from their beginnings.
2. In its initial set of definitions, for instance, Manitoba's recent legislation defines "abuse" but not neglect as the issue with which the child welfare mandate is to be concerned.
3. See Timpson (1990) for a thorough review of the development of special status for natives in child welfare legislation and practice.
4. See Breines and Gordon (1983) for an excellent review and discussion of the attribution and responsibility for family problems to the mother. Linda Gordon (1988) also deals extensively with this theme as it relates historically to child neglect.
5. An important exception is Linda Gordon's (1988) historical work on family violence, which includes chapters discussing child neglect from the perspective of mothers.
6. This is not to suggest that social workers fail to distinguish between affection and parenting tasks. Data from my study show that workers are well aware of this distinction. However, the evidence that counts in court involves the completion of identifiable tasks. Workers are therefore required to turn attention to that issue.
7. For discussion of the complexity of meanings attached to the phrase "best interests of the child," see Goldstein, Freud, and Solnit (1973, 1979).
8. An exception is Barbara Ehrenreich's (1983) examination of the

"flight from commitment" of American men in the past few decades.

REFERENCES

Andrew, C. 1984. "Women and the Welfare State," *Canadian Journal of Political Science*, XVII, 67–83.

Aries, Phillipe. 1962. *Centuries of Childhood*. New York: Alfred A. Knopf.

Austin, Carol D. 1981. "Client Assessment in Context," *Social Work Research and Abstracts*, 17, 1: 4–12.

Barrett, Michele, and Mary McIntosh. 1982. *The Anti-Social Family*. London: Verso.

Breines, W., and Linda Gordon. 1983. "The New Scholarship on Family Violence," *Signs*, 8, 3: 491–531.

Callahan, Marilyn. 1985. "Public Apathy and Government Parsimony: A Review of Child Welfare in Canada," in Kenneth L. Levitt and Brian Wharf, eds., *The Challenge of Child Welfare*. Vancouver: University of British Columbia Press.

Cicourel, A.V. 1976. *The Social Organization of Juvenile Justice*. London: Heinemann.

Custer, Lawrence B. 1978. "The Origins of the Doctrine of Parens Patriae," *Emory Law Journal*, 27, 2: 195–208.

Dalley, Gillian. 1988. *Ideologies of Caring*. London: Macmillan.

Daniels, A. 1987. "Invisible Work," *Social Problems*, 34, 5: 403–15.

DeMontigny, Gerald. 1980. "The Social Organization of Social Workers' Practice," Master's thesis, Ontario Institute for Studies in Education.

Ehrenreich, Barbara. 1983. *The Hearts of Men: American Dreams and the Flight from Commitment*. Garden City, N.Y.: Anchor Books.

Falconer, Nancy, and Karen Swift. 1983. *Preparing for Practice*. Toronto: Children's Aid Society of Metropolitan Toronto.

Farina, Margaret R. 1982. "The Relationship of the State to the Family in Ontario: State Intervention in the Family on Behalf of Children," Ph.D. thesis, Ontario Institute for Studies in Education.

Garbarino, James. 1981. "An Ecological Approach to Child Maltreatment," in L. Pelton, ed., *Social Context of Child Abuse and Neglect*. New York: Human Sciences Press.

Garfinkel, Harold. 1967. *Studies in Ethnomethodology*. Englewood Cliffs, N.J.: Prentice-Hall.

Gil, D.G. 1970. *Violence Against Children*. Cambridge, Mass: Harvard University Press.

Giovannoni, Jeanne, and Rosina Becerra. 1979. *Defining Child Abuse*.

New York: The Free Press.

Giovannoni, Jeanne, and A. Billingsley. 1970. "Child Neglect Among the Poor," *Child Welfare*, 49: 196-204.

Goldstein, J., Anna Freud, and A. Solnit. 1973. *Beyond the Best Interests of the Child*. New York: The Free Press.

Goldstein, J., Anna Freud, and A. Solnit. 1979. *Before the Best Interests of the Child*. New York: The Free Press.

Gordon, Linda. 1988. *Heroes in Their Own Lives*. New York: Penguin.

Graham, H. 1983. "Caring: A Labour of Love," in J. Finch and D. Groves, eds., *A Labour of Love: Women, Work and Caring*. London: Routledge and Kegan Paul.

Griffith, Alison, and Dorothy E. Smith. 1987. "Constructing Cultural Knowledge: Mothering as Discourse," in J. Gaskell and A. McLaren, eds., *Women and Education*. Calgary: Detselig.

Hepworth, Philip. 1980. *Foster Care and Adoption in Canada*. Ottawa: Canadian Council on Social Development.

Horowitz, Bernard, and Isabel Wolock. 1981. "Material Deprivation, Child Maltreatment and Agency Interventions Among Poor Families," in Pelton, ed., *Social Context of Child Abuse and Neglect*.

Johnston, Patrick. 1983. *Native Children and the Child Welfare System*. Toronto: Canadian Council on Social Development in Association with James Lorimer and Company.

Jones, Andrew, and Leonard Rutman. 1981. *In the Children's Aid*. Toronto: University of Toronto Press.

Jones, J.M., and R.L. McNeely. 1980. "Mothers Who Neglect and Those Who Do Not: A Comparative Study," *Social Casework*, 61, 9: 559-67.

Kadushin, Alfred. 1967. *Child Welfare Services*. New York: Macmillan.

Katz, S. 1971. *When Parents Fail*. Boston: Beacon Press.

Korbin, Jill. 1980. "The Cultural Context of Child Abuse and Neglect," *Child Abuse and Neglect*: 3-13.

Lovell, M., K. Reid, and C. Richey. 1988. "Social Support Training for Abusive Mothers," in J. Garland, ed., *Social Group Work Reaching Out: People, Places, and Power*. Binghamton, N.Y.: Haworth Press.

Lubove, Roy. 1965. *The Professional Altruist*. Cambridge, Mass.: Harvard University Press.

Martin, Marjorie. 1985. "Poverty and Child Welfare," in Levitt and Wharf, eds., *The Challenge of Child Welfare*.

Marx, K., and F. Engels. 1947. *The German Ideology*, Parts I and III. New York: International Publishers.

McCord, Joan. 1983. "A Forty Year Perspective on Effects of Child Abuse and Neglect," *Child Abuse and Neglect*, 7, 3: 265-78.

Mnookin, Robert. 1973. "Foster Care – In Whose Best Interests?"

Harvard Educational Review, 43: 599–638.

New, Caroline, and Miriam David. 1985. *For the Children's Sake.* Harmondsworth, Middlesex: Penguin.

Noddings, Nell. 1984. *Caring: A Feminine Approach to Ethics and Moral Education*. Berkeley: University of California Press.

Pelton, Leroy. 1981. *The Social Context of Child Abuse and Neglect*. New York: Human Sciences Press.

Polansky, N., and N. Polansky. 1975. *Profile of Neglect: A Survey of the State of Knowledge of Child Neglect*. Washington, D.C.: U.S. Department of Health, Education and Welfare.

Polansky, Norman, *et al*. 1981. *Damaged Parents: An Anatomy of Child Neglect*. Chicago: University of Chicago Press.

Polansky, N., D. Borgman, and C. De Saix. 1972. *Roots of Futility*. San Francisco: Jossey-Bass.

Smith, Brenda, and Tina Smith. 1990. "For Love and Money: Women as Foster Mothers," *Affilia*, 5, 1 (Spring): 66–80.

Smith, Dorothy, E. 1987. *The Everyday World as Problematic: A Feminist Sociology*. Toronto: University of Toronto Press.

Spearly, J.L., and M. Lauderdale. 1983. "Community Characteristics and Ethnicity in the Prediction of Child Maltreatment Rates," *Child Abuse and Neglect*, 7, 1: 91–105.

Sutherland, Neil. 1976. *Children in English Canadian Society*. Toronto: University of Toronto Press.

Swift, Karen. 1988. *Knowledge about Neglect: A Critical Review of the Literature*. Working Papers on Social Welfare, Faculty of Social Work, University of Toronto.

Timpson, Joyce B. 1990. "Indian and Native Special Status in Ontario's Child Welfare Legislation," *Canadian Social Work Review*, 7: 49–68.

Treudley, Mary. 1980. "The 'Benevolent Fair': A Study of Charitable Organizations Among American Women in the First Third of the Nineteenth Century," in F.R. Breul and S.J. Diner, eds., *Compassion and Responsibility*. Chicago: University of Chicago Press.

Waerness, Kari. 1984. "Caring as Women's Work in the Welfare State," in H. Holter, ed., *Patriarchy in a Welfare Society*. Oslo: Universitetsforlaget.

Wald, Michael. 1976. "State Intervention on Behalf of Neglected Children: A Search for Realistic Answers," in M.K. Rosenheim, ed., *Pursuing Justice for the Child*. Chicago: University of Chicago Press.

Wolock, I. 1982. "Community Characteristics and Staff Judgments in Child Abuse and Neglect Cases," *Social Work Research and Abstracts*, 18, 2: 9–15.

Wolock, Isabel, and Bernard Horowitz. 1979. "Child Maltreatment and Material Deprivation Among AFDC Recipient Families," *Social Service Review*, 53 (June): 175–94.

Wolock, I., and B. Horowitz, 1984. "Child Maltreatment as a Social Problem: The Neglect of Neglect," *Journal of Orthopsychiatry*, 54, 4: 595–602.

Young, L. 1964. *Wednesday's Children*. New York: McGraw-Hill.

CHAPTER IX

From Community Care to a Social Model of Care

Sheila M. Neysmith

INTRODUCTION

The emotional and physical work inherent in responding to the needs of others characterizes much of the paid and unpaid labour that women do. The undervaluing of this work has a negative impact on the quality of life enjoyed by most women both in the domestic arena and in the labour force, whether they work as low-paid service-sector employees, as part of the pink ghetto of clerical staff, or as members of the female-dominated professions such as social work, teaching, and nursing. In addition, the commitment that women have to caring is often seen as actually contributing to social problems: the persistence of high poverty rates among single mothers and widows is often defined as resulting from their interrupted employment patterns; women are raised on patriarchal notions of an ideal family and then are blamed for not leaving violent partners; finally, in direct contradiction to earlier messages, women who have been caring for others all their lives are expected to be independent and self-sufficient and to make few demands on state and familial resources in their old age.

The conceptual separation of family life, labour market activity, and state responsibility has resulted in a segmented, fractured discussion of caring. Bits and pieces get addressed by policy-makers, academic disciplines, and service professionals, each using different language and contrasting theoretical frameworks for analysing the issues. In this chapter my aim is to gather together a number of these threads and suggest how they might be knitted together to form a design for a de-gendered, collective approach to caring. However, reframing the argument entails surmounting a number of obstacles. The ongoing debate around the purpose and organization of long-term care for the frail elderly will be used to illustrate the extent and nature of this challenge. The analysis serves as a springboard for considering structural features of existing caring arrangements that will need to be altered if the risks, as well as the benefits, of caring are to be more equitably distributed in Canadian society.

One of the purposes of this book is to expand our understanding of how caring shapes the experiences of women at various points in the life cycle. Although the particular persons women care for may change over time, caring itself is a constant. The continuity of caring in women's lives is obscured by academic disciplines that delineate areas of interest for detailed examination and/or social programs restricted to specific population groups.

The preceding chapters highlight the contradictions that women face as they provide both instrumental and emotional support to those around them. However, contradictions can present opportunities and conceptual spaces for mapping out pathways to change. In different ways each chapter has shown that women recognize the importance of caring for the well-being of both themselves and others. In no case has there been even a hint that women were trying to abdicate their caring roles. On the contrary, all authors portrayed how important this work is to women despite some of the negative consequences that accompany it. Thus, the accusation that questioning the premise of a family-based model of caring devalues the family in a selfish pursuit of the rights of women finds little empirical support when the attitudes and behaviour of women are examined. The research does document, however, that the price women pay in order that their loved ones do not suffer is very high (Land and Rose, 1985). It is also unfair because it is undervalued, less is asked and expected of men, and state support is minimal. It is unfair because both women and the dependent persons they care for are cast as victims or victimizers when they are neither.

Assessing possibilities for change necessitates an analysis of the relationships among the domestic sphere, the world of paid work, and the state. The nature of these bonds produces many of the contradictions facing women as they try to combine their public and private lives. The resulting dilemmas only "make sense" when viewed within the political economy of Canadian society. The impact on women is amplified in periods of fiscal restraint. Hernes (1987: 80) summarized it nicely when she said that:

> to the extent that the crisis [of the welfare state] is regarded as *financial* women will be affected more than men by attempts to solve the crisis through budget cuts; to the extent that it is regarded as a crisis of *legitimacy* it is women who, through their demands and support, can maintain belief in the state as opposed to the market as the problem solver; if one regards it as primarily a problem of government *overload* women will be affected if it is solved by transferring services back to the family and the market, a process that will affect women as clients, consumers and employees.

To some extent the attacks on social spending in Canada during the 1980s have resulted in all three.

THE ILLUSION OF COMMUNITY-BASED CARE VERSUS THE REALITY OF FAMILY-BASED CARE

The spectre of uncontrollable health and social service costs associated with an aging population has resulted in considerable efforts by provincial and local governments to find alternatives to expensive institution-based services. The pressure-cooker atmosphere within which policy-making for long-term care is occurring has made explicit assumptions about family responsibility. Under less pressing circumstances, these assumptions tend to remain submerged. For example, following is a list of seven principles that guided the reform of long-term care in Ontario (Sweeney, 1989):

1. The system of funding long-term care beds will be reformed so that funding will be based primarily on the care needs of the individual and be responsive to the level of care provided.
2. Services that complement and sustain families and friends as caregivers will be recognized as a fundamental part of the system.
3. The incentives in the system will encourage use of the most appropriate, cost-effective service suitable to the individual's and family's needs.
4. An increasing proportion of the elderly and people with physical disabilities who require health and social services will receive them in their own homes to avoid both inappropriate use of acute care beds and unnecessary growth in the number of extended and chronic care beds.
5. A single, integrated admissions process to long-term care beds and long-term community care will rely on an objective, multi-disciplinary review. It will encourage use of the least intensive care suitable for the person's needs.
6. Within the context of province-wide policies, there will be an enhanced local role in planning, establishing priorities, and managing services.
7. The long-term care system must be affordable and the costs shared appropriately among governments and consumers.

Provincial cost concerns are apparent in each of these objectives. The costs to women of such a family-based model of long-term care are absent.

The aging of our population was a major impetus in placing caregiving on the policy agenda in North America and Europe. These origins shaped the subsequent debate. As noted earlier, the costs of providing services to an aging population were starting to become apparent. Women's participation in the labour force was steadily increasing and thus it was feared that they would be less available for future domestic labour. At the same time the assumptions and organization of a market economy, which separates an employee from her larger social existence as mother, spouse, daughter, citizen, have remained virtually unchanged since the turn of the century. Women from all classes are experiencing increased demands on their caring services as the life expectancy of their parents and parents-in-law increases, as divorce rates rise (Biegel and Blum, 1990), and as women's track record for obtaining custody of their children is more successful than the state's ability to enforce support orders on fathers to provide for those children (Foote, 1988). Change is being demanded, but the direction these changes will take is not at all clear. As the stated goals on long-term care demonstrate, conflicting agendas abound! The current fiscal crisis of the state has resulted in strong pressure to locate responsibility for community-based services firmly in the bosom of the family. The statement of the objectives for a provincial homemaker program illustrates this:

> to assist the frail elderly and the adult disabled to remain in their own homes or in the community; and to sustain and expand the scope of the family's capacity to continue to care for its members. (Ministry of Community and Social Services, 1989: i)

This dynamic is also visible in the struggle over the reallocation of health resources. Acute-care patients are being released quickly and thus require closer supervision at home (Glazer, 1988); chronic-care patients are viewed as bed-blockers with constant pressure on social service staff and families to move them out (Aronson *et al.*, 1987). It is argued that this is a more efficient use of expensive beds, but the demands this budgetary decision imposes on family re-sources are not monitored. The result is a socially constructed intergenerational conflict where the needs of the elderly are pitted against those of younger generations (Tindale and Neysmith, 1987; Binney and Estes, 1988). When the focus is on health care expenditures, the elderly become the villians who use a disproportionate share of resources that are then not available to others. When the family is the focus of study, care of the elderly is viewed as a burden on the limited resources of younger members. Jane Aronson, in Chapter V, has documented how this definition is internalized in a mix-ture of anger and guilt experienced by both parties, those female kin who are doing the caring and the elderly women who are receiving care. Our discipline-bound tendency to isolate studies of public institutions from those of interper-sonal relationships makes it difficult to see the competing explanation that costs are being transferred from the public into the private domain. The apparent intergenerational war is actually a public-private one.

The scarcity of community-based services is widely recog-nized. However, the argument to be made goes beyond noting that the promotion of community services is frequently a response to financial pressure rather than a commitment to building an alternative service model. Of importance are the future ingredients under consideration for expanding commu-nity programs and services. Self-help groups, informal helping networks, neighbours, and volunteers are proposed as sources of aid to the frail elderly person and/or her kin carer. Together these actors are now called the "informal sector." It has been estimated that 80–85 per cent of care is given by informal sources, while 15–20 per cent is provided by formal programs and services (Chappell *et al.*, 1986: 80). Concern is expressed that the contributions of the informal sector must not be destroyed by allowing formal services to overpower them.

The reality is that the informal sector is often the care given by an aging spouse or by a daughter living elsewhere who fits parental care into other family and employment responsibil-ities. To refer to such individuals as a "sector" presents an illusion of substance. Discussion of how the formal and informal sectors might interweave into a total care package uses a language that conceals differences in power, resources, and information.

Public policy statements clearly envision family care as the ideal, with formal services representing a necessary alternative if family care is not available:

> Generally, family and friends provide the most *effective* support for older persons. Nevertheless, it must be recognized that traditional assistance patterns have been affected by changing social conditions. . . . Consequently, *some* families will require assistance to maintain their elderly members in the community and *some* older persons will need more support than family or friends are able to provide. Given these circumstances, a responsive community services system is a necessity. (Ontario, 1986: 10; emphasis added)

The effects on women of an ideology of kin care are now well documented (Brody and Schoonover, 1986; Dalley, 1988; Finch and Groves, 1983; Ungerson, 1987). Along with the idealization of the family as the appropriate locus for care, there is a tendency to assume that because caregivers express a willingness to continue providing care for family members, programs should encourage them to do so.

The idealization of family care also influences the type of service developed. Studies show that caregivers express a strong desire for respite care. Family respite is defined as: "a service that provides periodic, short-term care to a dependent person for the purpose of providing an interval of respite for that person's parents, spouse, children, or other primary caregiver" (Ministry of Community and Social Services, 1987: 4). Such services may relieve the stress that women bear but the conditions that gave rise to it remain unchanged. The model allows for time out or a holiday, but it does not question why women are doing the job and/or whether the job is organized in a just and equitable manner. This is not intentional. Most respite programs were set up after considerable lobbying and they are extremely popular (Neysmith, 1987; Canadian Mental Health Association, 1987).

Their strengths, however, should not distract from the fact that family care is seen as the natural form of care.

As home-care services expand, both their content and their coverage need to be monitored. It is useful to examine the experience of the U.S. in considering future policy directions for Canada. In a three-year study of the impact of federal and state funding policy on the delivery of health and social services to the elderly, Binney *et al.* (1990) found that in agencies providing services that could be reimbursed by Medicare, medicalized services were used with disproportionate frequency. The greatest number of unfulfilled requests were for home aides/homemakers, which were not covered but were available on a fee-for-service basis. Agencies not licensed to provide Medicare-financed services were much more responsive to this demand and supplied mostly low-cost home help, although they could also provide medical services on a fee-paying basis.

Such data are liable to several interpretations. One is that people will choose a cheaper service if they are paying for it. Another is that budget concerns will lead agencies to concentrate on the provision of services for which payment is guaranteed. Both interpretations fail to raise a far more fundamental question: why are medicalized services, which are expensive and do not reflect consumer preference, given priority over others in most insurance schemes? Binney *et al.* (1990) suggest that demand is shaped by service providers, not by consumers. This interpretation is consistent with the work of such Canadian health economists as Robert Evans (1983), who argues that people using health and social services are not free negotiators. The language of "consumer" and "provider" blurs the fact that health and social service professionals determine the organization of services as well as consumer/client decisions on the use of those services.

Professional interests have a powerful effect on the design of services. On the positive side, this has allowed female professions to lay claim to knowledge and expertise, which became the basis for demanding improvements in wages and working conditions. Unfortunately, there are also some negative consequences to the drive for professionalism on the part of these traditional female service groups, as Carol

Baines illustrates in Chapter II. Glazer's (1988) study of hospital nurses documents how the rhetoric of professionalization was used by managers to justify increases in the responsibilities of registered nurses while decreasing ancillary staff. For example, eliminating aides was justified by the need for nurses to provide "total care" if nurses expected to get the professional recognition they sought.

Another negative effect of professional credentialism is that the work of service personnel doing the concrete tasks of daily maintenance becomes more routine and lower paid. The people doing this work, the essence of home care, are the most disadvantaged members of the female labour force – immigrants and visible minorities (Tellis-Nayak and Tellis-Nayak, 1989). Poor working conditions are reflected in the annual turnover rate of homemakers, which is at least 50 per cent. The poignancy of the situation was captured in the *Report of the Interministerial Committee on Visiting Homemaker Services* (Ontario, 1989):

> Homemaking services represent one of the key programs in operation that is helping to maintain people in their communities. Services are provided for clients who are: elderly; physically disabled; chronically ill; acutely ill; children and families.
>
> While homemaking services are widely available across the province, the major barrier to receipt of service is the lack of available homemakers.
>
> Four key areas were identified to be addressed by the Committee:
> (1) Training programs and resources for homemaking
> (2) Low wages paid to homemakers
> (3) Annual agency rate setting process
> (4) Homemaker agency rate structure.

The issue of wages is a real if a somewhat underplayed component of the home-care discussion. In foster homes of all types there is the assumption that caring is done on an altruistic basis. Covering out-of-pocket expenses is appropriate, but somehow paying a wage for the work itself will "attract the wrong kind of people." This is quite a different perspective than that used in the labour force, where the dictum is to pay good wages in order to attract "good people." In the male-dominated service professions there is no question that the maxim "you get what you pay for" prevails. We do not question the motives or skills of physicians and lawyers because they demand a fee – on the contrary. Payment and care are not antithetical – payment does not negate caring just as non-payment does not guarantee it (Leat and Gay, 1987: 62). Therefore, one must conclude that resistance to paying for care springs from causes that lie elsewhere.

I would argue that this resistance springs from the same ideological source that turns community-based care into family-based care, supplemented by the free labour of friends and volunteers with the occasional infusion of expensive formal services. Providing care for their elderly relatives is a task that women will continue to do. Community input is needed in the decision-making process that determines what types of services are going to be developed and how they will be funded and distributed. Only if we introduce a new set of players will we get a different perception of priorities, one that does not reflect the professional interests of health professionals. Finally, it is the responsibility of the state, not of families, to ensure that Canadians have the resources they need in their old age.

The above is a type of community input not pictured in the debate about the relationship between formal and informal networks; too often we get a blending of family with community that obfuscates both. The resulting bundle of contradictions is both public and private, collective and individualistic, all at the same time (Bullock, 1990).

If the current situation is not what we had in mind when promulgating community care, then what was? What do we mean when we talk about social care?

VALUES SHAPING THE DISCOURSE ON CARING

Caring is pivotal to keeping the human enterprise going, yet its function is invisible in the organization of our daily lives.

When aspects of it do break into the public domain, only the task component is seen – and defined as unskilled labour and paid accordingly (Neysmith and Nichols, 1989). Each chapter has shown how caring is made up of hard practicalities as well as personal attention, warmth, involvement, and empathetic understanding. The difficulty in specifying or creating a "job description" for caring work, particularly the emotional labour inherent in it, is partly due to the minimal theoretical attention paid to it. This continues to be a challenge to current research. The effects of caring are recognized not when the outcome is right but on those occasions when it goes wrong. Like prevention, the product is invisible; it exists in the negative form of distress rather than in the positive form of adjustment. Furthermore, when emotional labour is employed but unrecognized it is incorporated into concrete tasks, which ensures that it remains hidden. The results are predictable: as resources become scarce, visible work is given priority, for example, meals delivered, baths given, sheets changed, etc. – tasks that can be counted. Emotional labour is slotted in only as time allows. Second, although women may be hired for these jobs because of their skills in dealing with people's feelings, they are given no credit for these skills (James, 1989).

At this time caring for others is seen by Canadian policymakers as a private responsibility. Occasionally it is expanded to include informal helping networks, self-help groups, volunteers, and even neighbours. This remains so even when the phrase "community care" is used. The language that is evolving is worthy of note. A "caregiver" refers to the family member, usually female, who assumes primary responsibility for the daily tending, support, and monitoring required by adults who are incapacitated in some way. This labour is truly given, and seldom is there any remuneration. "Care providers" is the term used to designate persons who are paid to deliver specific services. The term "caregiver" is seldom used in relation to the ongoing tending of children, where the concept of mothering is assumed to incorporate such activities. Similarly, the physical and emotional energy women put into caring for adult males is subsumed within and seen as integral to heterosexual relationships. The support given and received among friends is assumed to be covered in the definition of friendship.

In each case the words are different, but many attributes of the phenomena are similar. One commonality is that caring is seen as a feature of the private world of personal relationships. The public world of employment may acknowledge it as an ingredient in certain jobs, but its attributes are poorly defined – and even more poorly remunerated. From an employer's perspective the caring responsibilities of women are a private issue that may impinge on work performance, but those responsibilities are essentially an individual problem best handled through personal negotiations between an employee and her immediate supervisor. The idea of developing legislation around leave for family responsibility is strongly resisted by both large and small business firms (Labour Canada, 1988).

At the beginning of this chapter I suggested that the family, the state, and the labour market all have an interest in defining community care. The concept of community care implies a collective responsibility for protecting the welfare of vulnerable groups in our society, and this is at odds with present assumptions about the private family, a market-based economy, and a non-interventionist government. A social-care model would provide explicit recognition that care of vulnerable persons is not a family responsibility but rather that public services must be made available to people who need them as part of a social security system based on the rights of citizenship. The state would be actively involved in the development of a range of services and would guarantee that financial impediments did not discriminate against their use. Labour force policies would reflect the fact that employees have family responsibilities. Employment practices would not penalize those who assume family responsibilities; rather, they would ensure that both men and women had equal freedom and responsibility in decision-making about who does what in caring.

Recognition that such policies do not fit neatly into current assumptions about the respective responsibilities of our major social institutions does not designate them as unworkable or as naive idealism, but it does mean that change has to be seen as a long-term endeavour that inevitably will be riddled with compromises. History also suggests that progress toward such goals may be more feasible in certain periods than in others. This is quite a different stance from one arguing that structural change in the economy is pivotal and necessary before we can proceed. Concrete examples demonstrate that antithetical values can co-exist and become the starting points for change. The Scandinavian countries possess a market economy, yet they have been able to realize a collective responsibility through the idea of the welfare state. The resulting policies and programs have a very different profile from those found in Canada, the U.K., or the United States. As Hokenstad and Johansson (1990: 255) observe in their recent assessment of Swedish long-term care policy:

> Debate about the relationship between formal and informal care has a different point of departure in Sweden than in the United States [and Canada]. The accepted policy position is that publicly provided care is a citizen's right, and should be available to any individual or family who needs it. The decision regarding the mix of informal and formal care is a choice which rests with the family. In fact, the issue of care substitution is framed very differently in Sweden. There, the discussion is centered around the question of how much formal care is necessary so that no family is forced to substitute informal care for formal care. Families are not statutorily required to take care of the elderly, but the government does have this obligation.

This is a long way from the starting position of many Canadian policies. Nevertheless, European feminist scholars note than an active welfare state has not been successful in turning caring into a non-gendered issue. In such countries women still do most of the caring labour (Showstack Sassoon, 1987); men do proportionately less. The situation has not changed because the ethic of care, i.e., the set of standards or rules by which behaviour is assessed, is still gender-specific. Women are socialized to care and, when all is said and done, they assume *responsibility* for ensuring that loved ones get what they need. However, countries that invest the state with the power to tax and develop services engage in activities that reflect a collective ethos, which challenges an ideology of familism and possessive individualism.

Familism is the idealization of what we think a family should embody: a conflict-free private domain where emotional and physical needs are tended to. Although the concept, by definition, includes one or more persons with extrafamilial status and responsibility, these are dropped at the front door. Supposedly, once one enters the home, tranquility replaces the strife of the outside world; consensus is achieved on important family goals; equity exists in the pursuit of these goals by family members.

Substantial empirical evidence supports other realities of family life, as Imogen Taylor's chapter on abused women graphically illustrates. However, knowledge about a contrary reality does not detract from the power of images. It remains the ideal against which all other forms of meeting emotional and physical needs of people are compared – and usually judged inferior without even the benefit of trial.

The results, as we have seen throughout this book, are policies that are residual, programs that are limited in content and coverage, families that cope rather than thrive. Thus, a frail old woman living isolated in an apartment receiving homemaker service three hours per week (the average for recipients of the Integrated Homemakers Program in Ontario in 1989) is said to be *living* in the *community* thanks to a *home-care* program. The words ring hollow. Children are moved from foster home to foster home in frustrated attempts to realize a family model in circumstances that are most unfamily-like (Dalley, 1988: 26). Perhaps most importantly, other ways of doing things are jettisoned before they are considered because they do not fit within the parameters of the ideology of family. As Anne Bullock (1990: 75) comments:

The notion of a community that relies on the "family" for its existence is a contradiction. Community implies egalitarian social organization that benefits all of its members. Family implies a privatized, hierarchical and gendered work organization that does not equally benefit its members and also foments the differences among families who are thought to comprise "the community".

The following section looks at some factors essential to developing a social model of care. They have been gleaned from a variety of writers who approach the issue in different ways. Some focus on the kinds of obstacles that need to be overcome while others make recommendations for policy change. They do not, therefore, provide a blueprint for change but hopefully will clarify some of the key ingredients needed.

A SOCIAL MODEL OF CARE: CONSIDERING THE ESSENTIALS

1. Guaranteeing Services

As women moved into the labour force some services and resources were made available to aid them with their domestic responsibilities. Day care, maternity leave, pay equity legislation, and affirmative action are examples of policies explicitly geared to the needs of women employees. It is important to note, however, that not all women benefit equally from them. Pay equity and affirmative action operate within the parameters of a labour market designed by men for men. These programs may help some women obtain a better deal within current models of paid employment, but they do not address the problems women face in blending family and employment responsibilities. Day care and maternity leave do cross this divide. They address women's home labour and thus present an implicit challenge to the ideals of familism and individualism. Their growth, however, has been agonizingly slow. The resulting paucity of services means that they are explicitly rationed. Certain groups receive priority: childcare spaces, for example, are sometimes reserved for single mothers, and scarce homemakers go to persons who are living alone or where the kin carer is not a woman. To question the priorities is to run the risk of having one's claim to a social conscience questioned!

No one is suggesting that today's special needs groups

should *not* receive service, but two-parent low-income families and elderly persons who have a female relative judged capable of providing care are pushed further back in the queue because of the accidents of family structure. In situations of such scarcity, to talk of a mother or daughter choosing to stay home to care for a dependent family member ignores the fact that choice assumes the existence of options. Consumers can access the commercial market for some services, but obviously this market is only available to those who can pay. Many needed services are also staffed by volunteers. This means that their existence rises and falls on the availability of people, usually women, who fit volunteer work into days already filled with caring for others. Both approaches reflect a residual perspective of social welfare, i.e., services are set up to fill in gaps when the preferred model of family care breaks down. The result is that income groups and family types are played off against the other. Evelyn Ferguson, in Chapter III, has documented the way this occurs in child care. I have outlined the influence of similar forces on the options available, or unavailable, to women caring for elderly family members.

If voluntary and for-profit services continue to be seen as major components of our future community service structure, it will affect the welfare of all women. Volunteers cannot staff services that people have a claim to by virtue of being Canadian citizens. Similarly, for-profit agencies are in business to make a profit, not to guarantee that services are universally available to those needing them. Unless a funding regulation for community-based services is put in place, similar to that found in the Canada Health Act, which guarantees universal access while disallowing an individual or organization from receiving both public and private fees for service, we can anticipate the emergence of a two-tiered community care system – underfunded minimum-level public services for those with limited resources, and a multi-choice private market of services available to those who can pay.

2. Co-ordinating Services – Who Will Be in Charge?
The organization of care in the domestic sphere is marked by

flexibility and attention to individual preferences; criteria for receiving services are particularistic, e.g., claims are made on the basis of personal relationships (Ferguson, 1984). However, public services are housed in bureaucracies that, by definition, rationalize, delegate authority, are hierarchical, and stress efficiency and effectiveness; the criteria for receiving service are universalistic, e.g., claims are made on the basis of citizenship. Recognition of the contradiction that the content and organization of public services do not necessarily fit with the particular needs of individuals has sometimes led to the suggestion that families become the case managers for services received in the home (see, for example, Seltzer *et al.*, 1987). The initial attractiveness of such schemes fades as one examines the dynamics of co-ordination.

A cursory look at community-based services reveals great variability from province to province in the types of services available, their organizational features and regulations, and their funding bases and access criteria. Such differences are an historical "fact of life" in Canada because health and social services are a provincial responsibility. Furthermore, some provinces, for example Ontario, have actively encouraged communities to take the initiative in developing services. Whatever the strengths of this model for promoting service designs that meet local need, the seemingly complex mix of services it produces is confusing to the uninitiated.

Take, for example, a woman in her early seventies who is caring for her spouse in the early stages of Alzheimer's disease. This is a progressive condition where the services appropriate at one stage will differ from those needed later. On the positive side, increased public awareness of how exhausting it is to care for such persons means that this woman will probably be given priority for such services as respite care. However, the types of respite available vary across the province. She must expend time and energy in exploring what services exist, accessing them, and then must use considerable creativity in adapting these bureaucratic/ universal services to the specific/particularistic needs of the person she cares for. In the "family as case manager" scenario, it would be primarily the responsibility of this elderly woman to steer her way through myriad services, each characterized by its own set of rules and regulations. Any potential empowerment, or sense of control, to the kin carer envisioned by this model has to be weighed against the costs to her in terms of time and energy. In addition, the model assumes that a family member has the knowledge, experience, and skill to perform this managerial function in a way that will maximize benefits to her. Although family may be best positioned to meet the social support needs of its members, information and contacts are a form of knowledge and a source of power that professionals have to a far greater degree than most kin carers.

3. Moving from Private to Public Dependence
In countries with a well-developed welfare state, it is often noted that women have moved from a position of dependence on individual men to one of dependence on the state. It can be argued that it is a moot point as to whether this has furthered their welfare. Pat Evans in Chapter VI has shown that the Canadian version of the welfare state has had mixed benefits for women. It is also likely that this shift in dependence has made much more visible the dependency of women and the power imbalance within families. We are now far more wary of the monolith of the family (Eichler, 1983).

Bullock (1990: 76), in her review of community care in Canada, is at best ambivalent about the consequences for women of the shift from private to public dependency. She notes that women and their dependants, along with their advocates, have to interact with the state on its terms. Doing this decreases the possibility of questioning the rules of the game:

> The state organization of women's work as care-givers in the community mitigates against developing a politics of care. The reliance of the state on an ideologically constructed family/community category to meet its own financial and administrative priorities reinforces and deepens the forms of inequality mentioned earlier – particularly those arising out of gender. Women are not only bearing the brunt of the state's requirement to divest itself of expensive long-term care responsibilities; many of them are also rendered more dependent on a male wage as a result – even middle-class

women. That economic dependence can be more "silencing" than even the "invisibility" of the work itself.

In contrast, Borchorst and Siim (1987), in reviewing the Scandinavian situation, argue that the shift from dependency on one man to receiving service from the state has benefited women. They acknowledge that women have indeed become dependent on publicly funded day care and home helps. However, as a result of their time in the labour force, women had improved their position when the cutbacks of the eighties began to take their toll. The public nature of child care in Sweden was widely accepted and thus it was more difficult to return it to the private sphere of the family. Child care had become a universal service rather than a selective one, and women could exercise a right of citizenship rather than make client-based claims subject to a means test.

Recent assessments of preferences for and use of home help services in Norway show a dramatic increase since the 1960s. Daatland (1990) concludes that the growing preference for public services reflects their increased availability, not a decrease or weakening of the intergenerational solidarity, that we may have been confusing what was possible with what was wanted. Such findings from countries with well-established public services raise questions about the context within which the current North American preoccupation with family-based models of care should be viewed. A recent national survey in Norway found that nearly half of the people saw themselves as responsible for sick parents but only 20 per cent wanted their children to care for them in old age. Daatland's (1990: 10–11) conclusion captures one of the themes permeating this book:

> The contrast between what responsibility an adult child will accept for old parents, and the responsibility the elderly are willing to impose on their own children, may go to the core of the issue. . . . Parents are afraid of overloading their children, and use alternatives when they have a reasonably good choice. Like all persons, young and old alike, they find it easier to give than to receive; easier to be the independent

provider than the dependent receiver. One sided dependency has probably never been productive for good family
relations.

4. Changing Professional Models

Moving into the public domain allows us to look at what it
means to be a client, a consumer, and a service provider.
Women populate all three of these positions today, and the
same person might occupy each at different points in her life
cycle. This forces us to look at several important issues. First,
it has become popular to speak of recipients of service as
consumers rather than clients. Does this designate a change
in the way we think of service recipients as discussed in the
preceding section? Does it reflect a material change in the
social conditions of these women's lives? Does changing a
client into a consumer indicate that the person has more
choice or autonomy over what service she uses? Or is it an
example of co-opting language, with business proceeding as
usual? It was noted earlier that the expression "community
care" only meant that people were no longer being housed in
institutions, not that an alternative policy was being actively
pursued, as the term suggests.

Second, women who are professionals in the bureaucracies
delivering services have a different set of interests from those
who are seen as clients or consumers. It therefore behooves
us to look at the models of professionalism that are being put
forward today. In Chapter II Carol Baines has documented
how this has been an ongoing arena for struggle in the
helping professions. Authoritative relationships are inherent
in Western models of professionalism. Authority is granted on
the basis of claims to special knowledge and skills. Practice is
regulated by codes of ethics designed to control self-interest
and define acceptable behaviour between professional colleagues and for interactions with service recipients. Even
regulation within this narrow definition has been subjected
to increasing criticism. Because professional organizations are
made up of peers that reflect professional orthodoxies, the
perspective of the client is, at best, in a minority at disciplinary hearings. At its worst, the professional organization

functions as a guardian of rights and privileges rather than ensuring the optimal performance of its members (Wilding, 1982; Friedson, 1983).

In addition to concerns about ethical behaviour, the structure of current professional models raises significant issues. These models are consistent with a market economy that rewards individuals who possess certain skills, knowledge, education, and experience, what economists refer to as "human capital." These are the same attributes used to specify qualifications for membership in a profession. It is consistent, then, to allow such assets to be used with the same freedom, and subjected to the same restrictions, that Canadians impose on other forms of personal possessions. In effect, this transforms professional credentials into property rights that have a financial value to the person possessing them. As the U.S. Medicare example used earlier illustrates, prestigious professions are usually more successful in ensuring that the services they provide are defined as essential and thus given priority in funding decisions. Whatever the financial benefits such professional "turf-guarding" might have for certain groups of women, it is an obstacle to developing programs that envision a more egalitarian and collective approach to caring for others.

5. Gender Desegregation of Caring

Most discussions of equity concern women's position in the labour force and focus on determining criteria and procedures for ensuring equal pay for work of equal value and/or eliminating features of the labour market that lead to job segregation. An even more fundamental issue is the unequal allocation between men and women of opportunities and responsibilities in the public world of employment and the private world of family life.

Hooyman (1989: 6) makes the point that the ideology of separate spheres has meant that our major institutions are not founded on the tenet of helping others to develop.

> The ideology of separate spheres accepted profit as the sole operating principle of the market place and exonerated the public sphere from obligations of social responsibility. Care-

giving values, thus removed from the mainstream of public life, were sequestered in the home as an antidote to the public sphere of the marketplace rather than a central force in shaping it.

Thus the idea of community responsibility versus family obligation was resolved along gender lines, neatly avoiding the necessity to deal with inherent inequities. Having entered the private realm of the home, caregiving becomes invisible. It runs on a different clock than the world of employment. Both these characteristics make it difficult to see it as work when the definition of work is so firmly market-related. Work that isn't seen isn't valued, except when it isn't done!

One of the biggest barriers to redistributing the costs and benefits of caring is the definition of what constitutes full-time employment in our market economy. This phenomenon has been the focus of inquiry by feminist scholars in all Western industrialized countries, as much in the social democracies of northern Europe as in the free enterprise milieu of the United States. During the 1930s when unions and industrial owners were defining the nature of the relationship between labour and capital, women were not invited. Workers and managers were men, and there were certain shared assumptions held by both sides. One of these was that the world of the factory and the world of the family were quite separate. How men arrived at the workplace and how they handled family responsibility after hours were issues outside of the agreement. The existence of a private life was only reflected in the concept of a family wage, that is, that salaries had to be sufficient for a man to support his wife and children. This helps us understand why most unions, until quite recently, did not have a strong track record in promoting women's issues, even when their membership was primarily female. Maternity leave and child-care dropout clauses in pension schemes were viewed as divisive and liable to jeopardize important items like salaries, working conditions, and pension entitlements (Hernes, 1987).

The unchanging nature of the labour force has had some interesting effects on the whole discussion of payment for care, exploitation of the paid and unpaid labour of women, and what Waerness (1987) has referred to as the rationality of caring. Men, although they may be viewed with sympathy, are praised for going beyond the call of duty when they take on familial caring responsibilities. Women, although they may be lauded for doing their duty, are expected to care. This reflects not only our differing expectations of men and women, but also our assessment that the actions of such men are particularly praiseworthy because the decision is usually more costly for the male carer in terms of forgone earnings. As a consequence, not only is such a person viewed as having a greater claim to relief, but it is assumed that there must have been a very important reason for his making such a choice. A similar status of active decision-maker is not accorded to women. Being socialized to care seems to remove the element of choice in decision-making and any consequent claim to moral worth. If a woman does say that she chose to care, this does not lead to a reassessment of the woman as actor but rather suggests irrationality (Waerness, 1987). Why would she not try to escape the burden of caring? Her claim is not to be believed because, given the situation, such a decision makes no sense if one has any options. Underlying this argument is the image of economic man (specifically not woman) who weighs the pros and cons of action and then decides in his best interest. To do otherwise is irrational. Women have fewer opportunities in the labour market and thus have less to lose by withdrawing. To choose to care for a dependent family member under these circumstances is seen as less costly. Thus both moral and financial claims are weakened. The result is that a person's worth in the labour market influences the assessed value of her/his contributions in other spheres of life.

CONCLUSION

Much social policy discussion presupposes the separation of the public from the private, the family from the state, production from reproduction, even when our daily experience causes us to question the concept of separate spheres. Change is hampered by the discourse available to us, which is concerned with the relations of power and control in our society as they are embedded in our policy documents, service structures, and professional practices. An examination of the relationships among the family, the paid labour force, and the state as they are being played out in the development of community care services for the elderly illustrates how this occurs. It was argued that the contradictions that this examination revealed can open up possibilities for resistance and change. The notion of resistance emerged in Jane Aronson's chapter on aging women and Marge Reitsma-Street's chapter on girl delinquents. Current community care and delinquency discourses offer little opportunity for either group to define itself differently from the dominant view of them as dependent old women or sexually promiscuous females.

In contrast, the discourse around domestic violence has undergone considerable modification in the last decade. This area is a current example of how a change in language (wife abuse, marital rape) allowed women to restructure their experiences, think of them in a new way, and suggest alternatives that were not possible before. However, as this newly legitimized social problem demanded responses in the form of resources to meet the needs of these women, the language and structure of the "problem" again changed. In order for the legal system to respond, charges had to be laid against a husband/partner – a contradiction to dominant ideas about how family disputes should be handled. In order to obtain funding, shelters had to fit into funding categories originally designed for hostels – thus the need for housing was seen as temporary until "something" could be worked out. To access counselling services wife abuse was renamed "domestic" or "family" violence – thus making invisible again the source of the abuse and returning it to the private sphere of the family, unhooking its link to other structures in our society that condone violence.

A decade later one might indeed ask, "Was this what we envisioned and worked so hard for?" The answer will depend on the standpoint of the questioner. In terms of decreasing the risk of violence to Canadian women, probably little has changed. However, from another perspective one might argue that the image of the private family as an oasis of tranquility has been shattered. The relationship of theory to practice is not just contingent and instrumental, it is conceptual and constitutive (Ferguson, 1984: 196). Thus, thinking about something in a different way *is* change – it is a necessary step to action. Understanding state/family/market relations is central to understanding our social construction of caring. The emotional and physical work is done in both private and public spheres. The state is a participant as actor, arbitrator, and definer.

An analysis of caring highlights the importance of crossing the micro/macro schisms that permeate both theory and practice in the helping professions. A dual perspective is needed to juxtapose the contradictions more sharply than has been possible with traditional separatist approaches to policy and clinical practice. The realities of women's lives do not fit into these professional boxes.

There are no fixed, universal meanings of caring as it relates to community and family. But, as Weedon (1987: 109) points out, "Particular discourses also offer different positions. While it will offer a preferred form of subjectivity it will imply others and thus the possibility for reversal." Until now the discourse on the nature of the welfare state has excluded the voices of women. The feminist discourse on caring offers a vision of community based on connectedness rather than one based on the possessive individualism that underlies familism.

REFERENCES

The research upon which this chapter is based was made possible through grant #472-86-0017 from the Social Sciences and Humanities Research Council, Ottawa.

Aronson, J., V. Marshall, and J. Sulman. 1987. "Patients Awaiting Discharge from Hospital," in V. Marshall, ed., *Aging in Canada: Social Perspectives*, Second Edition. Toronto: Fitzhenry & Whiteside.
Biegel, D., and A. Blum. 1990. *Aging and Caregiving: Theory, Research and Policy*. Newbury Park, Calif.: Sage Publications.
Binney, E., C. Estes, and S. Ingman. 1990. "Medicalization, public

policy and the elderly: social services in jeopardy?" *Social Science and Medicine*, 30, 7: 761–71.

Binney, E., and C. Estes. 1988. "The retreat of the state and its transfer of responsibility: the intergenerational war," *International Journal of Health Services*, 18, 1: 83–96.

Borchorst, A., and B. Siim. 1987. "Women and the advanced welfare state – a new kind of patriarchal power?" in A. Showstack Sassoon, *Women and the Welfare State*. London: Hutchison.

Brody, E., and C. Schoonover. 1986. "Patterns of Parent Care When Adult Daughters Work and When They Do Not," *Gerontologist*, 26, 4: 372–81.

Bullock, A. 1990. "Community care: ideology and lived experience," in R. Ng, G. Walker, and J. Muller, *Community Organization and the Canadian State*. Toronto: Garamond Press.

Canadian Mental Health Association. 1987. *Needs Assessment Study on Respite Care*. Toronto: Metropolitan Toronto Branch.

Chappell, N., L. Strain, and A. Blandford. 1986. *Aging and Health Care: A Social Perspective*. Toronto: Holt, Rinehart and Winston of Canada.

Daatland, S. 1990. "What are families for? On family solidarity and preference for help," *Ageing and Society*, 10: 1–15.

Dalley, G. 1988. *Ideologies of Caring: Rethinking Community and Collectivism*. London: Macmillan.

Eichler, M. 1983. *Families in Canada Today: Recent Changes and Their Policy Consequences*. Toronto: Gage.

Evans, R. 1983. "Incomplete Vertical Integration in the Health Care Industry: Pseudomarkets and Pseudopolicies," *Annals of the American Academy of Political and Social Science*, 468: 60–87.

Ferguson, K. 1984. *The Feminist Case Against Bureaucracy*. Philadelphia: Temple University Press.

Finch, J., and D. Groves. 1983. *A Labour of Love*. London: Routledge and Kegan Paul.

Foote, C. 1988. "The Economic Outcomes of Marriage Breakdown in Canada: Construction of a Social Problem through Law and Policy," paper presented at the Learned Societies Conference, Windsor, Ontario, June 7.

Friedson, E. 1983. "The Theory of Professions: State of the Art," in R. Dingwell and P. Lewis, eds., *The Sociology of the Professions: Lawyers, Doctors and Others*. London: Macmillan.

Glazer, N. 1988. "Overlooked, overworked: women's unpaid and paid work in the health services' 'cost crisis,'" *International Journal of Health Services*, 18, 1: 119–37.

Hernes, H. 1987. "Women and the welfare state: the transition from private to public dependence," in Showstack Sassoon, *Women and the Welfare State.*

Hokenstad, M., and L. Johansson. 1990. "Caregiving for the elderly in Sweden: program challenges and policy initiatives," in Biegel and Blum, *Aging and Caregiving.*

Hooyman, N. 1989. "Gender, Caregiving and Equity: A Feminist Perspective," paper presented at the Annual Meeting of the Council of Social Work Education.

James, N. 1989. "Emotional Labour: Skill and Work in the Social Regulation of Feelings," *Sociological Review*, 37, 1: 15–42.

Labour Canada, Women's Bureau. 1988. *Leaves for Employees with Family Responsibilities.* Prepared by Monica Townson Associates Inc. Ottawa.

Land, H., and H. Rose. 1985. "Compulsory altruism for some or an altruistic society for all?" in P. Bean, J. Ferris, and D. Whynes, *In Defence of Welfare.* London: Tavistock.

Leat, D., and P. Gay. 1987. *Paying for Care: A study of policy and practice in paid care schemes.* Research Report No. 661. London: Policy Studies Institute.

Ministry of Community and Social Services. 1987. *Guidelines for Family Respite Programs.* Toronto.

Ministry of Community and Social Services. 1989. *Evaluation of the Integrated Homemaker Program.* Final Report, March. Toronto: Price Waterhouse.

Neysmith, S. 1987. *SPRINT'S Respite Care Program: An Evaluation.* Toronto: Senior Persons Resources in North Toronto.

Neysmith, S., and B. Nichols. 1989. "Home Help: Who Pays When Caregivers Become Care Providers," paper presented at the Annual Meetings of the Canadian Association on Gerontology, Ottawa, October.

Ontario, Senior Citizens' Affairs. 1986. *A New Agenda: Health and Social Services Strategies for Ontario's Seniors.* Toronto.

Ontario. 1989. *Report of the Interministerial Committee on Visiting Homemaker Services.*

Seltzer, M., J. Ivry, and L. Litchfield. 1987. "Family Members As Case Managers: Partnership Between the Formal and Informal Support Networks," *Gerontologist*, 27, 6: 722–28.

Showstack Sassoon, A. 1987. "Women's new social role: contradictions of the welfare state," in Showstack Sassoon, *Women and the Welfare State.*

Sweeney, John. 1989. *Long Term Care for the Elderly and People with Physical Disabilities.* Statement to the Ontario Legislature by the Minister of Community and Social Services. Toronto, June 7.

Tellis-Nayek, V., and M. Tellis-Nayek. 1989. "Quality of Care and the

Burden of Two Cultures: When the World of the Nurse's Aid Enters the World of the Nursing Home," *Gerontologist*, XXIX, 3: 307–13.

Tindale, J., and S. Neysmith. 1987. "Economic justice in later life: A Canadian perspective," *Social Justice Research*, 1, 4: 461–75.

Ungerson, C. 1987. *Policy Is Personal: Sex, Gender and Informal Care*. London: Tavistock.

Waerness, K. 1987. "On the rationality of caring," in Showstack Sassoon, *Women and the Welfare State*.

Weedon, C. 1987. *Feminist Practice and Poststructuralist Theory*. Oxford: Basil Blackwell.

Wilding, P. 1982. *Professional Power and Social Welfare*. London: Routledge and Kegan Paul.

Index

Author Index